Management of Multinational Companies

Management of Multinational Companies

A French Perspective

Edited by

Ulrike Mayrhofer
IAE Lyon (Institut d'Administration des Entreprises), Magellan Research Centre,
Jean Moulin Lyon 3 University, France

palgrave
macmillan

First published in France as *Le Management des Firmes Multinationales* by
Editions Magnard-Vuibert, Paris 2011.

This edition first published 2013 by
PALGRAVE MACMILLAN

Palgrave Macmillan in the UK is an imprint of Macmillan Publishers Limited,
registered in England, company number 785998, of Houndmills, Basingstoke,
Hampshire RG21 6XS.

Palgrave Macmillan in the US is a division of St Martin's Press LLC,
175 Fifth Avenue, New York, NY 10010.

Palgrave Macmillan is the global academic imprint of the above companies
and has companies and representatives throughout the world.

Palgrave® and Macmillan® are registered trademarks in the United States,
the United Kingdom, Europe and other countries.

ISBN 978–1–137–02388–9

This book is printed on paper suitable for recycling and made from fully
managed and sustained forest sources. Logging, pulping and manufacturing
processes are expected to conform to the environmental regulations of the
country of origin.

A catalogue record for this book is available from the British Library.

A catalog record for this book is available from the Library of Congress.

10   9   8   7   6   5   4   3   2   1
22   21   20   19   18   17   16   15   14   13

Printed and bound in the United States of America

Contents

List of Tables, Figures and Boxes

Tables

Figures

Boxes

Foreword

It is a pleasure for me to endorse this original and thoughtful analysis of multinational companies (MNCs) active in the French economy. Two sets of MNCs are studied in this book. There are French MNCs like Accor, Danone, LVMH (Louis Vuitton Moët Hennessy), L'Oreal and Renault, and also foreign MNCs such as Volkswagen and Google. These studies make a major contribution to the field of international business, since they take the MNC as the key unit of analysis.

Today, in a world of globalization, it is important to understand the strategies of MNCs and the nature of relationships between the parent company and its subsidiaries. In the French academic context, this focus on the MNC as the unit of analysis for international management adds a new dimension to the more traditional economics and finance focus upon country-level factors. While the latter are important in explaining trade patterns and the macroeconomic infrastructure, it is the strategies of MNCs which now explain the majority of international business. For example, I have found that the world's 500 largest companies undertake more than half the world's trade, and account for over 90 per cent of the world's stock of Foreign Direct Investment (FDI). These 500 MNCs are roughly divided into three groups, correlated broadly with the regions of Europe, North America and Asia, and they average 75 per cent of their sales in their home region.

The first chapter by Ulrike Mayrhofer applies this thinking to the world's largest MNCs and introduces my regional framework, as well as the global factory of Buckley and Ghauri. This chapter, and the others in Part I, serve to better align research on MNCs in France, and French MNCs with mainstream research on the regional nature of MNCs.

In Part II, several chapters examine the nature of parent company and subsidiary relationships. Here, the basic framework of economic integration and national responsiveness is used and applied for the first time to analyse the organizational structures of French-based MNCs. Other chapters examine the role of distance for the implementation of subsidiaries, as well as innovation processes and human resource management issues in MNCs, again in a French institutional context.

In Part III, several chapters examine partner relationships of MNCs. Network analysis can be used to study both intra-firm and inter-firm linkages. This approach is applied in an original manner to examine the multiple partnerships developed by French MNCs and MNCs from other countries.

Overall, the chapters in this book offer new and exciting research on the role of MNCs in France. It is interesting to note that, contrary to the critical thinking about MNCs by Servan-Schreiber in 1967 in *Le Défi Américain*, today the evidence is that foreign MNCs transfer technology and help to upgrade the macroeconomic infrastructure of France. In turn, a major set of French-owned MNCs have become world leaders, serving to develop cross-country networks and supply chains that enhance the growth and prosperity of France. Thus MNCs serve to better integrate France into the world economic system.

Alan M. Rugman
Henley Business School, University of Reading

Acknowledgements

This book has benefited from the financial support of the Magellan Research Centre, IAE Lyon (Institut d'Administration des Entreprises) and Jean Moulin Lyon 3 University.

The authors wish to thank Collette Drifte, Dominique Lachkar, Thierry Artzner, Leandro Di Domenico and John Laxton for their precious help in the translation of the book.

Notes on Contributors

Lusine Arzumanyan is Assistant Professor of Management at IAE Lyon (Institut d'Administration des Entreprises, School of Management), Jean Moulin Lyon 3 University. She holds a master's degree in international management from IAE Lyon, and is currently preparing a doctoral thesis on the implementation of communities of practice in the field of innovation in MNCs. The empirical study of her doctoral thesis is based on the case of the French Groupe SEB.

Pascale Berthier worked as a human resource manager in various companies, and is now Affiliated Professor at EM Lyon Business School. She teaches human resources and personal development, to both students and managers in MNCs. She received her doctorate in 2010 from Jean Moulin Lyon 3 University. Her research focuses on the international mobility of managers and competency transfer on the repatriation of top executives.

Jean-Baptiste Cartier is Associate Professor of Management (specializing in organizational finance) at IAE Lyon, Jean Moulin Lyon 3 University. An alumnus of ENS (Ecole Normale Supérieure) in Cachan, where he graduated in economics and management, he obtained his doctorate in 2004. The subject of his thesis was the improvement of company performance following a change in legal structure. He has published several articles on the relationship between legal structures and the organization of subsidiaries.

Ludivine Chalençon is Assistant Professor of Management at IAE Lyon, Jean Moulin Lyon 3 University. She is currently preparing a doctoral thesis on location strategies and value creation in mergers-acquisitions. She teaches finance at IAE Lyon.

Paul Marc Collin has held management positions in MNCs, and is now an associate professor of Management at IAE Lyon, Jean Moulin Lyon 3 University, as well as the director of the Master's Degree in International Management (EPAS – European Programme Accreditation System – accredited by EFMD, European Foundation for Management Development) programme. His lectures and research concern the fields of strategic management and international business.

Claire Faverjon is Associate Professor at IAE Lyon, Jean Moulin Lyon 3 University. She currently teaches corporate finance, financial theory and corporate valuation. She is in charge of a master's programme in corporate finance at IAE Lyon. She conducts research on the link between strategy and finance, and more specifically between specialization strategies and shareholder value creation and between credit rating and specialization strategies.

François Lantin is Associate Professor of Management at IAE Lyon, Jean Moulin Lyon 3 University. He is involved with the Master's in Accounting-Controlling-Audit programme and mainly teaches international financial reporting standards (IFRS) and the analysis of consolidated financial statements. His main research theme concerns credit rating and its impact on stock prices and corporate strategies.

Simin Lin is a doctoral student in management at IAE Lyon, Jean Moulin Lyon 3 University, where she was awarded a master's degree in innovation management. Her major research themes concern international business and innovation management.

Yves-Frédéric Livian studied at the University of California at Berkeley and holds a doctorate in sociology and a master's degree in political sciences. He is Professor Emeritus at IAE Lyon, Jean Moulin Lyon 3 University, and conducts research at the Magellan Research Centre. His research themes focus on career management, organizational change and intercultural management. He teaches in the Czech Republic, China and West Africa, and is the author of 25 books or book chapters and 30 journal articles.

Ulrike Mayrhofer is Professor of Management at IAE Lyon, Jean Moulin Lyon 3 University. She is the director of the Magellan Research Centre, where she also heads the international management research team. She is Vice-President of Atlas/AFMI (Association Francophone de Management International – Francophone association for international management). Her teaching activities concern international management, strategic management and international marketing. She has published several books and case studies, as well as many journal articles on internationalization strategies of multinational companies.

Christopher Melin is Assistant Professor of Management at IAE Lyon, Jean Moulin Lyon 3 University. He is preparing a doctoral thesis on intra- and inter-organizational relationships and is conducting a field study on the Renault Trucks company (Volvo group). He teaches entrepreneurship and marketing to master's degree students.

Catherine Mercier-Suissa is Associate Professor of Economics at IAE Lyon, Jean Moulin Lyon 3 University, and is the director of the CFIMI (Centre Franco-Italien de Management International, Franco-Italian centre for international management). She received her doctorate in economics from Paris I University and has written several books and journal articles on internationalization strategies.

Sylvaine Mercuri is Assistant Professor of Management at IAE Lyon, Jean Moulin Lyon 3 University. She is currently preparing a doctoral thesis at the Magellan Research Centre on corporate social responsibility (CSR) and the role of middle managers. She teaches accounting, organization theory and marketing.

Emna Moalla is a doctoral student in international business at the Magellan Research Centre of IAE Lyon, Jean Moulin Lyon 3 University. Her research focuses on the impact of distance/proximity on the development of inter-firm linkages. She worked as an assistant professor at Grenoble School of Management and at IAE Lyon.

Aline Pereira Pündrich is Assistant Professor of Management at IAE Lyon, Jean Moulin Lyon 3 University. She holds a master's degree in international management and is preparing a doctoral thesis at the Magellan Research Centre. Her research concerns the fields of crisis management and corporate social responsibility.

Catherine Pivot is Professor of Economics at IAE Lyon, Jean Moulin Lyon 3 University, where she teaches industrial economics and the economics of quality. Her research concerns agriculture and the agrifood industry. She works in collaboration with institutions of higher education and professionals in the wine industry. She is a member of both the Amorim Academy, which assigns awards to young researchers working on the wine industry, and of the UNESCO (United Nations Educational Scientific Cultural Organization) 'Wine and Culture' Chair.

Maha Raïs is Assistant Professor of Management at IAE Lyon, Jean Moulin Lyon 3 University, where she is preparing a doctoral thesis at the Magellan Research Centre. Her research focuses on internationalization strategies of small- and medium-sized enterprises (SMEs) and alliances between SMEs and MNCs. She previously worked for two years as an assistant at the Faculty of Law, Economics and Political Sciences of Sousse.

Jérôme Rive, Dean of IAE Lyon, Jean Moulin Lyon 3 University, is Associate Professor of Management. His teaching and research activities concern human resource management, and in particular job forecasting. He has contributed significantly to the development of the study of international relations at IAE Lyon, and created the Master's programme in International Management, for which he received the EPAS (European Programme Accreditation System) accreditation (EFMD, European Foundation for Management Development).

Alain Roger is Professor of Management at IAE Lyon, Jean Moulin Lyon 3 University. He is a former director of the Magellan Research Centre, and is now in charge of the human resource management research team. His teaching and research activities are centred on human resource management, with a focus on career management and a special concern for international mobility.

Fabrice Roth is Professor of Management at IAE Lyon, Jean Moulin Lyon 3 University, where he is in charge of the Master's programme in the Management of International Activities. His research focuses on corporate governance, relationships between top management and middle management, the link between corporate governance systems and corporate strategies and the management of cultural diversity.

Dora Triki is a doctoral student in international business at the Magellan Research Centre, IAE Lyon, Jean Moulin Lyon 3 University. Her doctoral dissertation analyses the performance of international joint ventures based in the Mediterranean region. She holds a master's degree in International Management from IAE Lyon. She teaches marketing and entrepreneurship and has worked as an Assistant Professor at IAE Lyon and at ESC Saint Etienne (Ecole Supérieure de Commerce, Graduate School of Management).

Introduction

Ulrike Mayrhofer

Multinational companies (MNCs) play a major role in the process of globalization, and they contribute significantly to the creation of wealth in
national economies. According to data provided by the United Nations
Conference on Trade and Development (UNCTAD), there are about
82,000 MNCs in the world which own 810,000 subsidiaries located in
different countries. As a result of a vast concentration movement the
economic and financial power of MNCs has considerably increased.
In 2009, the total sales generated by the 20 largest MNCs in the world
amounted to 3801.5 billion US dollars, while the gross domestic product (GDP) of France totalled 2555.4 billion US dollars. In the same year,
the American group Wal-Mart, the world's largest MNC generated 408.2
billion US dollars total sales, and the Axa group, the largest French
MNC, 175.3 billion US dollars (see Chapter 1).

In a rapidly changing context, MNCs raise numerous questions. What
are these MNCs which have a larger economic and financial power than
even some countries? What are their strategies and how do they operate?
What are their managerial practices enabling to succeed on international markets? What are their plans for the coming years? Despite their
importance in the French economy, MNCs have not been widely studied in academic research in France. However, business practice reveals
that the management of MNCs remains highly contextualized, and that
it is necessary to renew concepts and tools likely to guide managers.
Against this perspective, researchers and doctoral students from the
'International Management' research team of the Magellan Research
Centre at IAE Lyon (Institut d'Administration des Entreprises) School
of Management, Jean Moulin Lyon 3 University, took the initiative to
write this collective work on the management of MNCs. In the context
of their investigations, the authors focused on French MNCs and foreign
MNCs which have established themselves in France. Their analyses are
based on the latest advances in international business research and are
illustrated with numerous examples and case studies.

The first part of the book deals with new challenges faced by MNCs in
the present environment. In the first chapter Ulrike Mayrhofer describes
the place and the characteristics of MNCs in a globalized economy and
examines the changes in their organizational configurations. Given the

importance of emerging markets, Catherine Mercier-Suissa highlights the development opportunities provided by BRIC (Brazil, Russia, India, China) countries following the economic and financial crisis. From an industry perspective, Catherine Pivot focuses on the wine industry which has been thoroughly restructured and is marked by the emergence of new MNCs. The question of governance is addressed by Fabrice Roth who analyses recent changes in government systems introduced by MNCs listed at the Paris stock exchange, CAC 40. Claire Faverjon and François Lantin emphasize the impact of credit rating on the development strategies of MNCs.

The second part of the book is dedicated to different aspects of internal management, and more precisely to relationships established between headquarters and subsidiaries. Given the geographic dispersion of activities and the fragmentation of the value-chain, headquarters–subsidiaries relationships have become a strategic issue for MNCs. Ludivine Chalençon and Emna Moalla explain how MNCs locate their subsidiaries, illustrating their analysis with the case of the Accor group. Jean-Baptiste Cartier and Christopher Melin stress the importance of the legal context for the coordination of headquarters–subsidiaries relationships, and focus on the legal framework adopted by two French banks, Société Générale and Crédit Agricole. Lusine Arzumanyan and Christopher Melin study innovation processes in MNCs, with an analysis of Groupe SEB. Human aspects, which play a crucial role in headquarters–subsidiaries relationships, are then addressed with Jérôme Rive and Paul Marc Collin advocating the creation of an observatory of international professions and Pascale Berthier and Alain Roger showing how the international mobility of managers may foster competence development and transfer.

The third part of the book deals with the management of partnerships. Many MNCs have developed networks of relationships that include different types of actors located around the world. However, the management of partnership relationships is complex and delivers contrasted results. Emna Moalla and Dora Triki identify factors that enable MNCs to have more successful partnerships, and they analyse the case of GL events. Yves-Frédéric Livian examines the impact of national culture on the management of several emblematic inter-firm alliances: Alcatel-Lucent, EADS (European Aeronautic Defence and Space Company), Renault-Nissan and Danone-Wahaha. Paul Marc Collin explains, through the example of the banking sector, how MNCs can build inter-organizational networks, including a multitude of actors. Maha Raïs and Simin Lin highlight the possible benefits of partnerships between French MNCs and Chinese companies. Finally, Aline Pereira Pündrich and Sylvaine Mercuri broaden the concept of cooperation to include different stakeholders of MNCs; the analysis of Google allows them to explain how to develop a corporate social responsibility policy.

Part I
New Challenges of Multinational Companies in a Rapidly Changing Global Environment

1
MNCs in the Global Economy

Ulrike Mayrhofer

How We Compete: What Companies around the World are Doing to Make it in Today's Global Economy – this is the title of the book published by Suzanne Berger in 2005, which is based on a survey of 500 companies in North America, Europe and Asia, conducted by a group of researchers from the Massachusetts Institute of Technology (MIT). This analysis emphasizes the diversity of responses given by multinational companies (MNCs) to meet the challenges of market globalization. It shows that increased global competition does not impose one single model of economic organization, both at the level of companies and at the level of countries. The observations made by the MIT research team highlight that if companies need to adapt to changes in the global environment, development pathways are numerous, and performances vary, even within the same industries.

MNCs are particularly affected by changes in the global economy in which they play a major role. In fact, the strategies they develop and the decisions they make contribute to shape the globalization process (Pesqueux, 2010). Over the past few years, many MNCs have tried to diversify their international expansion by reinforcing their presence in new geographic regions, particularly in emerging markets. At the same time, one can observe a fragmentation of the value-chain, marked by a growing geographic dispersion of production and marketing activities, as well as of research and development (R&D) activities (Mayrhofer and Urban, 2011).

These trends raise many questions. What are the characteristics of MNCs in a context of economic globalization? How do management modes of MNCs develop? How do organizational configurations adopted by MNCs evolve over time? How do MNCs succeed in managing activities located throughout the world?

In order to respond to these questions, the boundaries of MNCs in a globalized economy will first be examined. Then, new organizational forms which allow dealing with the fragmentation of the value-chain will be analysed.

1.1 MNCs in a globalized economy

According to figures provided by the United Nations Conference on Trade and Development (UNCTAD, 2010), there are about 82,000 MNCs in the world, which own 810,000 subsidiaries located in different countries. The majority of MNCs have their headquarters in developed countries, but this trend is decreasing (92% in 1992, 79% in 2000 and 72% in 2008). In 2009, the Wal-Mart group was the first MNC in the world, followed by Royal Dutch Shell and Exxon Mobil. Nine European companies (three French, two German, two Dutch, one British and one Italian group), six US companies, two Japanese and three Chinese companies appear in the ranking of the world's 20 largest MNCs, published in *Fortune Global 500*, in 2010 (see Table 1.1). The recent period is characterized by the growing weight of MNCs from emerging countries, which also aim to expand on the world market (Ghemawat and Hout, 2008).

1.1.1 The diversity of MNCs

MNCs cover an important variety of companies, ranging from small companies owning several subsidiaries abroad to large groups managing subsidiaries in a large number of countries. The MNC and its characteristics have been widely studied in the international business literature. In fact, organizational configurations of MNCs are diverse, and their degree of geographic dispersion changes following the opportunities offered by international markets. According to Dunning and Lundan (2008), an MNC may be defined as an enterprise that engages in foreign direct investments (FDI) and which owns or, to a certain extent, controls, value-added activities in several countries. These activities generally take place within subsidiaries.

Today, many MNCs have to manage a 'portfolio' of subsidiaries located in different countries. There are two forms of subsidiaries: (1) where the company owns the majority or the entire share capital (wholly owned subsidiaries); they can be created *ex nihilo* or result from the acquisition of a local company; (2) where the company shares its capital with another company; this may take the form of minority equity stakes in the capital of local companies or joint ventures developed with other companies. Because of the geographic dispersion of activities, the

Table 1.1 Classification of the world's largest MNCs (total sales 2009)

Rank/Company	Country	Industry	Total sales (in billion US dollars)	Net income (in billion US dollars)	Number of employees
1. Wal-Mart	United States	retail	408.2	14.3	2,100,000
2. Royal Dutch Shell	Netherlands	petroleum	285.1	12.5	101,000
3. Exxon Mobil	United States	petroleum	284.7	19.3	102,700
4. BP (British Petroleum)	United Kingdom	petroleum	246.1	16.6	80,300
5. Toyota Motor	Japan	automobile	204.1	2.3	320,590
6. Japan Post Holdings	Japan	services	202.2	4.8	229,134
7. Sinopec	China	petroleum	187.5	5.8	633,383
8. State Grid Corporation	China	power	184.5	−0.3	1,533,800
9. Axa	France	insurance	175.3	5	103,432
10. China National Petroleum Corporation	China	petroleum	165.5	10.3	1,649,992
11. Chevron	United States	petroleum	163.5	10.5	64,132
12. ING (Internationale Nederlanden Groep – international Dutch group)	Netherlands	financial services	163.2	−1.3	107,173
13. General Electric	United States	diversified	156.8	1.1	304,000
14. Total	France	petroleum	155.9	11.7	96,387
15. Bank of America Corp.	United States	bank	150.5	6.3	283,717
16. Volkswagen	Germany	automobile	146.2	1.3	368,500
17. Conoco Phillips	United States	petroleum	139.5	4.8	30,000
18. BNP Paribas (Banque Nationale de Paris)	France	bank	130.7	8.1	182,459
19. Generali Group	Italy	insurance	126	1.8	154,069
20. Allianz	Germany	insurance	126	6	153,203

Source: Based on data provided by Fortune Global 500 (2010).

coordination of subsidiaries has become more complex. Companies thus need to consider the diversity of national environments (language and cultural barriers, time zones, legislation, and so on) and managerial practices in different countries (Beddi, 2008; Jaussaud and Schaaper, 2006). Relationships that are established between headquarters and subsidiaries are closely linked to the concept of management chosen by MNCs. The EPRG model, proposed by Heenan and Perlmutter (1979) identifies four conceptions of management: ethnocentrism, polycentrism, regiocentrism and geocentrism.

The ethnocentric approach refers to a centralized management mode that is based in the home country culture of the MNC. The headquarters play a predominant role and set strategic objectives, which are deployed at the operational level in local subsidiaries. Values and managerial practices of headquarters are transferred to subsidiaries, and the control exercised by headquarters appears to be strong. Important positions within the group are held by employees of the headquarters. The managerial teams of subsidiaries are composed of expatriates who previously gained experience at the headquarters. This option is favoured by MNCs which aim to develop a concept (or a brand) that can be standardized at the global level.

The polycentric model reflects a decentralized concept of management, where an MNC grants considerable autonomy to its subsidiaries in order to take into consideration specific characteristics of foreign markets. Strategic objectives are determined according to the characteristics of each country. Subsidiaries develop their own organizational culture and are frequently managed by local managers. Control by the headquarters is limited. Foreign subsidiaries can be regarded as 'local' companies, and are highly integrated into the local economic environment. This management mode is preferred by companies which operate in a limited number of markets and which adapt the characteristics of their products to the specificities of each country.

The regiocentric approach is based on a division of the world in geographic regions which correspond to groups of countries characterized by a certain degree of homogeneity (Europe, North America, and so on). The management and control of subsidiaries by the headquarters take place at the regional level. Regional headquarters enjoy a strong autonomy with regard to the world headquarters of the group. They set strategic objectives at the regional level and coordinate activities of several national subsidiaries. Their strategy is based on similarities between countries belonging to the same region, and decisions tend to be standardized at the regional level. Mobility of managers within the same region is significant. This concept of management is used by companies which regroup their markets into several geographic regions.

Geocentrism represents a concept of management that aims to integrate headquarters and subsidiaries in a global decision-making process. Relationships between headquarters and subsidiaries are characterized by a strong interdependence, and each entity participates in the definition and the implementation of strategy. The geocentric model is based on the organization of a network made up of subsidiaries and headquarters. Relationships between different entities follow the logics of cooperation rather than hierarchy. Managerial teams are generally composed of persons with different nationalities, and the international mobility of managers is important. The geocentric approach is chosen by large MNCs which attempt to reconcile global integration requirements with local differentiation.

Since the pioneering work accomplished by Heenan and Perlmutter (1979), many authors have studied the development of organizational configurations in MNCs. It seems important to emphasize that, in many industries, hierarchical organizational structures, characterized by the central role played by headquarters, have progressively been replaced by more flexible structures, called network structures. Several scholars have analysed MNCs that are organized in networks. For example, Bartlett and Ghoshal (1991) conceptualized an organizational form, called the transnational company that goes beyond the centralization/decentralization dialectic. A system of internal differentiation defines different roles and responsibilities for subsidiaries of the same group. This management system aims to improve the company's learning capacity and reinforce its competitiveness at the international level. It is based on a strong interdependence between the different units belonging to the same company. More recently, Doz et al. (2001) introduced the meta-national company, which is a company whose competitive advantage is built through the knowledge acquired by subsidiaries located in different countries. The authors hold the view that in a knowledge economy the major challenge for companies is to innovate, thanks to their capacity to learn in different parts of the world. The meta-national company has three major competences:

1. It is the first to identify new knowledge that is developed throughout the world.
2. It is able to innovate by using this knowledge before its competitors.
3. It creates value through innovation by an efficient production and marketing process at the global level.

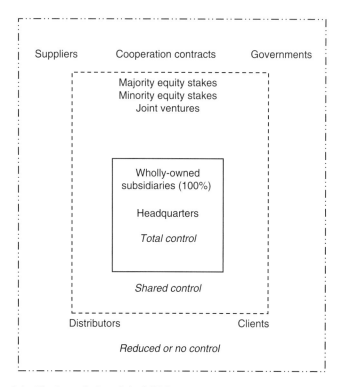

Figure 1.1   The boundaries of the MNC

Whatever typology is used to characterize organizational structures of MNCs, it is necessary to highlight their heterogeneous and changing character. Today, the boundaries of the MNC have become unclear. Local subsidiaries can thus form partnerships with other companies, and interact autonomously with other actors in their local environment (suppliers, distributors, clients, government, and so on) (see Figure 1.1). Given the embeddedness of subsidiaries in local networks, the MNC plays an increasing role in the economic environment of the country where it operates (Hennart, 2009). It thus seems necessary to examine the geographic origin of MNCs and the destinations of their investments.

1.1.2   The place of MNCs in the world economy

In the past, the world economy was dominated by MNCs from Triad nations (Western Europe, North America, Japan), who carried out most of their activities in their home country and in other developed countries. Today one can observe the growing importance of emerging markets, which offer interesting growth opportunities and whose companies also aim to conquer new markets. One can thus observe the emergence of new MNCs (e.g., Lenovo in China) which compete with companies from developed countries, both in the local and foreign markets (Ghemawat and Hout, 2008).

Data provided by UNCTAD (2010) illustrates this phenomenon. Since the new millennium, developing countries contribute more significantly to FDI, both as destinations and as investors. In 2009, 25.4 percent of FDI originated from developing countries and 49.2 percent of them were received by these countries. Table 1.2 indicates the world's top investing countries in 2009. It shows that the US ranked first (22.5% of outward FDI), ahead of France (13.4%) and Japan (6.8%), but that several emerging countries have become particularly active in terms of FDI. For example, China contributed 4.4 percent and the Russian Federation 4.2 percent to outward FDI.

Table 1.2 The world's top investing countries (2009)

Rank/Country	Value of FDI (in billion US dollars)	% of outward FDI
1. Unites States	248.1	22.5
2. France	147.2	13.4
3. Japan	74.7	6.8
4. Germany	62.7	5.7
5. Hong Kong, China	52.3	4.8
6. China	48	4.4
7. Russian Federation	46.1	4.2
8. Italy	43.9	4
9. Canada	38.8	3.5
10. Norway	34.2	3.1
11. Sweden	30.3	2.8
12. British Virgin Islands	26.5	2.4
13. Ireland	20.8	1.9
14. United Kingdom	18.5	1.7
15. Australia	18.4	1.7
16. Netherlands	17.8	1.6
17. Spain	16.3	1.5
18. Denmark	15.8	1.4
19. Switzerland	15.5	1.4
20. Luxembourg	15	1.4
Other countries	110.1	9.8
Total	1101	100

Source: Data provided by UNCTAD (2010), pp. 167–71.

Table 1.3 presents the first 20 countries that received FDI in 2009. It shows that the US ranked first (11.7% of inward FDI), ahead of China (8.5%) and France (5.4%). BRIC (Brazil, Russia, India, China) countries also attract a significant part of investments: Brazil received 2.3 percent, the Russian Federation 3.5 percent, India 3.1 percent, and China 8.5 percent of FDI (see Chapter 2).

The growing number of countries which invest and receive a significant amount of investments demonstrates the proliferation of MNCs and their subsidiaries. Over the past few years, many MNCs have chosen to accelerate their international expansion with the objective of acquiring dominant positions in the world market. Therefore, they have multiplied international alliances and mergers-acquisitions, despite the risks associated with these operations (Barmeyer and Mayrhofer, 2008; Meschi, 2008). Inter-firm linkages have been initiated by MNCs from developed countries, and also from emerging markets. One can mention the Indian groups Mittal Steel and Tata who

Table 1.3   The world's top FDI recipient countries (2009)

Rank/Country	Value of FDI (in billion US dollars)	% of inward FDI
1. United States	129.9	11.7
2. China	95	8.5
3. France	59.6	5.4
4. Hong Kong, China	48.4	4.3
5. United Kingdom	45.7	4.1
6. Russian Federation	38.7	3.5
7. Germany	35.6	3.2
8. Saudi-Arabia	35.5	3.2
9. India	34.6	3.1
10. Belgium	33.8	3
11. Italy	30.5	2.7
12. Luxembourg	27.3	2.5
13. Netherlands	26.9	2.4
14. Brazil	25.9	2.3
15. British Virgin Islands	25.3	2.3
16. Ireland	25	2.2
17. Australia	22.6	2
18. Canada	18.7	1.7
19. Singapore	16.8	1.5
20. Spain	15	1.3
Other countries	323.2	29.4
Total	1,114	100

Source: Data provided by UNCTAD (2010), pp. 167–71.

recently acquired several Western companies. Are MNCs becoming global companies?

1.2 From 'regional' MNCs to 'global' companies?

In the context of market globalization, MNCs aim to diversify the geographic location of their activities with the objective of increasing their global performance. One can observe the growing internationalization of production activities, and also of research and development activities. Specialists forecast a further development of observed trends (UNCTAD, 2010).

1.2.1 The regional focus of MNCs remains important

At the beginning of the new millennium, Rugman (2005) conducted a study on location strategies of the world's 500 largest MNCs. The collected data showed that most MNCs represented regional or bi-regional groups, characterized by a strong presence in their home region. Global companies appeared to be rare. The author proposed a 'regional' matrix, which allowed differentiating between possible location strategies.

The horizontal axis of the matrix corresponds to the geographic scope (regional or global) of firm-specific advantages. These advantages, which refer to factors that allow the development of a competitive advantage, for example, technological or marketing competences, can be exploited at the regional or the global level. For example, the geographic scope of a firm-specific advantage can be based on a European patent. To have a global scope, firm-specific advantages need to become global standards or global brands, or they need to generate global integration benefits, thus allowing economies of scale and experience effects.

The vertical axis represents the geographic reach of location advantages of a firm. These advantages relate to exogenous factors that determine the locus of the company's competitive advantage. Location advantages can be based on various elements such as natural resources, the legal system, infrastructure, workforce qualification or local demand. They can have a regional or global reach. For example, at the regional level, the geographic reach of a company can be influenced by location advantages linked to national or regional government regulation; at the global level it can result from the legal context determined by international organizations like the World Trade Organization (WTO) or the International Monetary Fund (IMF).

According to these two criteria, companies can be divided into four categories:

1. Companies that possess firm-specific advantages with a regional focus and location advantages with a global scope.
2. Regional companies where firm-specific advantages and location advantages have a regional reach.
3. Global companies which can benefit from the global scope of firm-specific advantages and location advantages.
4. Bi-regional companies whose firm-specific advantages have a global reach, but whose location advantages remain regional; they have a strong presence in two geographic regions.

A study focusing on location strategies developed by companies in the automotive industry confirms these trends. It shows that most European car manufacturers have chosen to locate an essential part of their R&D and production activities in the European Union, which is also their major market. They can therefore be considered as regional companies, because their presence in other geographic regions remains limited. Conversely, most US and Japanese groups can be considered as bi-regional groups, because they have developed R&D and production activities in both their home region and in another geographic region. For example, the Ford group has a significant presence in the North American market, and also in the European market. The same applies to the Honda Group, which focuses most of its activities in Japan and North America (Colovic and Mayrhofer, 2011).

If the regional focus of MNCs seems to remain important, it is worth mentioning that over the past few years many MNCs have reinforced the geographic diversification of their activities, giving preference to emerging countries. This choice allows them both to conquer markets that offer an important growth potential and to cut production costs. For example, PSA Peugeot Citroën has recently strengthened its presence in China by increasing its production capacities and opening a research and design centre. These trends may also be observed in other industries: the Danone group, which first developed in the European market, currently pursues its expansion in more distant countries. In 2009, the company carried out 53 percent of its total sales outside Western Europe: 13 percent in Central and Eastern Europe, 13 percent in Latin America, 13 percent in the Asia-Pacific region, 9 percent in North America and 5 percent in Africa/Middle East. 123 out of 159 production units of the group are located in other geographic regions.

The company has also created research centres in different geographic regions in order to better adapt to specificities of local markets (Hertrich et al., 2011). The same applies to L'Oréal. In 2009, in the field of cosmetics (without the Body Shop chain store and dermatology), the company carried out 57 percent of its total sales outside Western Europe, 23 percent in North America, 13 percent in Asia, 8 percent in Central and Eastern Europe, 7 percent in Latin America and 6 percent in the region 'Africa, Middle East, Pacific'. The group, which currently targets emerging countries with a strong growth potential, has also established production and research and development units for mass-consumer goods abroad. Conversely, luxury products continue to be produced in France (Collin and Rouach, 2009).

1.2.2   ...but the fragmentation of the value-chain becomes reality

The geographic dispersion of activities developed by MNCs is in line with the increasing fragmentation of the value-chain. In fact, activities located abroad not only concern production and marketing but also research and development (UNCTAD, 2010; Dunning and Lundan, 2008). Subsidiaries in different countries contribute to the global value-chain, but they may also establish links with local actors (Hennart, 2009). The model of the 'global factory', proposed by Buckley and Ghauri (2004), allows a better understanding of the fragmentation of business functions throughout the world. The authors argue that a growing number of companies develop flexible production systems in order to respond to the evolution of customer expectations in different countries. The global factory is organized around several key functions, which are generally controlled by the company's head-quarters: design, engineering, brand strategy and marketing. Certain features linked to these central functions such as research and development or design and engineering, may be subcontracted to other companies. The production function is frequently outsourced to suppliers producing different components of the products; their assembly may be carried out by the company or subcontracted. This system allows producing closely to final clients, reducing fixed costs and adapting products to the expectations of local markets.

The fragmentation of the value-chain is also emphasized in the study conducted by the MIT research team. Berger (2005) compares the modularization of production to Lego: the same pieces can be used in different ways to produce different forms, according to market trends. Berger underlines that information and communication technologies facilitate this modular organization which allows distributing business functions around the world. In the past, almost all functions were coordinated within MNCs, but today they are frequently outsourced to independent companies, located in various countries. An example is provided by producers of sporting goods like Adidas, Puma and Nike, who have chosen to subcontract a certain number of their activities to a network of suppliers throughout the world.

1.3 Conclusion

MNCs play a major role in economic globalization and contribute to the growing interdependence of national economies. At the same time, they need to adapt to changes in the global environment (Milliot and Tournois, 2010). The competitiveness and performance of MNCs are based on their capacity to acquire dominant market positions that allow them to create prosperous conditions for growth. They also need to keep on reducing costs and increase their capacities for innovation. One response to these challenges is to optimize the organizational configuration of their activities (Mayrhofer, 2011).

Available studies show that the regional focus of MNCs remains strong, but it is worth noting that many MNCs have aimed to diversify their geographic expansion, namely in emerging markets. They have not only located their production and marketing activities in these countries but also their research and development activities. This trend leads to an increasing fragmentation of the value-chain which requires the implementation of specific coordination mechanisms. Cohesion between the various units seems necessary for the 'global factory' to function satisfactorily.

In a rapidly changing environment, MNCs need to maintain their competitive advantage, by outsourcing several business functions and trying to anticipate market trends. The development of new MNCs from emerging countries is likely to challenge the positions acquired by MNCs from developed countries on the world market. The constant evolution of MNCs seems to become reality.

References

Barmeyer, C. and Mayrhofer, U. (2008) 'The Contribution of Intercultural Management to the Success of International Mergers and Acquisitions: An Analysis of the EADS Group', *International Business Review*, 17 (1), 28–38.

Bartlett, C. and Ghoshal, S. (1991) *Managing Across Borders: The Transnational Solution* (Boston, MA: Harvard Business School Press).

Beddi, H. (2008) 'Contribution à l'analyse de la diversité des relations siège-filiales au sein des firmes multinationals', unpublished doctoral dissertation (Paris: Université Paris Dauphine).

Berger, S. (2005) *How We Compete: What Companies around the World are Doing to Make it in Today's Global Economy* (Random House: Doubleday Broadway).

Buckley, P. J. and Ghauri, P. (2004) 'The Globalisation, Economic Geography and the Strategy of Multinational Enterprises', *Journal of International Business Studies*, 35 (2), 81–98.

Collin, B. and Rouach, D. (2009) *Le modèle L'Oréal. Les stratégies clés d'une multinationale française* (Paris: Pearson Education).

Colovic, A. and Mayrhofer, U. (2011) 'Optimising the Location of R&D and Production Activities: Trends in the Automotive Industry', *European Planning Studies*, 19 (8), 1481–98.

Doz, Y., Santos, J. and Williamson, P. (2001) *From Global to Metanational: How Companies Win in the Knowledge Economy* (Boston, MA: Harvard Business Press).

Dunning, J. H. and Lundan, S. M. (2008) *Multinational Enterprises and the Global Economy*, 2nd edn (Cheltenham: Edward Elgar Publishing).

Fortune Global 500 (2010) *Ranking of the World's 500 Largest Companies* (New York: Fortune Magazine).

Ghemawat, P. and Hout, T. (2008) 'Tomorrow's Global Giants. Not the Usual Suspects', *Harvard Business Review* 86 (11), 80–8.

Heenan, D. and Perlmutter, H. (1979) *Multinational Organization Development* (Boston, MA: Addison Wesley).

Hennart, J.-F. (2009) 'Down with MNE-Centric Theories! Market Entry and Expansion as the Bundling of MNE and Local Assets', *Journal of International Business Studies*, 40, 1432–54.

Hertrich, S., Kalika, M. and Mayrhofer, U. (2011) *Danone: A World Leader of the Food-Processing Industry* (Paris: Centrale de Cas et de Medias Pedagogiques, Case-Study Clearing House).

Jaussaud, J. and Schaaper, J. (2006) 'Entre efficience, réactivité et apprentissage organisationnel: une étude qualitative sur le cas des filiales françaises en Chine', *Management International*, 11 (1), 1–14.

Mayrhofer, U. (2011) 'La gestion des relations siège-filiales: un enjeu stratégique pour les firmes multinationales', *Revue Française de Gestion*, 37 (212), 65–75.

Mayrhofer, U. and Urban, S. (2011) *Management International. Des pratiques en mutation* (Paris: Pearson Education).

Meschi, P.-X. (2008) 'Impact de la corruption d'Etat sur l'évolution des participations européennes dans les coentreprises internationales', *M@n@gement*, 11 (1), 1–26.

Milliot, E. and Tournois, N. (eds) (2010) *The Paradoxes of Globalisation* (Basingstoke: Palgrave Macmillan).

Pesqueux, Y. (2010) 'What is Globalisation? The Paradoxes of the Economic and Political Substance of Markets' in E. Milliot and N. Tournois (eds) *The Paradoxes of Globalisation* (Basingstoke: Palgrave Macmillan) pp. 6–23.

Rugman, A. M. (2005) *The Regional Multinationals. MNEs and 'Global' Strategic Management* (Cambridge: Cambridge University Press).

UNCTAD (2010) *World Investment Report 2010* (New York/Geneva: United Nations Conference on Trade and Development).

2
Growth Opportunities for French MNCs in Emerging Markets (BRIC)

Catherine Mercier-Suissa

In 2009, the two G20 summits, in London and in Pittsburgh, highlighted the need for the participation of at least three new economic powers, China, India and Brazil, in the world's major economic policy decisions, in which Russia already takes part through its participation in the G8 forum. These four countries, which have a high growth potential, are grouped under the acronym BRIC (Brazil, Russia, India and China). They have large populations, are eager to consume and attract foreign direct investments (FDI). Investing foreign companies conduct a commercial and production strategy, seeking to take advantage of both high demand and favourable production conditions (low labour and raw material costs). Brazil and Russia have raw materials, mainly oil and gas; China and India have a population that exceeds one billion people. But beyond these common characteristics, the four countries have followed different models of economic development. China is characterized by outstanding performance in exports, especially of manufactured goods, and seems more affected by the slowdown in global demand. India has opened its market to FDI, particularly in the area of services (computers), and has a growth driven and borne by domestic demand. Brazil, the driving force in the *Mercado Comun del Cono Sur*, or Southern Cone Common Market (MERCOSUR), exports energy-producing raw material, agricultural products and foodstuffs, like Russia. The financial crisis of 2008 has had a different impact on each country. Even though most governments have taken measures to boost their economies, the effects of these stimulus plans have varied. Since the 2008 crisis, emerging countries have become the world's growth engine. There have been important signs of growth recovery, especially for India and China. New opportunities thus emerge for multinational companies (MNCs) of traditional industrialized countries, including French MNCs.

In the first section of this chapter, the main characteristics of the economic development model followed by BRIC countries after the 2008 crisis will be presented. In the second section, new investment opportunities for MNCs will be analysed, following measures adopted by governments to boost the local economy. The study will focus on market entry strategies chosen by French MNCs in the luxury and automotive industries.

2.1   General description of the crisis and its effects on some industries

The financial and economic crisis has affected both developed and emerging countries, but the latter began to suffer from its consequences with some delay. Their relatively low direct exposure to sub-primes meant there was no reason to expect a strong impact on their economies. However, these countries have been affected by both lower international liquidity and a collapse in global demand aggravated by a fall of commodity prices in exporting countries. Since BRIC countries have adopted different models of economic development, the effects of stimulus packages introduced by governments have not had the same impact on their economies.

2.1.1   BRIC: Effects of the crisis on each economy

Although Russia has recently been regarded as a newly industrialized country with a relatively high gross domestic product (GDP) per capita, China, India and Brazil are slightly different, owing to their huge, poor rural population. Russia is a rent economy, dependent on oil and suffering from the 'Dutch disease', the apparent relationship between the exportation of natural resources and the decline in the manufacturing sector. China, India and Brazil have a more diverse industrial base, a developing middle class willing to buy consumer products, a slow unequal growth and major regional disparities (see Table 2.1).

2.1.1.1   *Brazil: Growth driven by domestic consumption of an emerging middle class*

In 1985, after 20 years of military dictatorship, Brazil experienced a long period of hyper-inflation, up to 2800 per cent for the year 1990. Therefore, specific policies were adopted to fight inflation, with interest rates sometimes reaching 15 per cent, at the expense of investment in subsequent years. However, in 2003 a growth cycle developed. In 2007, an investment plan in infrastructure was launched to accelerate growth. As shown in Table 2.2, economic indicators improved.

Table 2.1   Economic characteristics of BRIC countries (2009)

	Brazil	**Russia**	**India**	**China**
% of world GDP (in US$)	2.6	2	2	8.1
GDP per capita in 2009 PPA*	10,400	15,300	3,000	6,500
Population in millions	196	141	1,125	1,326
Exports in 2009 (billion US$)	153	303	164	1,204
Currency reserves in December 2009 (billion US$)	238	439	275	2,422
GDP growth rate in 2009 in % (US$)	− 0.20	− 7.9	+ 7.4	+ 9.1
Budgetary deficit in 2009 (billion US$)	80	72.5	84.4	109
National debt in % of GDP	60%	6.3%	58%	40%
Doubtful accounts held by banking system	no	yes	no	yes

Note: *GDP per capita: Gross Domestic Product per capita in Purchasing Power Parity (PPP).
Source: IMF (2009).

Table 2.2   Brazil, economic indicators (annual average in %)

	1995–2002	2003–9
GDP	2.3	3.4
GDP per capita	0.7	2.7
Inflation	14.9	6.6

Source: *Le Monde* (2010) 'Brésil, un géant s'impose', 11 September.

Public finances were restored and the external vulnerability of the Brazilian economy was reduced. Growth was first driven by exports, and then by domestic demand. Brazil has an opening rate (exports/ GDP) of around only 15 per cent, but it benefited from capital inflows (8% of GDP in 2007) which covered part of the financing needs of the country. In 2008, growth reached 6 per cent. The macroeconomic environment of rising commodity prices (50% of exports) and increasing global demand for industrial products partly explain the good performance of the economy. But the 2008 crisis stopped growth. The Brazilian economy was severely affected. Exports fell by half between the third quarter of 2008 (60 billion US dollars) and the first quarter of 2009 (32 billion US dollars). However, based on the experience of previous financial crises, Brazil had accumulated large foreign exchange reserves (over 200 billion US dollars). These reserves have been seen as insurance against any form of reversals in international capital inflows, and to some extent, as guaranteed independence from the International Monetary Fund (IMF). Brazil's accumulated reserves and limited debt in foreign currency therefore allowed the devaluation of its currency, the *real*, without incurring the wrath of investors (in contrast to Argentina in the 1990s). The *real* was devalued by more than 50 per cent against the dollar between August and September 2008, but reserves were sufficient to launch a recovery plan, as in traditional industrialized countries.

Thus if the Brazilian government accepted a foreign exchange adjustment, it targeted tax cuts for companies, particularly taxes on industrial production, which boosted consumption. In addition, it cut taxes on basic foodstuffs, and increased spending on vulnerable groups in society (a minimum wage increase with an impact on pensions, upgrading of social programmes, salary increase for civil servants). By promoting these broad-based social measures, such as the 'Bolsa Familia', which was financial aid for child schooling and medical care, the number of families which could benefit increased from 3.6 million in 2003, to 12.4 million in 2009. Overall, 19.5 per cent of Brazilian families received a financial subsidy. Within a few years, 32 million citizens were lifted out of poverty.

Brazilian society can be divided into five broad categories:

Classes A and B: The upper social classes with more than 1900 Euros income per month.
Class C: The middle class with 439–1900 Euros income per month.
Class D: The lower class with 317 Euros income per month.
Class E: The excluded with less than 317 Euros income per month.

In 2002, Classes D and E accounted for 43 per cent of the population, and Class C for 44 per cent. In 2009, Classes D and E accounted for only 32.5 per cent of the population, and Class C for 52 per cent. The latter is composed of new consumers who have access to credit and boost domestic consumption. The recovery plan therefore stimulated the market. In 2009, the automotive industry registered a growth rate of 11.4 per cent, and the GDP growth rate remained positive at +0.2 per cent. Brazil proved resilient thanks to its domestic market and dynamic exports, boosted by a recovery of commodity prices.

2.1.1.2   *Russia: A rent economy suffering from the 'Dutch disease'*

Economically, Russia has a relatively low GDP, which represents only 2 per cent of the global GDP. While its standard of living per capita remains incomparably higher than in the other BRIC countries (see Table 2.1), it is nevertheless more vulnerable. As well as the fact that it has been hit badly by the world recession, Russia today also suffers from deep-seated weaknesses: a lack of diversification in exports, huge population and health problems, and an urgent need for modernization. The country remains a rent economy, suffering from the 'Dutch disease' (Mercier-Suissa, 2009). It remains dependent on oil sales (60% of its export earnings) and has been heavily impacted by falling prices on the world market. Between July and December 2008, the decline in oil prices, which fell from 133 dollars to 41 US dollars, impacted on Russian oil revenues. In addition, the decline in global demand for hydrocarbons caused the collapse of the market capitalization of major Russian companies (Gazprom, for example).

The Russian economy has recorded high growth rates between 1999 and 2008, whereas in 2009, GDP fell by 8.7 per cent. In 2008, it still had a growth rate of 5.6 per cent. We have to look back to 1994, when GDP plunged by 12.7 per cent, to find another such decline. While the Russian budget generated a surplus each year since 2001, in 2009 the country ran a 6.3 per cent GDP deficit (Mankoff, 2010). The need for additional stimulus measures in the context of lower tax revenues from the energy industry is likely to widen the budget deficit. The Russian economy has also suffered a credit contraction, related to shrinking cash reserves, which has forced many companies into bankruptcy. All sectors were affected (construction, hotels, manufacturing, and so on) because many companies had based their development on credit. During the summer of 2008 foreign investors started to withdraw their assets when the government threatened companies suspected of tax arrears. Capital flight accelerated in August after the invasion of Georgia by Russia. In September 2008, stock markets and real estate speculative bubbles burst, foreign capital fled the country, local banks experienced cash shortages, and the announcement of amounts owed by Russian companies to foreign banks (437 billion US dollars) caused increased panic. By the end of 2008, nearly 130 billion US dollars had left the country, so the government had to take action. To bail out companies and banks and stabilize the Russian rouble, it used international reserves, which fell from 597 billion US dollars in August 2008 to 386 billion US dollars in February 2009. Then in early 2009, the government lowered interest rates and attempted to limit the budget deficit, but the lack of long-term financing explains the low rate of investment and the slow progress in the key area of industrial diversification. Russian authorities recognized that the country needs to diversify its economy, but with the gradual rise in oil prices that began in March 2009, only limited efforts could be made. The new price increase held out the prospect of improving current accounts. International reserves reached 412 billion US dollars in early July 2009.

In the third quarter of 2009 the country rose out of recession, the peak of the crisis was over and the decline in interest rates in Western countries was conducive to Russia's economic recovery. However, several structural weaknesses hindered this recovery. The crisis had more severely affected highly industrialized regions such as the Urals or 'mono cities' (460 *monogoroda*) which were created during the Soviet period around a single company which, in many cases, was no longer competitive. The government had chosen to support these basically uncompetitive companies to avoid social unrest, thus delaying necessary reforms; for example, the car manufacturer AvtoVAZ (*Volzhsky Avtomobilny Zavod*, Volga automobile plant) and the Rusal aluminium conglomerate in Pikalevo. The other problematic area is the banking sector, undermined by doubtful and uncollectible debts, in particular from the heavily indebted private sector. Thus the financial capacities of Russian banks are limited, and the confidence the Russian population seems to have in their country's economy is low. The Russian oligarchs invest heavily outside the country and the birth rate declines from year to year. All these factors indicate that the economic crisis in Russia is not likely to end, unlike in other emerging economies.

2.1.1.3 India: An unequal domestic growth driven in part by FDI in the tertiary industry

Before the crisis, India's gross saving rate reached 36 per cent of GDP. In 2008 the opening ratio to GDP was the same as China's in 2003. India is dependent on foreign supplies of raw material, in particular energy supplies, importing 75 per cent of its raw material needs. It mainly exports services (computer services being 16% of total exports), and the pharmaceuticals that many foreign companies produce locally. The private sector is dependent on foreign capital. India has also specialized in labour-intensive industries (jewellery, textiles, and so on). Between 2004 and 2008 the country received FDI of 50 billion US dollars, and it entered the crisis late. The annual rate of growth was still 7.6 per cent until the end of December 2008. The economic elite had confidence in India's performance and prospects, but their members agreed that reforms were needed in the following areas: infrastructure, agriculture, labour regulation, banking, energy, education and retail trade. In the wake of the financial crisis, a series of stimulus measures (public investment, lower taxes) were taken. With 300 million Indians living below the poverty line, the government decided to increase its expenditure in the social sector. The infrastructure sector received public investment of almost 28 billion US dollars. Another priority was to support agricultural production. Taxes on household incomes were cut to boost consumption. From the second quarter of 2009 these measures took effect, the economy recovered and, in early 2010, India seemed to regain the prosperity of the years prior to 2008. However, the stimulus measures had a cost. The national budget deficit increased from 2.6 per cent of GDP in 2007–8, to an interim rate of 5.9 per cent in 2009. The budget for the 2010–11 fiscal year (starting 1 April 2010) targeted the reduction of public deficits. The method used gives priority to increase in budget revenues over cuts in public expenditure.

2.1.1.4   China: An outward-oriented growth led by exports and investments

In 2010, China was the largest creditor worldwide, with over 2400 billion US dollars of foreign exchange reserves, and accounted for 8 per cent of the global GDP. During the last 30 years, China's growth has been significant, reaching 5–10 per cent annually. The introduction of competition and the opening of Western markets to Chinese goods accounted largely for this rapid economic takeoff. While until 2007, US domestic demand accounted for nearly one fifth of global growth, China's growth was based on exports and investments: from 2000 to 2007, public consumption as a percentage of GDP fell from 45 per cent to 35 per cent, that is to say to half the US ratio. The development model of the Chinese economy is based on outward-oriented growth led by exports (boosted by fixed exchange rate policies), investments and, to a lesser extent, by domestic consumption.

At the end of spring 2008, the Chinese government established a competitiveness and recovery policy. It restored the fixed link between the US dollar and the Chinese yuan, stopping the slight move towards revaluation initiated between 2005 and 2008, and increasing the competitive advantage of companies producing in China. In November 2008, the authorities announced a support plan of 4000 billion yuan (about 470 billion Euros). To enable recovery, a large investment programme was launched, particularly in the infrastructure sector, and banks granted more credit for exports, companies, housing, cars, and so on.

While credit flows doubled between 2008 and 2009, the acceleration at the beginning of 2010 doubled them again. The credit bubble and the gradual recovery in world trade enabled China to have a growth rate of over 9 per cent. However, there is a significant reset risk as bad loans are weighing on the solvency of banks, and causing insolvencies and personal bankruptcies.

Finally, the impact of the crisis has damaged public finances. While it is commonly reported that the Chinese public debt does not exceed 20 per cent of GDP, which is one of the lowest debt levels for a large country, this figure might be misleading. It does not take into account the situation of local governments that bear the brunt of the recovery plan. The central government collects 53 per cent taxes and is responsible for only 20 per cent of public expenditure, the rest being borne by the provinces. Regional authorities are not allowed to issue bonds and are financed through local public enterprises which borrow from banks on their own account. So if the expenditures of provinces are included, Chinese public debt reaches 40 per cent of the country's GDP. In addition, the Chinese banking system is weakened by the large number of bad loans.

2.1.2 Main areas of convergence within BRIC countries

BRIC countries were affected by the crisis later than mature economies. The crisis mainly spread by international trade channels, in particular due to the collapse of goods and services trade in Asia, which reduced national income. But like Brazil, this region had large currency reserves and relatively developed local funding markets. Asian and Latin American banks have been spared compared with European banks because they were well capitalized and made use of local capital markets (Banque de France, 2010). In emerging markets, governments took supportive measures to limit the negative impact of deleveraging and risk aversion; they have primarily sought to stimulate consumption and enhance investment in priority sectors.

2.1.2.1 *Governments seek to increase domestic consumption*

Growth patterns of BRIC countries are showing more resilience to the crisis at the time of writing, thanks to the development of domestic demand in these countries (except Russia), although domestic consumption is lower than forecast, more particularly in China. Following recovery plans, the growth patterns of these economies, mainly based on exports of manufactured goods for China, services for India or raw materials for Russia and Brazil, have changed at least for three of them. Domestic demand benefits from stimulus package measures in each country and drives growth. But the effect on consumption varies from one country to another. Owing to the consolidation of public finances, Brazil and Russia have benefited from lower interest rates. With the decrease of borrowing costs, households are taking on more debts, especially in Brazil. This development is advantageous for banks, real estate and consumption. In Russia, the rent economy is still very dependent on hydrocarbons, and consumption recovery remains weak. Access to credit is limited, partly due to Russia's underdeveloped banking system. Brazil, however, despite being a major exporter of raw materials, saw the emergence of a middle class, Class C, eager to consume, although the growth of the economy is largely based on the development of domestic consumption in classes A, B and C (*L'Expansion*, 2010).

In China, until the 2008 economic crisis, low access to credit for the population, especially in rural areas, accounted for the weak consumption and hence the high level of exports. China's household savings rate is one of the highest in the world, with around 30 per cent of income. It should be emphasized that these high saving rates often result from the need for households to have short-term precautionary savings because of poorly developed health insurance, and long-term savings to compensate for low pensions. But the lack of social protection is nothing new and cannot account solely for the decline in consumption between 2000 and 2007. The explanation may be found in changes to credit access during this period. During the 1980s and the early 1990s, taking out a loan was common. Some form of credit, formal or informal, was used by 70 per cent of families. Then, over the period 1995–2002, the percentage dropped almost by half (*Les Echos*, 2010). Regarding formal banking credits, the decline may have been the result of the new credit policy of public banks aiming to support investments of large state enterprises. Thus, to boost domestic consumption, it would only be necessary to develop household credit. Following the recovery plan, public banks facing bad loans, did not develop personal credit. The recovery resulted from investment, including infrastructure financing, rather than from consumption. Thus, even though emerging markets account for half of the world's automobile demand (a quarter for China), China became the world's largest automotive market in 2009, before the US. The social security system is still nascent and households must finance their own retirement pensions and health insurance, which explains why saving rates are still high. Finally, the crisis reduced efforts to cut company subsidies or create a labour law, another reason for the necessity of precautionary savings.

2.1.2.2   Investment opportunities according to policies of public investment and support for priority sectors

Following deleverage of banks and indebtedness of states, support plans were established in all BRIC countries to help specific industrial sectors (car, energy, the environment, and so on) and public investments were made in infrastructure and telecommunication. In India, the government planned to sell part of its shares in public companies, and to launch a public tender for the allocation of third generation (3G) phone licences. In Brazil, the lack of infrastructure hindered the development of some industries; for example, in the region of Minas Gerais, many mines did not open because the roads were congested and there were not enough railways. This should provide a host of development opportunities for foreign companies. In China, the government implemented support programmes with lower taxes for the automotive industry. Chinese consumers and local authorities which renewed their fleet of official cars, bought 13.5 million cars. In rural areas, another 730 million US dollar subsidy encouraged farmers to trade their polluting cars for mini-vans, and this contributed to the increase in domestic sales. At the beginning of the millennium, when energy consumption soared in China, the government launched several initiatives to limit this trend. For example, to improve the energy efficiency of industrial small- and medium-sized enterprises (SMEs) and cities, China implemented new energy management solutions in buildings, infrastructure and transports. Technological cooperation programmes with Western companies developed in the construction industry. In Russia, nearly half of subsidies went to support industries hit by the crisis, such as the automotive industry, the metal industry, the banking sector and the defence industry. But Russia's main industrial sectors are composed of private companies connected to the political environment and huge corrupt state conglomerates. The model is based on the connection between political and economic elites which take advantage of the situation. Yet, the government recognized the dependence of Russia on natural resources, and called for a dismantling of state corporations, and a focus on the development of high-tech industries. Furthermore, the private sector accounts for 65 per cent of Russia's GDP, while the contribution of state corporations is lower. There are few state companies which are profitable, and most of them are indebted, partly owing to loans taken out abroad to finance currency speculation, or to buy rival companies before foreign MNCs can do so. The private sector offers many opportunities for cooperation with foreign MNCs. Therefore, there are real opportunities for investments in these four countries for Western and French MNCs in the short term and in line with industrial priorities.

2.2 Growth opportunities for MNCs thanks to recovery plans set up by BRIC governments

The financial and economic crisis caused a decrease in FDI flows in the BRICs, with MNCs reducing operating costs and abandoning non-core activities as part of a whole-industry restructuring. However, they have recognized important growth opportunities in BRIC countries; for example in the luxury and automotive industries where French MNCs play an important role.

2.2.1 Shift of FDI flows towards emerging countries

In developed countries affected by the financial crisis, FDI flows declined in 2008, whereas they continued to increase in developing countries and transition economies. Then, 2009 saw a general decline in all countries. In 2008 emerging countries were much more resilient to the crisis, since their financial systems were less embedded in the US and European banking systems. Even in BRIC countries, FDI increased between 2007 and 2008 (see Table 2.3). In Russia and in Brazil, economic growth continued, thanks to higher primary commodity prices. FDI fell only in the first quarter of 2009 as a result of the global crisis. In China, rates dropped by 20.6 per cent on a full year basis in the first quarter of 2009. Over the same period in 2008, they rose by over 61 per cent. A similar trend can be observed in Russia (UNCTAD, 2009). However, available statistics show that FDI in emerging countries recovered more rapidly than those in mature markets (UNCTAD, 2010).

In 2009, MNCs deferred their foreign investment plans. By contrast, medium-term prospects improved and MNCs started increasing their investments in 2010, especially in BRIC countries (UNCTAD, 2009, 2010). Michalet (1979) introduced a typology of MNCs, including primary

Table 2.3 FDI in BRIC countries (in billion US$)

Countries	2007	2008	2009
China	138.4	147.7	95
Russia	55.1	75.5	38.7
Brazil	34.6	45.1	25.9
India	25.1	40.4	34.6

Source: IMF (2009) and UNCTAD (2009, 2010).

companies, companies with commercial strategies, global companies and financial companies, and described the role of foreign subsidiaries. There were also supply, production and sales subsidiaries (Mercier-Suissa and Bouveret-Rivat, 2007). This typology both identifies the major internationalization strategies of MNCs and highlights the current determinants of internationalization strategies in BRIC countries:

- primary MNCs wishing to ensure an adequate supply of raw materials
- MNCs with commercial strategies which seek new opportunities and establish themselves in order to penetrate new markets
- MNCs with productive strategies which produce more cheaply by lowering their costs globally
- integrated MNCs with geographically dispersed value chains.

(Buckley and Ghauri, 2004; Colovic and Mayrhofer, 2011)
(see Chapter 1)

One reason for internationalization is to control the production or distribution of scarce resources. The goal of primary MNCs is to ensure, at a low cost, the supply of raw material that the home country is lacking. In addition, in some sectors, such as mining, the crisis did not really slow down the move towards concentration and thus FDI. Three factors may explain this trend:

- Falling stock markets.
- Commodity price recovery.
- China's need for raw material.

Falling stock markets have put large companies within the reach of buyers. For example, the market capitalization of the British company Rio Tinto, a world leader in finding, mining and processing mineral resources, fell from 159 billion US dollars in December 2007, to 40 billion US dollars in February 2009 at the peak of the economic turndown. Thus, Rio Tinto announced a partnership with the Anglo-Australian mining group BHP (Broken Hill Proprietary) Billiton (Cyclope, 2009). The rise in commodity prices has brought back to commodity futures markets investors who sought to diversify their holdings beyond real estate, stock exchange and financial sectors. Finally, the stimulus plan in China has allowed Chinese importers to rebuild commodity stocks at low prices, thus allowing Chinese investors to enter the capital of mining companies.

MNCs with productive strategies target areas where labour conditions are favourable. At this stage, it does not matter if the local market enjoys high demand: the company re-imports its relocated production to sell on markets where demand is buoyant. The aim is to reduce production costs, mainly labour and social costs, thanks to labour market flexibility. It is worth mentioning that to improve their price competitiveness, MNCs may also have to invest in countries which use some form of price dumping. Indeed, a country with a weak currency compared with the currency of the home country increases its attractiveness for at least two reasons: first, the company that relocates its business is interested in paying its employees in local currency; and second, the export price of components or final products from relocated units becomes automatically more competitive. Finally, FDI which take the form of takeovers of existing companies, or creation of assets in the host country in the local currency, are relatively cheap. This is the case of China, which increasingly attracts European companies, thanks to its low labour cost policy and the weak yuan.

MNCs with commercial strategies seek to maintain their sales, or enter a new market previously subject to protectionist tariffs such as customs, quotas, or technical, sanitary, veterinary or environmental standards. Demand is the decisive factor for FDI. Thus, areas less sensitive to business cycles, and operating in markets where demand is stable (agro-industry or services, for example), and those with long-term growth prospects (e.g., pharmaceuticals or water) also benefit from recovery of FDI. In Brazil, the oil company Petrobras awarded contracts for the construction of plants to treat and recycle water from its new oil rigs, to French companies; for example, Veolia and Suez. With the resumption of growth in BRIC countries, the exit of public government funds from ailing industries will possibly trigger a new wave of mergers and acquisitions favourable to foreign investors. For example, at the end of 2009, Vivendi acquired Brazilian Global Village Telecom (GVT) for 2.8 billion US dollars. The telecommunication operator and Internet access provider has become the bridgehead of the French company in Latin America. Finally, when companies trust institutions, they seize opportunities available to them, insofar as the areas in which they operate receive aid and support from governments. This is the case, for example, of the Chinese automotive industry. In Brazil, the government social housing programme, *Minha case, minha vida* ('my home, my life'), benefits the French company Nexans, the number one cable business in Brazil, and also Saint Gobain's windows and pipe works. In BRIC countries, both types of strategies – production strategy (search for lower production costs) and commercial strategy (search for market opportunities) – are often complementary, and emerging economies can offset the weakness of more mature markets. MNCs seek to reduce uncertainty and market risks so that they can plan their production and sales. To reduce the number of uncontrolled variables, they may integrate production and commercial activities (vertical integration) and/or bridge the gap between production and sales cycles due to differing national circumstances, by diversifying their assets geographically. Therefore, the crisis imposes new constraints on companies, but also provides new opportunities. This will be illustrated in the following discussion about luxury goods and the automotive industry.

2.2.2   FDI in the luxury goods industry

Following the financial and economic crisis, the luxury goods industry seems to have recovered, partly thanks to the growing Chinese demand. In 2009 the total sales in the luxury goods industry decreased by 7.2 per cent in Europe and by 13.5 per cent in the US. In Asia, the decline reached 8.2 per cent in Japan, against a 10 per cent growth rate in China. LVMH (Louis Vuitton Moët Hennessy), the world leader in the luxury goods industry, was very cautious concerning the year 2010 and so reduced its costs. The company preferred to renovate its stores rather than open new ones. China accounts for 6 per cent of the group's total sales. For the Swiss Richmond group, number two in the luxury goods industry, China and Hong Kong have been the main new sources of growth, with a 25 per cent sales increase. The Italian Gucci Group (42% of its capital is owned by the French PPR group – Pinault-Printemps-Redoute) continued to invest in emerging markets. In 2004, the group had only four stores in China, but had 30 by 2009; its sales in China increased by 46.3 per cent in 2009. In 2010, 60 per cent of the group's investments were made in the Asia-Pacific region, the company's second largest market after Europe. The company clearly focuses on emerging countries, which represent almost one third of its sales (32.8% in 2009). China, Latin America with Brazil and, to a lesser extent, Eastern Europe, offset the weakness of more mature markets.

Thus, in time, China is likely to overtake mature markets, to establish itself as the first global luxury goods market. The number of Chinese millionaires is rapidly increasing. These consumers are relatively young, aged between 25 and 35 years. The appeal of luxury goods such as cars, clothing, leather goods, chocolate, wine, spirits, cosmetics and perfume is becoming evident. These new consumers are very focused on family and children. They save a lot. Purchasing luxury goods is a way of showing their wealth, but also that they care for their families. Finally, well-off households, which earn more than 25,000 Euros per year, were estimated at 1.6 million in 2008, and are expected to reach 4 million in 2015. Such figures allow forward-looking growth estimates in this emerging market. However, the downside of this explosion in luxury goods sales is a very strong increase in counterfeit production. Thus Western MNCs may break with the principle of home production, with design and production being done locally. In 2004 L'Oreal bought Yue Sai, a brand of luxury skincare and make-up, and this trend is likely to continue. In 2010 Hermès created Shang Xia, its own brand of Chinese furniture, art objects and clothing. Sales outlets were opened in China as well as in Paris, to provide international recognition to the brand. This strategy of circumvention associates local producers, managers, creators and employees in a cultural, legal and political fight against counterfeiters. The daughter of a leading Chinese architect, Jiang Qiong Er, is the designer of the Shang Xia brand. She holds a minority stake in the company and is thought to use her influence to protect the trademark. It is a questionable response to the French employment situation, but it preserves the brand and a large part of its added value. When taking advantage of recent opportunities in the Chinese luxury goods market, MNCs are forced to adapt their business model to specific constraints.

2.2.3   FDI in the automotive industry

Another sector that offers important growth opportunities is the automotive industry. Like governments of mature economies, the Chinese government supported the automotive industry with soft loans to increase car purchases by both private households and institutions and to renew fleets of official vehicles. The end of these temporary measures will not prevent the sector from growing in the coming years, as car manufacturers are investing in these new markets.

In China, vehicle sales in 2009 increased by 45 per cent over the previous year, boosted by support programmes of the State. With 13.6 million vehicles sold, the country became the world's largest automotive market, before the US. This spectacular increase concerned all car manufacturers, and particularly the German Volkswagen group, which kept its lead position in the Chinese market before General Motors. In 2009, the Volkswagen group sold 1.4 million vehicles in China, which represented a yearly increase of 36.7 per cent. Chinese manufacturers specializing in cheap cars have also experienced a sharp increase of sales. Sales growth is expected to continue, enabling China to maintain its position as the largest world market before the US.

China has only 35 cars per 1000 inhabitants compared with 850 in the US. The development potential is huge, as well as the environmental and mobility challenges generated by this development. To meet these challenges, the French PSA Peugeot Citroën group plans to develop models using new technologies; for example, hybrid cars and electric vehicles. In 2008, the company opened a research and development centre in Shanghai to develop models for the local market. The current economic environment of emerging countries provides incentives to invest locally, or to relocate to meet the demand of the local market. This is the case for MNCs with commercial and productive strategies, which maintain their global leadership by entering Asian, South American and Russian markets. Car manufacturers will have to renew their offer with products specifically dedicated to these markets, and it is for this purpose that PSA Peugeot Citroën intends to form new partnerships. It is worth noting that the specific demands of foreign markets may be considered as cultural barriers. The way to overcome these entry barriers has been widely studied in the marketing field, which explains potential benefits of product adaptation to local consumer behaviour. This is why so many FDI are targeting BRIC countries. PSA Peugeot Citroën expects the recovery of the still-damaged Russian market and is considering entering the Indian market, where the company has already established links with the car manufacturer Tata Motors. The adaptation of production to local demand in BRIC countries impacts the worldwide organization of the value chain of MNCs, especially the design of production platforms.

The automotive industry illustrates the adaptation efforts that companies must make in order to develop in emerging markets, in which new customers emerge, competition increases and the decision-making process is multi-polar. The advantage of operating in these markets is that they represent reference markets for other emerging countries. That is why MNCs study partnership opportunities with companies in emerging countries, either to enter these markets or to export to other markets.

2.3 Conclusion

Beyond the differences that emerge from the analysis of each country's model of economic development, the four BRIC markets have established themselves on the global stage. Like traditional industrialized countries, they have been affected by the financial crisis and its effects on the funding of their development process.

The growth model of these economies, mainly based on exports of manufactured goods or raw materials, has changed for three of them. Local demand, benefiting from recovery plans implemented in each country, has driven growth. Only Russia remains dependent on hydrocarbon sales, particularly on natural gas. It is therefore in this area that foreign companies could cooperate to diversify Russian operations, in exchange for the energy imported. Thus, BRIC countries are primarily involved in specific national strategies with often diverging economic paths and political interests. The 2008 economic and financial crisis hit them all, but unlike traditional industrialized countries, they regained their growth rate in 2009, with the exception of Russia. The financial and economic crisis both tested the resilience of these economies and strengthened their attractiveness for foreign MNCs. Well beyond exceptional opportunities such as, for example, in China, the Shanghai World Expo (2010), and in Brazil, the World Soccer Cup (2014) and the Olympic Games (2016), these countries all have a very high potential for the development of their local market, including the areas of transport and communication infrastructure, water, energy, equipment and consumer goods. They remain promising clients for foreign MNCs who know how to benefit from this new environment.

References

Banque de France (2010) 'De la crise financière à la crise économique', *Documents et Débats*, 3, 35.

Buckley, P. J. and Ghauri, P. (2004) 'The Globalisation, Economic Geography and the Strategy of Multinational Enterprises', *Journal of International Business Studies*, 35 (2), 81–98.

Colovic, A. and Mayrhofer, U. (2011) 'Optimising the Location of R&D and Production Activities: Trends in the Automotive Industry', *European Planning Studies*, 19 (8), 1481–98.

Cyclope (2009) *Les marchés mondiaux: vertiges et déboires* (Paris: Economica).

IMF (2009) *Yearbook* (Washington: International Monetary Fund).

Le Monde (2010) 'Brésil, un géant s'impose', 11 September.

Les Echos (2010) 'Crédit à la consommation et déséquilibre entre l'Amérique et la Chine', 11 January.

L'Expansion (2010) 'Le Brésil, l'Eldorado français', 751, 38–63.

Mankoff, J. (2010) *Quelle sortie de crise pour la Russie?* (Paris: Institut Français des Relations Internationales).

Mercier-Suissa, C. (2009) 'Restauration de l'Etat de Droit ou captation de la rente pétrolière en Russie', *Revue d'études et de critique sociale*, 25, 69–85.

Mercier-Suissa, C. and Bouveret-Rivat, C. (2007) *L'essentiel des stratégies d'internationalisation des enterprises* (Paris: Gualino, Carré Rouges).

Michalet, C.-A. (1979) 'Etats, nations, firmes multinationales et capitalisme mondial', *Sociologie et sociétés*, 11 (2), 39–58.

UNCTAD (2009) *World Investment Report 2009* (New York/Geneva: United Nations Conference on Trade and Development).

UNCTAD (2010) *World Investment Report 2010* (New York/Geneva: United Nations Conference on Trade and Development).

3
Internationalization Strategies of MNCs in the Wine Industry

Catherine Pivot

Multinational companies (MNCs) are among the key players in the global economy. Their emergence from a wide range of diversified national production systems results from the globalization process and the proliferation of different forms of competition. One of their strengths is their capacity to produce virtually identical products worldwide, with production tools and methods that allow them to achieve economies of scale and therefore higher profits.

The food industry is also affected by the general process of globalization, in particular because of the important growth of food demand in many emerging countries. Within this industry the beverage sector has developed, thanks to the emergence of companies which significantly increased their critical market size and entered the race for internationalization. However, the profitability in this sector varies: while the beer and spirits industry is profitable at the global level, the wine sector is much less profitable due to chronic over-production and a structural decline of consumption in traditional consumer countries (France, Italy, Spain) (Xerfi, 2008). Two major events marked a turning point in this sector: first, a strong reorganization of distribution structures worldwide which placed a predominant emphasis on the marketing of beverages and second, the integration of wine activities in the restructuring process of the beverage industry.

Until the 1980s, the wine sector had not been affected by the global restructuring of the world's beverage industry. France and Italy were still the undisputed world leaders in the wine sector. But in the last 30 years, the importance of the different 'worlds of wine' has considerably evolved, mostly at the expense of the 'old world of wine'. Today, although a major part of the wine supply still comes from traditional wine producing countries, vineyards are rapidly expanding in new parts of the world that hitherto did not produce wine (in China and Brazil for example), and the increase in consumption has shifted towards countries that did not previously produce much wine and where consumers were hardly wine connoisseurs (see Table 3.1).

It was not until the 2000s that wine became the subject of globalization, with two notable exceptions: champagne, a product which was included at an early stage in the restructuring process of global firms in the beverage sector; and premium wines ('vintages') that have long enjoyed a high demand by connoisseurs worldwide.

The gradual internationalization of the wine industry is due to the fact that the supply and demand which structure the wine industry are still strongly determined by the geographic origin and specificities of the product (at the national or even regional level, or 'terroir'). However, following the chronic surplus of supply in traditional producer countries, the internationalization of activities has become a necessity, and therefore a strategic goal for many actors in this sector.

The aim of this chapter is twofold: to explain the determinants of the internationalization of companies in the wine industry and to outline the characteristics of MNCs which are newly emerging in this sector. The first section of the chapter deals with the specificities of production and marketing structures of the wine industry worldwide.

Table 3.1 The worlds of wine and their development trends, 1980–2010

	Size of vineyards		Production volume		Consumption volume	
	1980–4	2010	1980–4	2010	1980–4	2010
Old world of wine: France, Italy, Spain, Portugal, Germany	45.50%	40.39%	58.00%	52.96%	53.30%	35.86%
Southern hemisphere: Argentina, Australia, Chile, New Zealand, South Africa	6.30%	10.14%	12.40%	18.25%	11.90%	9.53%
United States	3.10%	5.27%	5.20%	7.53%	7.20%	11.47%
Rest of the world	45.10%	30.43%	34.40%	21.26%	27.60%	43.14%
World total	100% 9912 Mha*	100% 7550 Mha	100% 344 Mhl**	100% 260 Mhl	100% 260 MhL	100% 236 Mhl

Note: * Mha = millions of hectares, ** Mhl = millions of hectolitres.
Source: Statistics provided by the International Organization of Vine and Wine (OIV) (2010).

The second section provides an analysis of the determinants concerning the internationalization of companies in this sector. Finally, the chapter highlights the international expansion of wine industry leaders.

3.1 A fragmented global production of wine but concentrated marketing

The diversity of grapes grown throughout the world makes it a non-standard raw material with respect to winemaking, and is further enhanced by production technologies which tend to strengthen this diversity.

Historically, the world of wine has been anchored in the world of agriculture. Thus the production structures of raw material (grapes) still strongly influence the production of the final product (wine). However, companies engaged in wine marketing distance themselves more and more from the upstream sector of the wine industry, in order to meet the expectations of consumers and to streamline their resources.

3.1.1 The structure of world wine production

All the levels of the food economy have been affected by the concentration of companies which has been taking place for roughly a century. This has led to an oligopolistic situation with 'fringes' dominated by very powerful MNCs (Nestlé, Unilever, Coca-Cola, Danone, and so on) (Rastoin, 2008).

Wine production professionals have traditionally structured the industry around the production of grapes through numerous vineyards having very heterogeneous structures and winemaking processes that are still very fragmented. This results in a variety of products, sometimes very 'ambitious' ones and seldom identified by a trademark. The wine industry therefore differs from other food industries, and even from the beverage industry, due to the limitations (natural or not) imposed by the soil and the grapes. Indeed, some wines are produced in areas and under constraints that lead to a relative scarcity and hence to an added value, thanks to the fact that they are unique, non-reproducible and available in limited quantity (Zalan, 2005).

Consequently, the world production of wine is generally very fragmented, with millions of vineyards in wine producing countries despite the move towards concentration which has started since the 1990s (e.g., 43,000 vineyards in France, 1.3 million in the European Union, 25,000 in Argentina). This fragmentation of production on the global scale explains the establishment of wine distribution structures through wine cooperatives, or trading structures which aim to gather raw material (grapes) and/or wine in bulk. In the wine industry, the term 'multinational companies' therefore stands for producing and marketing companies (that may own vineyards) rather than companies that transform grapes into wine.

3.1.2 Uneven concentration of marketing structures

There is a clear differentiation between the 'new world' and the 'old world' of wine: namely, that a single company often controls at least one quarter of the wine marketing in countries of the new world of wine, whereas a large number of companies are still involved in the marketing of wine in countries of the old world. Portugal is a special case insofar as port wine has long been a strongly internationalized product, traded on international markets.

It is noteworthy that, in some countries, there is a monopoly both on the distribution and the import of wine and alcoholic beverages. It is worth mentioning the existence of alcohol commissions in every province and territory of Canada (apart from Alberta) which monopolize the import and the distribution of wine and spirits; the state monopoly on alcohol sales in Sweden, in Finland or in Norway; the project to return to state monopoly in Russia; the Chinese National Cereals, Oils and Foodstuffs Import and Export Corporation (a state-owned company that holds a monopoly as wholesaler and distributor of alcoholic beverages).

3.1.3 World leaders of wine distribution

In ten years, the wine industry landscape has changed dramatically: some companies, such as Allied Domecq, Seagram's and Southcorp have virtually disappeared, while others, including Foster's and Pernod-Ricard, have improved their performance. If we compare the turnover of the world's top marketing wine company in 2008 (Constellation Brands: 5.2 billion US dollars) with that of the world's top multinational company in the same year (Wal-Mart: 378.4 billion US dollars), it appears that the world's wine leaders are comparatively of a 'small size'. Their market shares are still limited: the three top companies have control over only 10 per cent of the world's market. Companies from the new world have come out at the top of the rankings in the past few years. Only one firm from the old world seems to be able to compete: Pernod-Ricard (see Table 3.2).

Therefore, competition on the world market takes place between companies of all sizes in a fierce context, creating new 'winners and

Table 3.2   The world's wine leaders (2008)

	Groups	Country	Total sales million US$	Wine sales million US$	Ratio of wine sales/ total sales	Share of the world's wine market
1	Constellation Brands	USA	5216	2756	52.8%	3.7%
2	E & J Gallo	USA	2700	2700	100%	3.6%
3	Forster's Group	Australia	3595	1853	51.5%	2.5%
4	Louis Vuitton Moët Hennessy (LVMH)	France	20,208	1692	8.4%	2.3%
5	Groupe Castel	France	2640	1188	45.0%	1.6%
6	Pernod Ricard	France	8506	1070	12.6%	1.4%
7	The Wine Group	USA	735	735	100%	1.0%
8	Grands Chais de France	France	726	726	100%	1.0%
9	Freixenet	Spain	718	718	100%	1.0%
10	Oetker Gruppe (Henkell & Söhnlein)	Germany	1960	675	34.4%	0.9%
11	Diageo	United Kingdom	19,429	500	2.6%	0.7%
12	Casella Wines	Australia	486	486	100%	0.6%
13	Kendall Jackson Wine Estates	USA	440	440	100%	0.6%
14	Boizel Chanoine Champagne	France	422	422	100%	0.6%
15	Concha y Toro	Chile	405	405	100%	0.5%

Source: Adapted from Cuelho (2008).

losers'. As most of the current leaders were not topping the ranking only five years ago, the risk of non consumer-friendly agreements between companies is also virtually absent, since consumers can choose at all times from a wide range of products made by a large number of companies.

3.1.3.1   *Some major beverage holding companies*

Historically, the beverage industry's world leaders dealing in wine have two origins: France (Pernod-Ricard and Louis Vuitton Moët Hennessy) and the UK (Diageo, Allied Domecq). From the start, their strategies were clearly based on controlling premium wines and brands that enjoy a strong reputation throughout the world. For example, the Jacobs

Creek brand is held by Pernod-Ricard and made from Australian wines; another case in point is the Barton and Guestier brand which belongs to the Diageo holding and allows this company to export the largest volume of Bordeaux wine in the world (Green et al., 2003).

For these companies, wine is one of many assets; they follow a product portfolio logic by acquiring brands. The first stages of the wine production industry are of little importance to them. Instead, they develop strong marketing strategies and partnerships with distribution networks.

3.1.3.2   The growth of national companies specialised in wine

These companies usually include the wine industry as a whole, from production to sales. Most of them have forged their reputation on the market thanks to their starting position, which favoured economies of scale, and their efficient marketing strategy focusing on brands (premium wine segment, see Table 3.8).

Anglo-Saxon companies (Constellation, United States; E & J Gallo, United States; Foster's, Australia) have clearly gone for products that are varied, produced in wineries and belonging to the premium category, in order to cater for the Anglo-Saxon markets (Oceania, US, UK). Two powerful operational means are used: on the one hand, wine storehouses are bought in order to increase companies' commercial capacity and, on the other hand, partnerships with other Anglo-Saxon producers are established, in order to create distribution networks to help penetrate foreign markets (Green et al., 2003).

Thanks to their historical ties with national producers, European companies (Castel Frères, Grands Chais de France, Freixenet; and also Celliers des Dauphins in France, Torres – Osborne – Codorniu in Spain, Gruppo Italiano Vini – GIV – Caviro in Italy) have developed a diversified range of wines (from basic to super premium). They are now forced to adopt volume-based strategies in order to develop collective brands (such as 'vins de France' and 'vins d'Italie'). In Catalonia in Spain, companies have a competitive advantage insofar as they operate on specific markets where they can potentially internationalize their activities. These markets are distinct from Anglo-Saxon markets and those of the new world of wine. Contrary to Italy and France, where many cooperatives control large market shares, Spanish companies are often family-owned businesses that can be bought by MNCs.

The Chilean company Concha y Toro has increasingly diversified its markets after having acquired important market shares in the US; it has been able to develop on the European market.

3.1.3.3 Different business strategies

Two different business strategy models have therefore been developed in the past years: the core activity based strategy (specialization strategy) and the diversification strategy based on activities that are linked to each other (concentric diversification strategy) or on activities that are not linked to each other (conglomerate diversification strategy) (see Table 3.3).

The Castel group (concentric diversification strategy) is thus organized around three major areas: water, wine and breweries. It operates in the markets of bottled water through the Neptune holding (Thonon-les-Bains, Vichy, Cristalline, and so on), of breweries in Africa, and of sugar refineries. The company Grands Chais de France (specialization strategy) is focusing on wine making, maturing and bottling wines with two main priorities: the management of wine making processes by controlling each step of the process, from the vine to the glass, from the maturation of the grapes to the storage; and the partnerships with wine cellar owners and producers, in order to control the quality of its products; two logistical units also allow trade to develop across Europe.

So far, the decision of most of world's leading wine companies to diversify activities was motivated by the objective to increase their

Table 3.3 Business strategies developed by leading wine companies (2009)

Groups	Business strategy
Casella Wines	Specialization
Kendall Jackson Specialization	Specialization
Boizel Chanoine Champagne	Specialization
Concha y Toro	Specialization
The Wine Group	Specialization
Grands Chais de France	Specialization
Freixenet	Specialization
Constellation Brands (wine, beer, spirits)	Concentric diversification
E&J Gallo (wine, beer, spirits)	Concentric diversification
Groupe Castel (wine, beer, water)	Concentric diversification
Pernod Ricard (wine, spirits)	Concentric diversification
Forster's Group (wine, beer, cider, spirits)	Concentric diversification
Diageo (wine, beer, cider, spirits)	Concentric diversification
Louis Vuitton Moët Hennessy (LVMH) (perfume, fashion, beverages)	Conglomerate diversification
Oetker Gruppe (Henkell & Sohnlein) (transportation, food, beverages)	Conglomerate diversification

size, in order to have more weight on beverage markets and to spread marketing costs. But the downward wine price pressure throughout the world (given that the profit margins on wine are already far smaller than on other alcoholic beverages) led many diversified companies to revise their growth strategies and to carry out internal restructuring and sale of businesses in order to increase their profitability.

We must also expect the emergence of new actors in the years to come. In particular, Chinese companies will expand on existing markets, such as Changyu, Great Wall (majority shareholder: Saronno, Italy) and Dynastie Fine Wine Group (major shareholder: Remy Cointreau, France). They often benefit from state aid and favourable tax conditions. However, these newcomers represent only one aspect of the international development of many companies in the wine industry.

3.2 Strategic objectives of companies on international markets

The increasing number of companies in the wine industry which have developed internationally over the last few years mainly results from the saturation of national markets that were too small to absorb the entire national production, as well as from the decrease of local demand. Today, the internationalization strategy of companies of the wine industry meets various objectives:

- necessary search for new markets due to the frequent saturation of markets in traditionally producing countries;
- changes in market access conditions and adapting the existing product range to non-connoisseurs;
- reaching a critical size in order to benefit from economies of scale, and to increase the competitiveness of companies at an international level;
- acquiring greater bargaining power vis-à-vis distribution networks.

3.2.1 Necessary international openness

The strategy of international openness relies on the capacity of a company to implement its original activity abroad. The rise of international competition has forced most companies in the industry to shift from being 'ethnocentric' to becoming progressively 'polycentric' (see Chapter 1).

Over the period 1981–2009, the old world of wine (Germany, Spain, France, Italy, Portugal) was compelled to face tough competition on international markets with the new world of wine (Australia,

Argentina, Chile, South Africa, New Zealand and the US). Indeed, the share of global trade controlled by these new producing countries has risen from 1.6 per cent of world exports at the beginning of the period to 29.8 per cent at present. The terms of competition between companies have changed dramatically: the quality/price ratio, the impact of exchange rates and transportation costs have become critical factors in achieving success, alongside tradition and prestige (see Table 3.4).

However, Table 3.5 shows that only three countries really depend on their exports to reach a balance on their national market: Italy, Spain and France. In addition, France is the only country that is also a relatively important importer compared with the other major producing countries. The terms of integration in international trade are therefore very different according to the company's country of origin.

Nowadays, companies of the wine industry established in France and Italy must adapt their products to new markets and increase their competitiveness consistently on international markets in order to survive. By contrast, companies of the new world of wine are ahead in terms of the product specificities: simply with a favourable quality/price ratio on

Table 3.4   Evolution of the share of different groups of exporting countries in international trade in percentage

	Average 1981–5	Average 1986–90	Average 1991–5	Average 1996–2000	Average 2001–5	Average 2010
The old world of wine: the five top exporters of the European Union (Germany, Spain, France, Italy, Portugal)	75.6	78.8	75.5	71.2	65.1	55.9
The new world of wine: Southern hemisphere (Australia, Argentina, Chile, South Africa, New Zealand) and the USA	1.6	3.1	8.0	14.8	23.3	29.8
Central and Eastern European Countries (CEEC) and Maghreb	14.1	10.8	5.1	4.9	3.1	2.4
Other countries	8.7	7.8	11.4	9.0	8.5	11.9

Source: Statistics provided by the International Organization of Vine and Wine (OIV) (2010).

Table 3.5 International trade dominant countries (2010)

Top 10 importing countries			Top 10 exporting countries		
Country	Volume*	In %/world		Volume	In %/world
United Kingdom	12.5	12.9%	Italy	19.2	22.0%
Germany	11.1	11.3%	Spain	14.6	17.0%
United states	9.3	11.0%	France	12.6	14.0%
France	5.8	7.0%	Australia	7.7	8.9%
Russia	4.4	5.3%	Chile	6.9	8.0%
Netherlands	3.3	4.0%	United States	4.0	5.0%
Canada	3.2	3.9%	South Africa	4.0	5.0%
Belgium	3.0	3.7%	Germany	3.6	4.0%
China	2.1	2.3%	Argentina	2.8	3.3%
Denmark	1.9	2.0%	Portugal	2.3	3.0%
Total of the top 10	56.6	63.4%	Total of the top 10	73.7	90.2%

Note: * in millions of hectolitres.
Source: Statistics provided by OIV (2010).

Table 3.6 Chronic imbalance of the world's wine market (millions of hectolitres)

	2000	2005	2010
Production	280.4	279.9	263.0
Consumption	225.6	238.4	238.0
Gap between production and consumption	54.8	41.5	25.0

Source: Statistics provided by OIV (2010).

emerging markets and a consistent range of products – but they must manage to maintain their cost advantage.

Competition between countries and between companies has become stronger given that international markets have been permanently unbalanced for a number of years, and have therefore forced prices down (see Table 3.6).

3.2.1.1 *A major factor: The decline of traditional consumption and the change in demand*

Global consumption increased until the financial crisis of 2008, while the countries with the strongest production and consumption observed

Table 3.7   Trends in wine consumption in the world and in major consuming countries (million hectolitres)

	2000	2005	2010	
World	219.8	239.2	238.0	100%
France	34.5	33.5	29.4	12.3%
USA	21.2	26.8	27.1	11.3%
Italy	30.5	27.0	24.5	10.2%
Germany	19.5	19.8	20.2	8.4%
China		12,6	14.3	6.0%
United Kingdom	9.1	13.1	13.2	5.5%
Spain	13.8	13.8	10.9	4.5%
Argentina		10.9	10.0	4.2%
Russia		10.5	9.7	4.0%
Australia	3.8	4.5	5.3	2.2%

Source: Statistics provided by OIV (2010).

their consumption rate decrease rapidly. At the time of writing, France remains the world's top consumer, with an annual consumption of 29.4 million hectolitres in 2010. However, consumption has decreased steadily both because of the change of the place of wine in French society, and public health policies and anti-alcohol programs. In a year or two, the US will probably become the world leader in terms of wine consumption (see Table 3.7).

In recent years, the growth of world consumption has been driven by the imports of three countries: the US, which has become the second national market since 2007, Germany and the UK. However, on a global scale, the influence of the general economic crisis has reduced the demand in many countries that used to import wine. Currently, consumers tend to buy cheaper products, apart from some countries where the purchasing power and/or changes in consumption favour the purchase of more expensive wine. Hence, world consumption has dropped by roughly 10 million hectolitres in this sector between 2008 and 2010. However, all countries and market segments are not affected in the same way. Both small and large companies in the wine industry have had to adapt to this new situation by changing their product offering in the face of new consumer expectations and preferences.

3.2.1.2   The geographic trend of companies' potential markets

There are three major markets for wine in 2010: continental Europe (France, Italy, Germany, UK and Spain), US and China. Asian markets are the priority targets for wine exporting companies.

- While Asian markets as a whole are expanding drastically, they represent only 7 per cent of the world's wine consumption. But Asian markets are destined to grow quickly, not only for demographic reasons but also thanks to rising living standards. The emergence of the middle class in India and, above all, in China, will increase the demand for national and foreign wine, especially as partnerships between Chinese and foreign companies are developing. In China, wine already represents 2 per cent of alcoholic beverage consumption, but 8 per cent of alcoholic beverage purchase (OIV, 2010).

- The Chinese wine market, with an average growth of 30 per cent over the last five years, is undoubtedly the most attractive (see Box 3.1). China both produces and consumes wine. With a population above 1.3 billion, China represents a very important market. In 2010, the total consumption of wine reached 14 million hectolitres, that is 0.5 litres per capita and 6 per cent of the world's wine consumption. Wine consumption is becoming more widespread in large cities. Indeed, in the last ten years, the national consumption has risen by over 144 per cent and, during the last two years, the annual increase in volume has nearly reached 40 per cent, compared with 4.8 per cent worldwide. Chinese wine consumption relies mainly on national production, which is less valued than imported products, and involves resorting to imports of bulk wine: 94 per cent of the wine consumed is produced locally.

- The Indian market is a more recent development. However, the consumption and production growth should reach 25–30 per cent by 2015. This market is highly protected by Indian authorities because Indian companies are not yet competitive in terms of costs. This prevents foreign companies from entering the Indian market. We can also expect a variety of growth models given that domestic demand, strongly dependent upon wage developments, will be very diverse (Rabobank, 2009).

In practical terms, all companies that export wine must now be able to deal with very diverse commercial regulations and to offer products that are customized to meet a new demand. Joint ventures and local partnerships with local wine traders or distributors have often been set up to achieve these goals. Indeed, the multiplicity of opinions and viewpoints regarding wine and wine markets, as wine carries a huge cultural significance, makes it difficult to implement a brand policy.

Box 3.1   Strategy of the Castel group in China (2010)

NB: The French Castel group, historically established in Bordeaux and in Morocco, initially developed a strategy of progressive integration of production, marketing and distributing resources (e.g., the purchase of Nicolas stores in 1988, and the English company Oddbins in 2001), in order to supply consumers directly, especially for basic and premium wine.

Established in Asia for over ten years, with a subsidiary in China as well as a partnership with the Chinese market leader Changyu, the French market leader is consolidating its network through partnerships with ten importers who supply more than 1500 distributors in China. With 13 million bottles exported to China in 2009, Castel has confirmed the success of its development and expansion in Asia, a venture created in 1999.

Boasting a growth rate of more than 240 per cent in 2009, Castel has now established itself as the leading exporter of bottled wine to China. This is the result of a development strategy based on flagship brands for the Chinese market with wide ranges of products fully meeting the needs of Castel's clients.

Castel now conducts its strategy with collaborators who are home market specialists and are well-established locally, in order to develop privileged relationships with Asian wine professionals, for whom a human relationship remains paramount.

Today in China, the professionalization of the wine sector, with a public appetite for information, not to mention the existence of over 300 million wine drinkers to win over, heralds a bright future. The market appears among one of the ten foremost wine producers and consumers worldwide. Thus, Castel is investing heavily in product research and development, packaging, promotional campaigns, media relations, press campaigns and even television campaigns, the only 2009 French wine TV campaign having been renewed in 2010. These strategies have enabled Castel to gain very high visibility in China.

Source: Castel group press release (2010).

3.2.2   Changes in trading conditions

The global wine market is characterized by a wide range of products which stems not only from the multitude of small and medium sized producers – despite the emergence of large companies in the world of wine – but also from regulations that tend to protect the specificities of a large number of wines, in particular their regional identities (identifying their production origin, in particular in the countries of the European Union). In addition, the world of wine has not really questioned its business model, despite being in an environment where a process of permanent innovation constantly modifies the markets' balance of power (Pivot, 2008).

3.2.2.1 The increasing importance of the 'quality/price ratio' in international markets

There is no global consensus as to which criteria are to be met in order to describe a quality wine. Yet the success of companies from the new world of wine during the 1990s has led to the implementation of a quality grading system based on the combination of 'volume and price' which now determines the logic of trade and the segmentation of the world's wine markets. This segmentation is based on vertical market segmentation according to the 'quality/price' ratio (icon, ultra-premium, super-premium, commercial premium, basic) (see Table 3.8).

As a result, the companies that sell their products abroad must now integrate this practice and develop a system of brand ranges.

Table 3.8 The international segmentation of the world's wine markets according to product access criteria and consumption

Market segment	Icon	Ultra-premium	Super-premium	Commercial Premium	Basic
Price	>50 US$	14–50 US$	7–14 US$	5–7 US$	<5 US$
Consumer type	Connoisseur exceptional wines	Wine amateur expressive wines	Experienced consumer 'trendy wines'	Wine enthusiast Easy access	Consumer focused on price
Competition	Entry to the segment limited by strong barriers	Gradual increase of international competition	Growth driven by brands and 'quality/price ratio'	Explosive, more and more based on brands and prices. Role of marketing innovation.	Price war

3.2.2.2   Difficulties in transferring competitive advantages abroad

Currently, two distinct and opposed conceptions of what is wine quality can be distinguished:

- wines for which nature and *terroir* are the forces driving and determining quality: this conception prevails in traditionally producing countries, where the origin (*terroir*, or production area) constitutes the basis for the vertical segmentation of wines;
- wines for which the technological processes and the market are the key determinants of quality: this is the characteristic and prevailing point of view in the new wine producing countries, where the quality of wine is developed according to the analysis of consumers' expectations and purchasing power, as well as their commercial perception and definition of quality.

Given the globalization of behaviours of social categories that benefit from rapidly increasing living standards in some countries, and the existence of customer preferences associated with different consumer types (expert amateurs, young hipsters, new rich, wine enthusiasts or consumers searching for bargains) on both emerging countries' markets and traditional consumer markets, wine companies selling abroad must put a full range of products in the marketplace to ensure the various needs and preferences of every new market they enter are being met, while simultaneously securing the profitability of each segment of their product range. It is therefore common for a single company that sells abroad to own super premium, commercial premium and premium wines. The Gallo group is a case in point: it has a range of products that is tailored for each type of targeted region and market.

However, multi-beverage groups that have a concentric diversification based on some beverages have recognized expertise and important marketing resources to promote high-end wines. The LVMH group is a significant example of luxury goods management that has enabled it to market high-end champagne (e.g., Dom Pérignon and Krug), as well as prestigious wines (e.g., Château d'Yqem) with great skill. However, the development of high-end products is increasingly difficult, even abroad, due to the great number of intermediaries taking their margin, which tends to disadvantage these types of wines compared with other prestigious alcohol brands in the world.

3.2.3   Changes in access conditions to international markets

For many years, three sources of competitive advantages for companies selling abroad have been highlighted, namely, economies of scale, of scope and of know-how (Kogut, 1985; Ghoshal, 1987).

3.2.3.1   *Pursuing economies of scale*

The costs of globalization include economies of scale, adequate logistics, the effects of the experience curve and the costs of production development, as well as the speed of technological innovations (Yip, 2003). The first two factors have strongly influenced the wine industry over recent years:

- the pursuit of economies of scale has encouraged the standardization of products and the concentration of production (wine and winemaking represent 40% of the cost of a wine bottle), of bottling and packaging;
- the production conditions in each country can also be a source of more or less important economies of scale; in this regard, the fragmentation of production in continental Europe is detrimental to companies that are established in this area;
- the costs of transportation are also a source of differentiation in international competition; grape production and winemaking are often located in the same area, and wine trade makes sense only if the production is internationally marketable. However, it is possible to consider that international 'proximity' trade will develop in order to limit the costs of transporting 'raw material' (between Turkey and the European Union, for example).

Companies are committed to diversified location strategies according to countries and risks they incur, as well as attempting to benefit from emerging innovations and opportunities (Ghoshal, 1987). In parallel, a movement of mergers and acquisitions has taken place in order to benefit from economies of scale and finance innovation. The increase in production volumes, necessary both for the production of certain wines (low-end wines) and in order to access certain markets through brands (to China, for example) requires that the production scale and capacity be massively increased. A progressive financialization of the wine industry has thus developed in order that the necessary resources reach a size which could enable such operations. This explains why many world leaders go public, as they are then able to collect the necessary funds for such investments.

3.2.3.2   *The trend in international supply conditions*

Large volumes of wine are now necessary to place cheap wines on the market ('basic') and also to build international brands. Securing supplies is therefore becoming a priority in order to have a steady flow of raw material to supply international brands. It is noteworthy that inter-tropical vineyards are seen as having strong potential to play this role in the years to come, given that their climate allows for several harvests per year.

Besides, given the downward pressure on prices on almost all markets and on many market segments, the control of production costs has become a necessity for all companies. Yet the major part of wine is currently produced in areas where grapes are grown, due to several protectionist policies (especially in the 'old world of wine'). However, a rapid change in flows is underway with a progressive transfer of some stages of the production chain to the global level. This reflects the transition from production-centred winemaking to marketing-centred winemaking, a trend that has already taken place in the brewing industry. The first stage of this process is also already underway: bottling according to the market. For example, the Castel group has a plant in Russia that imports and bottles bulk wine. This wine can thus be sold at a more competitive price, and allows the French group to pursue its growth in spite of the current crisis (*Comité national des conseillers extérieurs de la France* [CNCE] National Committee of France External Counsellors) (2009). This trend accounts for the development of international exchange of bulk wine that will soon result in the modification of flows and trade conditions, since these wines complement the range of wines offered on lead markets, and sometimes benefit from favourable fiscal conditions. In the years to come, location strategies will increasingly take into account these facts to generate profit, and this may lead to a closer location of places of production and distribution.

3.2.4   Improving bargaining power vis-à-vis large-scale distributors

The essential role played by large-scale distributors in terms of homogenization of food sales has increased over the past few years. The distribution structures also reflect the phenomenon of the so-called global national consumer (Yip, 2003).

3.2.4.1   *The increasing weight of large-scale distribution*

In the global wine market, supermarkets and hypermarkets are the main buyers since they distribute the major part of wines in the world (37.5 per cent according to DataMonitor, 2010). Distribution channels still remain very different across countries. On markets where there exist important surpluses concentrated in a limited number of regions (e.g., Languedoc-Roussillon in France, Castile and Mancha in Spain), the progressive entry of increasingly recognized exporters (Australia,

Chile, the US, Argentina and perhaps also Brazil soon) has improved the bargaining power of large-scale distributors, and led to the development of specific brands that cater for the demands of distribution. In addition, this phenomenon has become readily appreciated by consumers, in particular those who are not connoisseurs, since it enables them to find a clear reference in a context of multiplication and diversification of wines.

Given that the economic crisis has had an impact on the wine trade not only in terms of volume, companies from exporting countries are now faced with two possible options: 'trying to maintain the flows and the demand level by lowering the average prices for distributors, or maintaining the current average prices while taking the risk that distributors will reduce their demand, given that the competition from companies that will have chosen (or been able to implement financially) the first option will have put a strong pressure on prices' (OIV, 2010, p. 6). This mechanism, combined with the growing awareness of environmental issues, allows distributors, equally affected by the crisis, to recover parts of their benefits by conditioning wine as close as possible to places of consumption at the expense of trading companies.

Today, improving one's bargaining power against distribution networks has become critical for wine marketing companies in order to survive, but also to meet the needs of large-scale distribution. As competition became tougher for companies and above all between markets, large scale distributors (such as Tesco in England) were prone to reduce their number of suppliers, and to favour those who provided the largest range of products (known as 'multi products' suppliers), and who owned a portfolio of brands in other activities or beverages. Pernod Ricard thus finds itself in a position of strength.

3.2.4.2   *The necessity for companies to build brand awareness*

All brands allow a symbolic differentiation for each product and thus a segmentation of customers for this product. The representation of a brand is primarily the representation of an individual belonging to a socio-cultural environment. Since wine is a product for which the consumer's environment and cultural background play a critical role, companies working in the field of wine have been forced, to varying degrees, to take this into account, even though the traditional professional community was not generally in favour of such a strategy in many countries of the 'new wine world'.

One issue needs to be stressed: while most products are marketed under roughly ten brands in supermarkets, there are often several hundred (sometimes even a thousand) brands of wine. The consumer's choice for wine is therefore more complex than for other products. So when the consumer looks for a wine, the brand name turns out to be a key factor that determines his or her decision (Lockshin, 2009), hence the growing importance of a brand strategy for all companies that intend to sell wine to large-scale distribution.

The creation of a brand abroad nonetheless relies on three conditions:

- regular availability of a large volume of wine, which requires a regular supply of raw material that meets precise specifications;
- cost control, in order to market wines at a relatively constant and acceptable price for the selected distribution networks;
- implementation of efficient and cheap logistics.

But companies do not compete on an equal footing to meet all these international challenges. It is mainly the world's leading companies that can streamline and mobilize the necessary resources to both carry out a strategic shift and meet the requirements to enter the new lead markets.

3.3   Growth patterns for leading companies in the world's wine industry

The previous section highlighted the existence of a process of the internationalization of companies in the wine industry. But can we really say that there are multinational wine companies? We can reply in the affirmative only if we refer to the definition used in this book, namely that a company is considered to be multinational if it makes foreign direct investments (FDI) and if it has, or to some degree, controls, value-added activities in several countries (see Chapter 1). Indeed, internationally successful companies generally make direct investments abroad in order to gain market share and facilitate access to local consumers.

3.3.1   Giving priority to external growth to access foreign markets

The world of wine has not been spared by the process of mergers and acquisitions that has developed throughout the world. Thus, since companies like Guinness and Grand Met amalgamated to create the giant Diageo in 1997, the industry has witnessed an unprecedented wave of consolidation. Each year, with the opening of borders and the liberalization of trade that has removed many entry barriers, national wineries and trading companies have been bought by foreign firms, trying to gain market shares to expand their brand portfolios and/or increase their power over domestic distribution channels.

3.3.1.1 *Using mergers and acquisitions as a priority*

Unfavourable market conditions in many countries, and the fact that many companies remain too small to be competitive on the markets, have frequently led to the buyout of companies by larger foreign groups: New Zealand's Montana and Spain's Bodegas y Bebidas were purchased by the British Allied Domecq in 2001; Australia's BRL Hardy was purchased by the United States' Constellation Brands in 2003; Britain's Allied Domecq was purchased by France's Pernod-Ricard in 2005; the United States' Gallo was purchased by another American company, William Hill Estate, and so on (see Box 3.2). Last but not least, in December 2010, Constellation Brands announced the sale of its wine-related activities to Australia's Champ for 230 million US dollars. The annual number of mergers and acquisitions increased from around 50 in 1998 to a maximum of 350 in 2007, before falling to 150 in 2008 (Hanin et al., 2010).

As the number of available and interesting targets has become scarce, this strategy is now more expensive and difficult to implement. Furthermore, the concentration of production assets and the search for the profitability of production tools required in future years militates against the race for external growth in order to increase company size on the market. Selecting potential units to be purchased is now necessary (Coelho and Rastoin, 2005).

3.3.1.2 *The acquisition of local production units*

Most leading companies of the new world of wine own a significant part of their supply structures (see Table 3.9). Thus the Chilean company Concho y Toro owns more than 40 per cent of the areas required for its supply. This vertical integration strategy has enabled it to control its production costs and to develop wines that match the expectations of new consumers. By contrast, in the old world of wine, only a few leading companies have significant control over their supplies.

However, in order to have greater control over their supplies, some companies of the old world of wine are gradually changing their strategies. For example, the Castel group has developed acquisitions of vineyards in North Africa, China and Russia.

Box 3.2 An example of Pernod-Ricard asset acquisition by the Brazilian group Mioloce, in 2009

The French company Pernod Ricard signed an agreement to sell its subsidiary Almaden to the Mioloce group, which became the leader in premium wines on the Brazilian market. The transaction took place in 2010.

With this acquisition, the total production of the new group reached 12 million litres and a turnover of 100 million reals (39 million Euros according to the exchange rate at the time). The acquisition of Almaden allowed Mioloce to own more than 1000 hectares of vines. The surface area rose from 575 to 1150 hectares of vines intended for wine production only.

Mioloce planned to revive the Almaden brand, which has a high reputation in Brazil. Its goal was to double its market share over the next ten years. Therefore, 12 million reals (4.7 million Euros) were invested in vineyards, marketing, technology and the promotion of a 'wine route' type tourist attraction. The acquisition of Almaden is part of the Mioloce group's growth strategy. Mioloce is also the leader of sparkling wine production (according to the champagne method) on the American continent and is number three for sparkling wines in Brazil, a market that is undergoing a strong expansion; it is also the Brazilian brandy leader thanks to a partnership with the Spanish company Osborne.

Source: http://www.lemoci.com/ (accessed 3 March 2012).

Champagne-producing companies represent a special category of companies in the old world of wine. They have developed integration strategies with upstream sectors of the industry since the nineteenth century and have enhanced their vineyards by introducing long-term grape purchase contracts. Very precise specifications between grape growers and wine merchants have been developed in this context. This growth strategy associated with a guaranteed price policy has attracted new companies previously involved in other business sectors, mainly in the luxury industry (e.g., LVMH).

The acquisition of vineyards is also a preferred investment strategy on the part of some foreign companies. Although the return is often low compared with other investments (1–2%) and extends on the long

Table 3.9   Wine world leaders and their international acquisitions (2008)

Rank	Groups	Wine production sites abroad
1	Constellation Brands	Australia, New Zealand, Italy, Chile
2	E&J Gallo	Australia
3	Forster's Group	United States, Chile, New Zealand, Italy
4	Louis Vuitton Moët Hennessy (LVMH)	United States, Spain, New Zealand, Australia, Argentina, Brazil
5	Groupe Castel	Morocco, Tunisia, China, Russia
6	Pernod Ricard	Australia, Argentina, Brazil, New Zealand, South Africa, China, Spain, United States, Mexico, Georgia, India
7	The Wine Group	Italy
8	Grands Chais de France	Germany
9	Freixenet	France, Australia, Uruguay, United States, Mexico, Argentina
10	Oetker Gruppe (Henkell & Sohnlein)	Hungary, France, Austria, Poland, Czech Republic, Slovenia, Rumania, Bulgaria, Ukraine
11	Diageo	United States, France, Argentina, Portugal, India
12	Casella Wines	Virtually none
13	Kendall Jackson Wine Estates	Argentina, Chile, France, Italy, Australia
14	Boizel Chanoine Champagne	Virtually none
15	Concha y Toro	Argentina

Source: Adapted from Cuelho (2008).

term, demand keeps growing. This is particularly the case of prestigious French vineyards, since the scarcity of their wines provides a favourable brand image to the company that owns them, as well as access to markets that have previously been closed to foreign companies. For example, the group Longhai International was the first Chinese company to have invested in a French vineyard by purchasing Chateau Latour-Laguens in 2008.

3.3.2   Building a brand portfolio

Whatever the business activity, the elaboration of a brand strategy concerns two aspects: the relationship between the product and the brand (product-brand pair) and the brand portfolio where arbitration takes place, particularly to set a hierarchy between the brands. According to Cegarra (1994), a brand may be used to designate a single product (product-brand), a set of homogeneous products (product-brand range, or product-brand line) or a set of heterogeneous products (umbrella-brand). A product may therefore have a specific name or share one with several other products, whether similar or very different. Moreover, the overall management of the brand portfolio is based on their interrelationships, since all the brands do not play the same role, and it reflects the market coverage strategy of the company. Generally, one brand is developed for each market segment in each country. For example, in 2010, the Constellation Brands group had seven brands for still wines in Australia, five in New Zealand, three in South Africa, six in Europe, 13 in Canada and 22 in the US.

Apart from champagne and sparkling wines, there were traditionally few brands in the European wine industry. But some companies of the new world of wine have been able to generate growth by launching brands of still wines on dynamic segments of the market in recent years. In addition, these brands have been sought after by the largest firms, to complete their wines and spirits portfolio. In this highly fragmented industry there is no predominant brand. Moreover, it seems difficult to draw comparisons in this sector due to the diversity of soils, grape varieties and wine-making techniques. However, large international groups have control over several brands of wine and have been able to consolidate their position in this area. The brands of the new world of wine hold a leading market position. All these brands are usually umbrella brands that enable companies to develop a range of brands and products suited for each country and each market.

Companies carry out more and more exchanges between brands for several reasons. They first search for young and innovative brands that can provide access to new consumers. But the necessity of cutting costs and finding new customers, who are therefore predominantly non-connoisseurs, has led companies to refocus on their 'stronghold' brands that generate profit and can withstand competition. Secondly, companies usually prefer acquiring local brands, especially when they try to establish themselves quickly on a foreign market. It is noteworthy that the current crisis has resulted in a decrease in the development of brands, and has led companies to focus on their strongest brands, sometimes those being the oldest and best known to consumers. Similarly, the era of very high-priced wines seems to be over. Finally, umbrella brands seem to prevail on the newest markets: the name of the wine's country of origin which is symptomatic of a shift towards simplifying the designation of wines and, in the end, standardizing the production.

3.3.3 Developing partnerships between companies

Partnerships in the wine industry concern both distribution and marketing. For example, since 2009, E & J Gallo wines have been distributed in France by Yvon Mau, a subsidiary of the Spanish Freixenet group which is very well established in traditional networks: this is a major advantage to the French market. These alliances are particularly conducive to market expansion, resource sharing and the increase of market power.

3.3.4 The duality of financing international growth

The world leaders of the wine industry are still often family-owned businesses in spite of important financial requirements that are now necessary to expand at the international level. But in the future, these companies will be easily integrated into multinational, publicly listed companies as a result of market downward pressure.

Business ownership also varies according to companies: family-owned businesses are still numerous in the old world of wine, whereas this is not the case anymore in the new world. Today, shareholders of leading groups in the wine industry are no different from shareholders in other industries; they expect a minimum return from their financial investments. The financialization of these companies takes place gradually, as borrowing is required in order to fund mergers and acquisitions on domestic and international markets. In the future, it is likely that the leaders of family-owned structures (E & J Gallo, Groupe Castel, The Wine Group, Freixenet, Oetker Gruppe, Casella Wines, Kendall Jackson) will be highly sought after, either for brand purchasing transactions, or to share production assets. This is especially true in the context of crisis in the world's wine industry, and the downward pressure on price levels that lead to lower corporate profitability and hence diminished sources of cash-flow investments.

The progressive financialization of leaders' governance of the world's wine industry was carried out first by Anglo-Saxon companies that sought primarily to maximize shareholders' profits. This suggests that divestment of businesses will doubtless expand more than acquisitions in the years to come in the context of financial crisis. 'Industry-finance' arbitrations will probably not favour the wine activities of these large groups. The reorganization of production structures will be more important than the acquisition of new assets. This will undoubtedly be an opportunity for specialized companies to strengthen their activities.

The notifications made by most companies at the end of 2010 suggest that the world's wine industry will indeed experience strong changes in the near future. A case in point is the sale of 80 per cent of Constellation Brands' wine division to the Australian company Champ Private Equity for 230 million Australian dollars (177 million Euros) in December 2010; the purpose of this sale was to reduce Constellation Brands' debt.

3.4   Conclusion

The wine industry is facing one of its biggest challenges of all times for several reasons:

- existence of a chronic surplus production for over 30 years lead-ing to the decline of prices and profit margins in most producing countries;
- market pressure which increases competition between companies, more often at the expense of companies in the old world of wine;
- rapidly changing consumer preferences leading to new marketing strategies as well as to technical and commercial innovations for wine producers.

International trading has become a necessity for most companies. A significant move towards concentration allowed the emergence of glo-bal groups until 2007. However, many small exporters, belonging both to the old and the new worlds of wine, can still take advantage of remaining entry barriers, and of opportunities offered by arbitrage, while large com-panies also try to make the most of these barriers through aggregation strategies, and other companies attempt to take advantage of opportuni-ties provided by both aggregation and arbitrage strategies (Zalan, 2005).

Two major factors now seem crucial to succeed on international markets:

- the access to distribution networks which represents a significant barrier when trying to enter foreign markets; companies must therefore reach a sufficient size in order to secure sustainable access to these networks;
- the segmentation of supply according to the targeted markets and according to local preferences; however it is worth pointing out that this phenomenon results in a paradox, namely, the possibility of endless supply diversification and an ever-tougher trade war.

In the end, it is still possible to ask whether the wine industry remains one of the food processing industries for which product socio-cultural specificities are a major obstacle to market globalization, the development of global companies and the production of standardized wines targeted for a 'global' consumer.

References

Cegarra, J. J. (1994) 'Gérer un portefeuille de marques', *Décisions Marketing*, 1 (3), 81–91.
Coelho, A. M. and Rastoin, J. L. (2005) 'Financiarization et gouvernance des multinationales du vin' in E. Montaigne, F. D'Hauteville, J.-P. Couderc, H. Hannin and E. Montaigne (eds) *Bacchus 2006* (Paris: Editions La Vigne – Dunod), pp. 53–73.
Comité National des Conseillers Extérieurs de la France (CNCE) (2009) *Le vin dans le monde à l'horizon 2050* (Paris: Rapport Prospectives).
DataMonitor (2010) *Company Profile* (New York: DataMonitor Reports).
Ghoshal, S. (1987) 'Global Strategy: An Organizing Frame Work', *Strategic Management Journal*, 8, 425–40.
Green, R., Rodriguez Zniga, M. and Pierbattisiti, L. (2003) 'Global Market Changes and Business Behavior in the Wine Sector', *Cahiers du LORIA*, Number 2003–02.
Hanin, H., Couderc, J. P., d'Hauteville, F. and Montaigne, E. (2010) *La vigne et le vin* (Paris: La documentation française).
Kogut, B. (1985) 'Designing Global Strategies: Comparative and Competitive Value-Added Chains', *Sloan Management Review*, 26 (4), 15–28.
Lockshin, L. (2004) 'La marque et le vin' in F. d' Hauteville, J. P. Couderc, H. Hanin and E. Montaigne (eds) *Bacchus 2005* (Paris: Editions La Vigne – Dunod), pp. 209–25.
Lockshin, L. (2009) 'Consumer Purchasing Behaviour for Wine: What We Know and Where We are Going' (University of South Australia: Working Paper Wine Marketing Research Group).
OIV (Office Internationale de la Vigne et du Vin) (2010) *Notes de conjuncture* (Paris: Publications de l'OIV).
Pivot, C. (2008) 'La syrah, un cépage dans la dynamique mondiale', *1st International Syrah Symposium* (Lyon: Edition Chantré), pp. 76–86.
Rabobank International (2009) *The World Wine Business* (market study) (Utricht: Rabobank International).
Rastoin, J. L. (2008) 'Les multinationales dans le système alimentaire', *CERAS – Revue Projet* (307) http://www.ceras-projet.com/index.php?id=3382 (accessed 4 March 2012).
Xerfi (2008) *Groupes alimentaires dans le monde* (Paris: Groupe Xerfi).
Yip, G. S. (2003) *Total Global Strategy* (Upper Saddle River, NJ: Prentice Hall).
Zalan, T. (2005) *Global, Local or Semi-Global? The Case of the Wine Industry*, Australian Centre for International Business, working paper (6).

4
The Governance of MNCs: Continuity or Breakdown?

Fabrice Roth

The governance of multinational companies (MNCs), especially through listed companies, is a major topic in management. From the 1980s, 'good' governance practices, largely based on the Anglo-Saxon model, have accompanied the development of firms in a context of globalization. Today, the successive crises of recent years raise questions about the continuity of this movement. Are we witnessing a simple break, or a reversal of trend? In this chapter, we will study the impact of the crisis on the governance mode of MNCs.

First, we will review the theoretical framework in order to understand the relationship between the company's environment and its Corporate Governance System (CGS). We will then present some salient features about practices of MNCs listed on the CAC 40 stock exchange.

4.1 The instability of the environment leads to a concentration of power

The state of the environment of MNCs is related to various factors. When a company faces a certain degree of instability in its environment, generating a situation of uncertainty for managers, a need for strong commitment and cohesion arises, resulting in a modification of the CGS, and especially of the ruling coalition.

4.1.1 The company's environment and governance system

4.1.1.1 Trends in CGSs

The economic literature on governance mechanisms is abundant, but the progress of these mechanisms during the development cycle of the company, in relation to its environment, has been studied only in recent times. This literature illustrates how the development of the organization is accompanied by changes in governance mechanisms, in particular in the features of the board of directors and in the ownership structure. This idea results from a classical contingent approach, according to which the structures of the organization adapt to the characteristics of the environment. In addition, the CGS must play different roles to meet the needs that correspond to each phase of the cycle. For example, the knowledge possessed by the members of the board will be determinant in the early phases of the company's development (Filatotchev and Wright, 2005). Gedajlovic et al. (2004) argue that the CGS needs to change in order to face up to new issues, and this necessary adaptation must be accompanied by a change in the resources used by the company, of these processes and its culture. This idea follows Jawahar and McLaughlin's framework (2001), according to which managers will conduct a risky strategy with respect to stakeholders when the company is threatened, in particular in the phases of emergence and transition/decline, leading to favour those who have the critical skills for ensuring the survival of the company. In summary, an effective CGS must be sufficiently dynamic to meet the needs of each phase of the cycle in relation to the environment of MNCs, rather than simply comply with a universal model.

By studying the development of the board of directors' characteristics during the development cycle of the company, Lynall et al. (2003) discuss several different but complementary theories. They find that the resource dependence theory is applicable to companies going through the first phases of their development cycle, and the agency theory to those in the last phases. This result is consistent with the work of Krafft and Ravix (2008), which points out that young companies should have a governance model based on cooperation and assistance in order to foster innovation, while mature companies should impose a governance model based on control of the executive team's actions in the interest of shareholders. In other words, the CGS should be based on a subtle mixture of guidance and control of the leadership team, which should change during the development of the company, according to the constraints of the environment. These proposals are not surprising if we consider that a mature company carries out its activities in a stable environment, while an emerging company is built in the context of an ever-changing environment. In the first case, priority must be given to striking a balance between the main stakeholders, while minimizing the costs of potential conflicts of interest, which is indeed the very essence of agency theory (Jensen and Meckling, 1976). In the second case, it is essential for the company to gain sufficient resources to ensure its survival in an ever-changing environment. This is studied in depth in the resource dependence theory (Pfeffer and Salancik, 1978).

MNCs, confronted with a major change of their environment, must thus face challenges associated with companies that expand, while taking into account their particular structure as mature companies.

4.1.1.2   *The crisis leads MNC to a reorganization of their activities*

Effectively managing a business activity portfolio is a classic question in strategy, and is the subject of recommendations generally presented as a set of matrixes (Boston Consulting Group, and so on). When a company must take into account emerging activities in one of its industries, generating high growth rates, or even disruptive innovations (Christensen, 1997), developed by new companies, its position may appear threatened. This may question the company's strategy even further if radical technological and financial changes affect the world economy. In other words, a crisis situation can accelerate the decline of a company and the managers' response must go beyond asset portfolio reallocation. A crisis therefore requires that the company redefines its strategy, relying on new skills, to generate sufficient growth in the future. These questions arose in almost identical terms in the 1970s for many industrial companies (e.g., BSN-Danone or Bombardier). These periods of intense reallocation of human and physical capital see companies either disappear or deeply modify the nature of their business (e.g., BSN-Danone), but also new companies start up (e.g., Microsoft), according to the principle of 'creative destruction', proposed by Schumpeter (1935). However, contrary to emerging businesses relying on the arrival of new technologies, existing companies must take into account their history. Where a new company invents itself, an existing company reinvents itself. This phase of reconstruction is therefore a strategic combination of revival by the executive team, in an economic context of uncertainty, and having respect for the company's historical trajectory, which necessitates taking into account existing balances between stakeholders.

This question is a classic one in the field of corporate governance, in particular when it comes to comparing models of governance. Thus, the Anglo-Saxon model, which favours an economic vision of the company, is expected to shorten these phases, allowing managers to more quickly draw a line under the past, promoting an 'exit' type governance model. Conversely, the German model, expected to be more consensual or 'voice' type, places more emphasis on a negotiated solution to the crisis, according to the concepts introduced by Hirschman (1970).

This debate around the convergence of models had lost some of its intensity until the recent economic crisis, where the positions of major governments brought to the forefront the different national approaches to governance.

4.1.2 Consequences concerning the internal coalition

Mintzberg (1986) defines the concepts of internal and external coalition to study the nature of power organizations. In this perspective, but in a context of corporate governance, it is necessary to specify the terms of the Management Team (MT) and Internal Coalition (IC), and to locate the latter, to estimate the impact of change on this decision-making centre.

4.1.2.1 *The internal coalition*

Charreaux (1997) specifies that his definition of corporate governance, 'centred on the top executives' key role, goes beyond the analysis of relationships between shareholders and top management, often privileged ... and replaces the problem of corporate governance in the framework of contracts and relationships that the company (and its managers) maintains with its multiple partners, who can be shareholders, but also bankers, employees, customers or public authorities' (p. 1).

However, this reference to top executives can be strictly limited to the organizational structures of governance and ignore a certain number of partners having an influence on the company. Indeed, the concept of top management refers, in France, to executives, brought together within a management board (*directoire* in French or *Vorstand* in German), whose names and positions appear under the heading 'executive committee' of an annual report. It therefore excludes members of the board of directors or the supervisory board who are not corporate executives, although they play an important role in strategic decisions, in particular with the proliferation of board committees.

The second category of important actors which is not taken into account in the current definition of corporate governance is that of 'inside shareholders' (Jensen and Meckling, 1976). These shareholders may influence corporate management, without having to hold a majority stake in the capital of the company. Indeed, the expression 'minority shareholder' is used for the sake of convenience, as having control of a company does not imply holding a majority equity stake. The Delaware Court of Justice confirms the existence of inside shareholders in one of its rulings which defines their rights. The role of these inside shareholders was underlined by La Porta et al. (1998), who showed that this category of shareholders had generally more power than just their rights with regard to cash flows, in particular through the use of pyramid-like structures, or through their active participation on the management team.

In fact, the majority of the other categories of stakeholders can be associated with all or part of the managerial decisions according to the nature of their relationship with the company. We may refer, for example, to financial creditors, like banks, but also to customers or companies' strategic suppliers, or even companies' employees. Le Maux (2008) defines the concept of inside coalition as follows:

• The management team: its strategic position within the company enables it to control the dissemination of company information and, in particular, to limit its availability to other agents. The concept of management team should be considered in the broad sense, as it includes members of the executives' team as well as members of the main control committee, who are also heavily involved in the coalition (board of directors or supervisory board).
• Important shareholders: 'important' refers to their share of capital, without mentioning any specified threshold; on the one hand, these shareholders are better informed than others, particularly because they can mobilize important resources more easily in order to control managers and protect their investments; on the other hand, they have a stronger power of influence within general meetings.

Thus the internal coalition includes all stakeholders who have control over strategic decisions which are taken inside the company. This internal coalition is made up of the management team, in the broad sense as defined by Le Maux (2008), and of a control group, including the support members of the management team, beyond the group of inside shareholders. In other words, the above defined internal coalition makes it possible to identify the decision-making and control centre of the company.

4.1.2.2   *The role of the Chief Executive Officer and the independence of the board of directors*

The internal coalition, headed by the top executive, exercises its power in certain specific areas within the corporate governance structure, such as the management board and the board of directors or supervisory board. The board of directors, or the supervisory board, is a key mechanism of the CGS, and if one looks closely at its operating mode, one can see that its degree of independence is one of the most discussed parameters.

The question of adapting the CGS to the environment and the development of the company business cycle leads to focusing particularly on the board of directors. Firstly, it has been widely studied within theoretical frameworks such as resource dependence theory and agency theory (Charreaux and Pitol-Belin, 1990). Secondly, it is addressed either from an internal point of view, in the case of agency theory, or from an external point of view, in the case of the resource dependence theory (Pfeffer and Salancik, 1978). Therefore, it is hardly surprising that the development of the composition of the board of directors has been studied in relation to the progress of the company's development cycle (Filatotchev and Wright, 2005). On this issue, the independence of the board from the management team is recommended in most of the codes of good governance, which logically corresponds to a willingness to control the management team's actions.

Set within the context of the business development cycle, this general assertion appears more relevant when the company has reached a mature stage. This seems fairly consistent with the profile of listed MNCs. What about this issue of independence for MNCs facing strong challenges in their market environment? In this case, strategic decisions become critical and engage the responsibility of managers, who must in turn be able to rely on the support of the internal coalition. In other words, the management team's discretionary space must be wider, which entails the search for greater flexibility.

In this perspective, it is also necessary to consider the company's degree of reactivity. In fact, a strong environmental instability leads the company to respond to external stimuli, which implies a short and effective decision-making process. We need to remember the meaning of the concept of flexibility, which requires human 'intelligence' for the understanding of external events. In addition, one may think that a small team and a less complicated governance structure would have a positive effect on the speed of reaction. Concerning the first point, small boards and committees will prevent the problems of 'free riding'. Concerning the second point, fewer committees and the choice of a unitary structure (board of directors) rather than a dualist one (management and supervisory boards) will reduce the number of discussion forums. Moreover, the question of merging or separating the functions of decision and control is a key question in corporate governance. It becomes particularly apparent with the combination of the positions of chairman of the board of directors and Chief Executive Officer (CEO). Again, the general recommendations advise a separation of these functions to avoid the same person being judge and jury.

However, if we assume that the manager allows the MNC to explore new avenues, and that he assumes full responsibility for the decisions taken, separation of the functions can be a burden. Obviously, all these mechanisms are complementary and substitutable, which makes a global analysis of the CGS necessary.

4.2   The concentration of power within French listed MNCs

To illustrate these various arguments with a sample of MNCs, we focused on 32 companies listed in the key market indicator of the Paris stock exchange, the CAC 40, which includes the 40 largest market capitalisations (see Table 4.1).

Firstly, the companies in this index can all be considered as MNCs, due to their specific features. In addition, their data are relatively accessible and homogeneous, which allows sufficiently in-depth statistical processing, and the ability to look back over several years. Secondly, comparisons can be made with other studies, as this sample of companies has often been analysed. Finally, the way the index was built leads to a certain economic homogeneity of the sample. We therefore studied

Table 4.1   Presentation of sample

Company	Industry	Company	Industry
Accor	travel and leisure	L'Oréal	consumer goods
Air liquide	chemicals	LVMH	consumer goods
Alcatel-Lucent	technology	Pernod-Ricard	food and beverage
Alstom	industrial goods and services	Peugeot	automobile
Axa	insurance	PPR	retail
BNP Paribas	banks	Renault	automobile
Bouygues	construction and materials	Saint-Gobain	construction and materials
Cap Gemini	technology	Sanofi-Aventis	health care
Carrefour	retail	Schneider Electric	industrial goods
Crédit Agricole	banks	Société Générale	banks
Danone	food and beverage	Technip	oil and gas
Dexia	banks	Total	oil and gas
EDF	utilities	Unibail-Rodamco	real estate
Essilor International	health care	Vallourec	industrial goods
France Telecom	telecommunications	Vinci	construction and materials
Lafarge SA	construction and materials	Vivendi	media

the differences between the various elements of governance presented above over a period of five years, by comparing the situation in 2005 and the one prevailing in 2010. This comparison was carried out firstly with all companies and secondly with the group of companies which merged their functions of decision and control.

4.2.1 The development of the CGS of MNCs

Firstly, we will examine the recent period, marked by the economic crisis, and see whether it has led to a significant development of the CGSs of the French-listed MNCs, focusing on the manager's discretionary space.

4.2.1.1 *The independence of board members and competency profiles in boards*

Most of the CAC 40 companies refer to the criteria recommended by the *Association française des entreprises privées et du Mouvement des entreprises de France* (AFEP-MEDEF) for judging the independence of board members. According to this code (2010), 'a director is independent when he or she has no relationship of any kind whatsoever with the corporation, its group or the management of either that is such as to colour his or her judgment. Accordingly, an independent director is to be understood not only as a non-executive director, that is, one not performing management duties in the corporation or its group, but also as one devoid of any particular bonds of interest (significant shareholder, employee, other) with them' (p. 13).

In this sense, 'the criteria to be reviewed by the committee and the board in order to have a director qualify as independent and to prevent risks of conflicts of interest between the director and the management, the corporation, or its group, are the following:

- not to be an employee or executive director of the corporation, or an employee or director of its parent or a company that it consolidates, and not having been in such a position for the previous five years
- not to be an executive director of a company in which the corporation holds a directorship, directly or indirectly, or in which an employee appointed as such or an executive director of the corporation (currently in office or having held such office going back five years) is a director
- not to be a customer, supplier, investment banker or commercial banker

- ○ that is material for the corporation or its group
- ○ or for a significant part of whose business the corporation or its group accounts
- not to be related by close family ties to an executive director
- not to have been an auditor of the corporation within the previous five years
- not to have been a director of the corporation for more than twelve years'.

(AFEP-MEDEF Code, 2010, p. 13)

Even if these criteria are questionable, their extended use makes comparisons a lot easier. On this basis, we will study the composition of the board of directors and the supervisory board over the years 2005 and 2010.

Some descriptive statistics carried out on the sample (see Table 4.2) show a great stability of the average number of board members (14) and independent board members (8) over this period. In addition, the gap between extreme situations has been closed. These results are consistent with the study of Russell Reynolds Associates (2009), conducted between 2006 and 2008. The coalition control does not seem to have been affected by the 'impact of the environment'.

Table 4.2 Summary statistics of the structure of the boards

	2010	2005
Board members		
Mean	14	14
Max	19	18
Min	10	7
Median	14	14
Independent board members		
Mean	8	8
Max	11	13
Min	4	5
Median	8	8
Dualist form		
% Sample	16.67	30
Monist form		
% Sample	83.33	70
Separation of functions		
% Sample	43.33	60

Table 4.3 Summary statistics of the characteristics
of the boards

	2010	2005
Age		
Mean	60	60
Max	65	65
Min	53	52
Median	60	60
Education Diversity Index*		
Mean	37.47	40.30
% Male*		
Mean	83.50	92.77
% French		
Mean	73.60	74.36

Note: * Statistical significance for differences between 2005
and 2010 at the 0.10 level.

The concept of independence, which implies taking a critical look at the management team's action, can also be related to the issue of diversity. Thus, a diverse board, in terms of age, education, nationality and gender, may at first have a favourable impact on the independence of the board.

To study the diversity of the boards, it is possible to calculate a Herfindhal index using board members' educational profiles (see Table 4.4, selected profiles).

Concerning gender and nationality, we refer to the proportion of male or female as well as of French board members (see Table 4.3).

The table shows an extremely stable age average and proportion of French board members over this period. However, the proportion of men clearly drops over the same period. This last result reflects the anticipated application, by some companies, of the law relative to a balanced representation within the councils, and to the introduction of a 40 per cent minimum quota of women in the six years following the enactment of the law (28 January 2011). Finally, the education diversity index also declines, which means a greater variety of profiles within the boards.

Education can be a powerful factor influencing board members' minds. We built the Herfindhal index by isolating, in a classic way, three typically French educational profiles:

- High engineering school (*Grande Ecole*) profile, for *Ecole Polytechnique* or *Ecole Centrale alumni*

- Civil service administrator profile, for National School of Administration (*Ecole Nationale d'Administration* or *ENA*) or Institut d'Etudes Politiques, Paris *alumni*
- Manager profile, for one of the top business schools in Paris, for example, Hautes Etudes Commerciales (HEC), Ecole Supérieure de Commerce de Paris (ESCP) Europe, or Ecole Supérieure des Sciences Economiques et Commerciales (ESSEC) *alumni*.

Table 4.4   Summary statistics of the weight of education profiles

	2010	2005
High engineering school profile		
Average weight	4.87	5.06
Civil service administrator profile*		
Average weight	4.27	5.93
Manager profile*		
Average weight	2.03	1

Note: * Statistical significance for differences between 2005 and 2010 at the 0.10 level.

The results (see Table 4.4) show a significant drop in the weight of the administrator profile, a significant increase in the manager profile and stagnation in the high engineering school profile. They reflect a search for more operational effectiveness, in coherence with a more demanding economic environment.

4.2.1.2   *The structure of decision-control bodies and the separation of functions*

The changes in the structure of the decision-control bodies, and the separation of the functions of control and decision, seem to become more significant (see Table 4.2). On the one hand, we observe that the percentage of companies choosing a dualist structure (management and supervisory boards) decreased by almost half over this period. On the other hand, we note a very clear increase in the percentage of companies combining the chairman and the CEO positions. In addition, approximately 27 per cent of the companies from the sample merged the two functions over this period, which constitutes a significant statistical trend. The search for more unified decision making is thus highlighted. Again, these results confirm those of Russell Reynolds study (2009) and show that the crisis in particular slowed down the movement towards separation of the functions initiated in the 1990s.

Table 4.5 Proportion of board members having same profile as managers (background and nationality)

	2010	2005
Same background*		
% mean	33.3	39.37
Same nationality		
% mean	71.4	71.3

Note: * Statistical significance for differences between 2005 and 2010 at the 0.10 level.

4.2.1.3   The trend in the managers' discretionary space

To appreciate the possible changes in the managers' discretionary space over this period, it is interesting to study how the composition of the boards developed in relation to managers' profiles. The idea is to find out whether managers seek identical board members' profiles, and what the trend is over this period. A strong homogeneity could thus reflect a less open-minded management team.

The results (see Table 4.5) show a very clear and significant decline of board members having the same educational profile as the manager, and no change in the proportion of board members having the same nationality. On the whole, management teams do not seem to shift towards greater cultural homogeneity. In summary, the analysis of the decision and control bodies over the period shows a trend towards greater concentration of power. However, the size and the degree of independence do not change, with a slight increase of diversity.

4.2.2   The companies having merged the functions of decision and control

We used the previous tests and distinguished between companies having kept the same structure of governance over this period (Group 1) and those having merged the functions of decision and control (Group 2). The objective was to study in more depth the development of boards which had concentrated the power.

4.2.2.1   The independence of boards

To study the progress of the boards' degree of independence, we focused on the percentage of board members for each group in 2005 and 2010 (see Table 4.6).

Table 4.6 Summary statistics of the independence of the boards

	2010	2005
Board members		
Average number Group 1	13.44	13.4
Average number Group 2	14.57	13.6
Independent board members		
% Group 1	64	61
% Group 2	59	61

Table 4.7 Summary statistics of the composition of boards in terms of diversity

	2010	2005
Age		
Mean Group 1	60.3	59.9
Mean Group 2	58.4	60.1
Diversity Index for Education		
Mean Group 1	39.8	42.6
Mean Group 2	30.9	31.1
Proportion of men*		
% Mean Group 1	84	93
% Mean Group 2	83	94
Proportion of French members		
% Mean Group 1	73	73
% Mean Group 2	74	74

Note: * Statistical significance for differences between 2005 and 2010 at the 0.10 level.

The results show a different trend in the two groups over this period. More precisely, the companies having merged the functions of control and decision (Group 2) also see the proportion of independent board members decline over this period, whereas it increases significantly for the other group. In other words, companies which merged the functions have a less independent board, which seems to indicate a trend towards more discretionary power for managers. We also recalculated the various diversity indicators for each group (see Table 4.7).

Few differences can be noted regarding the proportion of males, French board members or the board members' average age, even though, in this respect, the reduction in the board members' average age in Group 2 tends to confirm substantial board renewal within companies.

Table 4.8 Summary statistics of the importance of education profiles

	2010	2005
High engineering school profile		
Average weight Group 1	4.95	5.00
Average weight Group 2	6.14	6.14
Civil service administrator profile*		
Average weight Group 1	4.30	6.10
Average weight Group 2	5.00	7.71
Manager profile*		
Average weight Group 1	1.25	0.60
Average weight Group 2	3.00	1.71

Note: * Statistical significance for differences between 2005 and 2010 at the 0.10 level.

The results also show, as for the population as a whole, an increase in the diversity of education for Group 1 and a virtual stagnation of this index for Group 2. Companies having merged the functions of control and decision therefore report less 'open-mindedness' over this period, which, again, is consistent with the idea of a greater discretionary power for managers. When we take a closer look at the education profile (see Table 4.8), we notice a more important weight of managers within Group 2.

4.2.2.2 The managers' discretionary space

For a more detailed analysis of the development of mangers' discretionary space, we took a look at the board members' education and nationalities compared with those of the managers, in the two groups (see Table 4.9).

If we compare these results with those of the whole population (see Table 4.5), we notice that the percentage of board members having the same educational profile as managers remains relatively stable over this period for Group 2, while it decreases globally for the other group. In addition, Group 2 board members seem much more 'international' than those of Group 1.

In summary, if one refers to the principle of the 'free-rider', these various indexes tend to show that Group 2 companies have globally concentrated the power around a tightened management team, underlining the organizations' reaction to a more and more turbulent environment.

Table 4.9   Proportion of board members having the same origin as managers (background and nationality)

	2010	2005
Same background*		
% mean Group 1	33.60	38.50
% mean Group 2	30.30	31.40
Same nationality		
% mean Group 1	72.00	71.20
% mean Group 2	64.00	69.90

Note: * Statistical significance for differences between 2005 and 2010 at the 0.10 level.

4.3   Conclusion

MNCs have been confronted with a major economic and financial crisis for several years. Within the framework of the contingent organizational theories, it is assumed that an unstable environment leads to a tightening of management teams around a 'leader', combining the functions of control and decision in order to respond to the uncertainty generated by this unstable environment, while identifying pathways towards progress for the organization. Meanwhile, the degree of independence of the decision and control bodies must decrease.

These consequences go against the trend observed since the 1980s which show governance oriented towards managers' control, according to conclusions drawn mainly from the Anglo-Saxon model. It seems crucial to study governance modes of MNCs in a changing environment.

After the theoretical discussion of the subject, we presented some results from a study of MNCs listed on the Paris stock exchange. These results demonstrate and confirm a break in a long-term tendency to opt for a governance model based on managers' control, a break pointed out in several other studies. The results also show a shift towards greater concentration of power in favour of management teams in MNCs.

References

AFEP-MEDEF (2010) *Code de gouvernement d'entreprise des sociétés cotées* (Paris: AFEP-MEDEF).

Charreaux, G. (ed.) (1997) *Le gouvernement de l'entreprise: Corporate Governance, Théories et faits* (Paris: Economica).

Charreaux, G. and Pitol-Belin, J. P. (1990) *Le conseil d'administration* (Paris: Vuibert).

Christensen, C. M. (1997) *The Innovator's Dilemma* (Boston, MA: Harvard Business School Press).

Filatotchev, I. and Wright, M. (2005) *Corporate Governance Life-Cycle* (London and New York: Edward Elgar).

Gedajlovic, E., Lubatkin, M. and Schulze, W. S. (2004) 'Crossing the Threshold from Founder Management to Professional Management: A Governance Perspective', *Journal of Management Studies*, 41 (5), 883–95.

Hirschman, A. O. (1970) *Exit, Voice, and Loyalty: Responses to Decline in Firms, Organizations, and States* (Boston, MA: Harvard University Press).

Jawahar, I. M. and McLaughlin, G. L. (2001) 'Toward a Descriptive Stakeholder Theory, an Organisational Life Cycle Approach', *Academy of Management Review*, 26 (3), 397–414.

Jensen, M. and Meckling, W. (1976) 'Theory of the Firm: Managerial Behavior, Agency Costs and Ownership Structure', *Journal of Financial Economics*, 3 (4), 305–60.

Krafft, J. and Ravix, J. L. (2008) *Powerful Finance and Innovation Trends in High-Risk Economy* (Basingstoke: Palgrave Macmillan).

La Porta, R., Lopez-de-Silanes, F. and Shleifer, A. (1998) 'Law and Finance', *Journal of Political Economy*, 106 (6), 1113–55.

Le Maux, J. (2008) 'La "coalition de contrôle". Un outil au service de la gouvernance,' *Revue Française de Gestion*, 34 (181), 15–39.

Lynall, M. D., Golden, B. R. and Hillman, A. J. (2003) 'Board Composition from Adolescence to Maturity: A Multitheoretic View', *Academy of Management Review*, 28 (3), 416–31.

Mintzberg, H. (1986) *Le pouvoir dans les organisations* (Paris: Editions d'Organisation).

Pfeffer, J. and Salancik, G. R. (1978) *The External Control of Organizations: A Resource Dependence Perspective* (New York: Harper and Row).

Russell Reynolds Associates (2009) *Etude sur la gouvernance des entreprises du CAC 40: Réflexions sur l'impact de la crise* (New York & Paris: Russell Reynolds Associates).

Schumpeter, J. A. (1935) 'The Analysis of Economic Change', *Review of Economic Statistics*, 17, 1–10.

5
Impact of Credit Rating on the Strategies of MNCs

Claire Faverjon and François Lantin

> GDF Suez becomes a major actor in the electricity sector.
> Two years after the merger of Suez and Gaz de France,
> the French company announced yesterday the pur-
> chase of the British company International Power. ...
> Consequently, GDF Suez's debt will grow from
> 33.5 billion Euros to 42.4 billion Euros. So, Gérard
> Mestrallet's group plans 4 to 5 billion Euros asset sales
> to repay debt and to maintain a strong credit rating.
>
> *(Les Echos*, 11 August 2010, p. 1)

There is increasing evidence, especially in the business press, that credit rating agencies play an important role in the strategies of multinational companies (MNCs). With the globalization of the economy, corporate strategies must take into account the expectations of international portfolio investors. Hence, there must be refocusing plans, split-offs and other restructuring strategies. With the 'financialization' of strategies (Batsch, 1999), credit rating agencies play a key role by indicating to investors the probable default risks of companies. In particular, down-grades are the result of excessive debt and a lower capacity to repay it. The reduction of asymmetric information between managers and credi-tors and between managers and shareholders impede the capacity for some MNCs to launch major strategic operations.

The role and credibility of rating agencies have been discussed in relation to their independence, their direct financing by MNCs and also because rating announcements have a major impact on the bond market. They were much more criticized during the 2008 financial crisis and were accused, for example, of late downgrading and undervalua-tion of the risk for financial securities including sub-primes. From 2010 rating agencies have also been accused of hastily downgrading European countries and being responsible for high market speculation.

The literature on credit rating reports rather heterogeneous results, in particular regarding the influence of credit rating on equity capital markets and corporate strategies. This chapter has two objectives: first, to study the impact of downgrades on the French stock price and, second, to analyse the consequences of downgrades on the strategies of French MNCs.

To address these two questions, we used a standard event study methodology in order to assess the impact of 65 downgrades of 24 French MNCs announced by Standard and Poor's (S&P). We then analysed measures taken by companies following their downgrades: operational measures (cost-cutting, layoffs, asset sell-offs) and/or financial measures (debt restructuring, equity issues).

The first section of the chapter therefore presents a theoretical approach to credit rating. The second section then describes our research design, its methodology and the sample, and offers a discussion of the empirical results of the study. These will then be compared with the conclusions of the literature discussed in the first section of the chapter.

5.1   Theoretical framework of credit rating

5.1.1   Introduction to credit rating

5.1.1.1   *Role of rating agencies*
Investors in the bond market have difficulties estimating the real financial situation and credit risk of issuers. However, they can take advantage of the role of credit rating agencies, which is to evaluate the credit default risk of bonds. The agencies announce short-term and long-term ratings, which are considered as signals by investors, reduce information asymmetry and improve the efficiency of bond markets. The prices of bonds already issued and the stock prices are therefore modified almost instantaneously, to integrate changes in credit default risk and its consequences.

5.1.1.2   *Typology of ratings*
Credit rating should give the same level of credit risk at all economic periods, for stock markets and business sectors alike. It reveals the default rate and allows creditors to appreciate the level of risk for their investments. Ratings are listed according to credit quality. Standard and Poor's current scale comprises 21 long-term ratings (over one year)

from AAA to C, including or not a + or − sign. There are only seven short-term ratings because investors have a better knowledge of the short-term situation. Ratings are finally divided into two categories: investment grade (AAA to BBB−) and speculative grade (BB+ to D).

5.1.1.3 Types of rating announcements

Agencies can use three types of announcements to change the credit ratings of MNCs. The first type concerns downgrades and upgrades, which are limited to one or two notches in most cases. Issuers, whose rating decreases from investment grade (AAA to BBB−) to speculative grade (BB+ to D), are called fallen angels. Their debt is called junk bonds, also known as 'high yield bonds'. This downgrade has a serious impact because many fund managers cannot contractually invest in securities classified in speculative grade.

The second type of announcement concerns changes in outlook. Long-term credit ratings have a positive, stable or negative outlook (see Box 5.1) which defines the potential development over the following two or three years. The change in outlook results from the analysis of financial data provided by the company.

Box 5.1 Air Liquide rating changes

'Standard and Poor's (S&P) announced that Air Liquide credit rating would be placed in negative credit watch until the end of the acquisition process of British, German and North-American activities of Messer Griesheim. At that time, S&P had downgraded Air Liquide's long-term and short-term ratings respectively to A+ and A−1. After the acquisition, the financial ratios were not in line with the actual AA− rating. The outlook was negative and the long-term credit rating could be downgraded to A if the process of debt reduction was longer than expected' (*Les Echos*, 8 March 2004, p. 31).

Credit ratings had been downgraded with negative outlook on 6 May 2004 at the time of the final acquisition process of Messer Griesheim. The negative outlook was upgraded to stable on 7 April 2005: 'S&P raised its outlook on Air Liquide from negative to stable because of the improvement of the capital structure. The rating agency confirmed the long-term A+ rating and the short-term A−1 rating. "These ratings highlight the leadership of Air Liquide in the profitable and predictable industrial gas sector", explained S&P' (*Reuters*, 7 April 2005).

Being placed on credit watch (or rating watch) indicates that a particular event (merger, recapitalization) could change the credit rating in the near future (see Box 5.1). It can have a positive, negative or an indeterminate implication (evolutionary or neutral), depending on the nature of the strategy which determined the credit watch. This procedure is used when an event which will probably cause a change in credit rating, occurs unexpectedly. The agency releases the new rating once the study is completed. In the end, the rating may or may not differ from its previous level. The credit watch is not always due to a particular event, and it can also be a step towards future rating changes (Iankova et al., 2009).

5.1.1.4   Impact of capital structure on credit rating

In the final analysis, credit rating agencies lend greater importance to the 'net financial debt/cash flow or operating profit' cover ratio than to capital structure ratios like gearing (net financial debt/shareholders equity) (see Box 5.2).

The regressions, between credit rating and debt ratios, confirm empirically that companies with low financial leverage have the highest ratings (Paget-Blanc, 2003; Gray et al., 2006).

5.1.2   Effects of downgrades on the value of MNCs

The increase in the cost of the present and future debt is one of the main reasons for declines in the stock prices of downgraded companies (Holthausen and Leftwich, 1986). The magnitude of the reaction depends on the expected rise in interest rate spreads (the difference between the interest bond rate of a company and that of a state considered as having no credit risk). The spreads are greater when the rating is low. In addition, investors who have contract rating triggers may require immediate payment, when the issuer is downgraded to a

Box 5.2   Lafarge's debt ratios

Standard and Poor's (S&P) downgraded Lafarge's credit ratings following the 20 per cent acquisition of the English cement manufacturer Blue Circle. This acquisition undermined Lafarge's financial ratios: the additional debt has only been partly cancelled by the increase of the operating margin by 21.1 per cent in 1999 (20.1% in 1998). The credit ratings assume that the cash flow had totalled 30 per cent of the average net debt since 2001. Otherwise, a new downgrade could take place. (*Les Echos*, 22 May 2000, p. 47) speculative grade. In practice, these triggers lead to new negotiations which increase interest rates.

Since Holthausen and Leftwich's conclusions (1986), similar event studies have confirmed the average asymmetry of stock price reaction to credit rating change: there is a decrease in stock price when the company is downgraded, but no reaction when the announcement of the rating agency is neutral or positive. The US stock market seems to strongly reduce market capitalizations from -1 to -5 per cent over the period of $(-1, +1)$ days around a downgrade (Hand et al., 1992; Zaima and McCarthy, 1988). The results are similar on European stock markets (Norden and Weber, 2004; Iankova et al., 2009).

The reaction of stock markets is stronger when the downgrade is not contaminated by another event, when the original rating belongs to a speculative grade and when the announcement concerns a change which does not remain within the same class. Goh and Ederington (1993) show significant results occur only when profits, cash flows and future financial ratios have changed. By contrast, there is no significant reaction in the case of acquisitions or bankruptcies. These situations are often already foreseen by stock market analysts.

Finally, there is an emerging consensus on the fact that shareholder value declines following a downgrade. In our research, the first objective was to test whether stock markets in our sample reacted negatively to a downgrade and whether the reasons given in rating agencies reports had an impact.

Our second objective was to analyse the relationship between capital structure and strategy, in particular, the effect of excessive debt. Our study was the first to examine the impact of credit rating on corporate strategy, with the exception of Lantin and Roy (2009) who focused on only one MNC.

5.1.3   Relationship between capital structure and corporate strategy

Since Modigliani and Miller's studies (1958) about the existence of optimal financial structure, many authors have tried to identify the determinants of the financial structure of companies by using the characteristics of corporate strategy. Some papers examined the relationship between corporate strategy (level of diversification) and capital structure; others looked at the capital structure of MNCs.

5.1.3.1   *The optimal financial structure of MNCs*

Eiteman et al. (2007) report that MNCs may be in a better position than their domestic counterparts: MNCs are able to improve the liquidity of securities by gaining access to both domestic and foreign capital markets. Theoretically, international availability should allow MNCs to have a lower marginal capital cost than domestic companies, when significant amounts of new funds must be raised.

In addition, MNCs should be able to bear a higher debt ratio because their cash flows are diversified internationally (Shapiro, 2003), so, they would have a higher tax deductibility on interest and a lower capital cost compared with domestic companies.

However, empirical evidence may not support the theoretical positive effect of international diversification. Some empirical studies (Lee and Kwok, 1988; Burgman, 1996) show that US MNCs are less leveraged than their domestic counterparts. The weighted average cost of capital of MNCs is not always lower than in comparable domestic companies because of the additional costs for international financing: transaction costs, agency costs, foreign exchange risks, political risks and asymmetric information. Also, a company's debt ratio and overall financial structures are based on the financial structure standards expected by international portfolio investors, which are close to standards set by developed countries. Therefore, investors have difficulties accepting any higher debt ratio if a company wants to raise capital in the global market.

Other studies show that the relationship between a company's international activity and leverage is more complex. For example, Mansi and Reeb (2002) assume a nonlinear relation, whereas Low and Chen (2004) suggest that the results are different for US and non-US companies. Chkir and Cosset (2001) reveal a geographical diversification effect as well as an industrial diversification effect.

As for international diversification, product diversification is associated with a company's business risk reduction, and is thus positively related to high debt levels. The reduction of the volatility of earnings gives diversified companies greater debt capacity than specialized companies of similar size. Palard (2007) shows that by controlling the international diversification variable, exchange-listed European focused companies have lower debt than diversified companies. In addition, the 20-year long trend towards specialization is positively correlated to a decrease in financial leverage.

High leverage also has some effects on corporate restructuring; for example, the divestment of unrelated activities. Séverin and Dhennin (2003) suggest that leverage has an influence on the type of restructuring measures taken by French companies in response to significant stock price decline. In our study, we adopted a similar approach to look at the relationship between capital structure and restructuring measures, but we used rating downgrade as a proxy for high level of debt.

5.1.3.2 Bond rating downgrades and restructuring measures

Restructuring strategies cover many situations but all of them have the same goal: deleveraging the company directly by debt reduction, or indirectly through an increase in operating earnings. MNCs can take either or both operational and financial measures. First, operational restructuring measures include cost-cutting programmes, employee lay-offs and divestments. Cost reduction involves purchase rationalization and also a reduction in working capital. Lower costs as well as layoffs have an impact on cash flows. These measures can be taken by companies in financial distress but also after a merger.

Corporate divestments are often made by asset sell-offs; but we can also find plant or division closing, split-offs or equity carve-out. Divestment policies can have both financial and strategic impacts. From the financial viewpoint, divestitures can increase cash flows if divested activities support negative earnings, and they can also be used to reduce debt. From the strategic viewpoint, divestitures can allow the company to focus on its core business. To conclude, if divestitures can permit the company to honour financial commitments, they can finance value-enhancing projects when raising capital is impossible or expensive. Asset sales eliminate underinvestment problems described by Myers (1977) and increase growth opportunities gained through reaching a critical size in the core business (Faverjon, 2001).

Financial measures also involve debt restructuring, equity issues and changes in the dividend policy, and they must lead to a level of debt that is not excessive compared with equity. Private renegotiation of the company's debt modifies the terms of the debt in a new contract, in which at least one of the terms may be changed. For example, interest rates and/or the principal payments may be reduced, the maturity of the debt may be postponed and the creditors may buy some shares in the company. If private reorganizations concern MNCs in financial distress, MNCs could also reorganize their debt by refinancing it periodically on the debt market under better conditions. An alternative way to restructure is to issue shares. Raising equity capital allows a company to invest and/or to improve its financial structure. Finally, a company may change its dividend policy. However, we ruled this third financial measure out because of the difficulty in establishing a link with a downgraded company.

5.2 Impact of downgrades on stock prices and strategies of MNCs

5.2.1 Research methodology

The initial sample for our study was based on companies from the French CAC 40 *(Cotation Assistée en Continu)* and SBF 120 *(Société des Bourses Françaises)* indices. The database of Standard and Poor's was used to identify all downgrades between 1 January 1998 and 1 July 2006. The Bloomberg's Rating Change function (RATC) allowed us to check if a previous announcement had been made by Fitch and/or Moody's, other rating agencies. The final sample included 65 announcements for 24 MNCs affected by ratings (see Table 5.1).

5.2.1.1 Qualitative secondary data analysis

The empirical study was based on secondary data which traced the history of events and mixed several sources: reports from rating agencies

Table 5.1 Overview of the sample

Company	Industry	Company	Industry	Company	Industry
Accor	travel and leisure	Carrefour	retail	Renault	automobile and components
AGF (*Assurances Générales de France*)	insurance	Casino Guichard	retail	Rhodia	chemicals
Air Liquide	chemicals	Crédit Agricole	banking	Saint Gobain	construction and materials
Alcatel	technology	Danone	agri-food	Schneider	industrial goods and services
Arcelor	industrial goods and services	France Telecom	telecommuni-cation	Scor	insurance
ASF (*Autoroutes du Sud de la France*)	industrial goods and services	Lafarge	construction and materials	Sodexho Alliance	travel and leisure
Axa	insurance	LVMH (Louis Vuitton Moët Hennessy)	travel and leisure	Suez	utilities
Cap Gemini	technology	PPR (Pinault-Printemps-Redoute)	retail	Vivendi Universal	media

and articles from the financial and economic press. The qualitative data were the reports from S&P analysts, which provided justifications for downgrades of short-term and long-term ratings. The 'word frequencies' function of the qualitative data software, N'Vivo, was used to process the content analysis. In particular, we established, thanks to an analytical and a lexical reading of the reports, a list of concepts from the key words which helped us identify the reasons for downgrades.

The Factiva database provided additional secondary data from the French economic and financial newspaper *Les Echos* and the Reuters' database. The restructuring processes were identified in the year following a downgrade. In the case of a previous rating watch, we also considered restructuring measures taken between the rating watch and the downgrade.

Cost-cuttings, reduction in working capital, layoffs and asset sell-offs of MNCs were revealed when the databases disclosed such information. We also noted if divestments were presented as refocusing asset sales. Moreover, we identified the willingness of companies to reduce investments according to their objectives or, conversely, their wish to carry on with acquisitions and internal growth. We finally noted debt restructuring and made a distinction between equity issues and share sales to employees.

5.2.1.2 Event studies

The study was based on the estimate Abnormal Return (AR) at the time of the rating event. This is equal to the difference between the real stock price and the expected price estimated on the historical value during the estimation period. Figure 5.1 shows the case of an event, dated

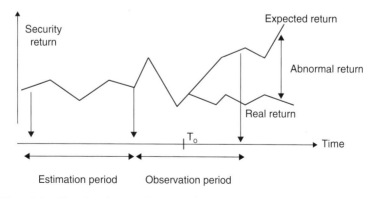

Figure 5.1 Negative abnormal return calculation

T_o, which leads to a decline in the stock price. The difference between the real return on stock markets and the expected return, is a negative abnormal return.

Stock prices of MNCs and indices are reported by the Datastream financial database. The real stock return (Rit) is compared with the expected return (Rit*), estimated by the market model based on the following equation:

$$Rit* = \alpha i + \text{ß}i \, Rmt + eit$$

with Rit* = expected return of security i at time t; αi = intersection of the market line; ßi = beta of security i; Rmt = market return; eit =random errors. The market index corresponds to that of the company studied (CAC 40 or SBF 120). Parameters αi and ßi is estimated on the 240 previous days before the observation period of $(-1,+1)$ stock exchange days around the announcement.

For each security i and each date t of the observation period, an abnormal return (ARit) is calculated with the Excel Visual Basic software. It computes the coefficient value ßi prior to estimate abnormal returns:

$$ARit = Rit - Rit*$$

with Rit = abnormal return of security i at time t.

Finally, Cumulated Abnormal Returns (CARs) are computed as:

$$CARit = \Sigma \, t/k = 1 \, ARik$$

with ARik = abnormal return of security i at time k.

5.2.1.3 *Descriptive analysis of the sample*

Our sample aggregated announcements which changed an initial rating in investment grade (AAA to BBB−), or in speculative grade (BB+ to D) (see Table 5.2).

Table 5.2 Sample distribution by rating class

Rating class	AAA	AA	A	BBB	BB	B	Total
		Investment			Speculative		
Number	0	15	23	24	3	0	65
%	0.0%	23.1%	35.4%	36.9%	4.6%	0.0%	100%

AA = Rating class AA including ratings AA+, AA and AA−.

The median of the sample was in rating class A (A−, A and A+), while the European median published by rating agencies was in class BBB, because our sample included the most important French capitalizations. Owing to their size, these companies can have a better rating than middle capitalizations, even with a low level of debt. Lastly, there was a large data cluster: 78.5 per cent of the companies in the sample had only five different ratings (AA−, A+, A, A− and BBB+) out of 21 existing ratings.

The speculative grade was weak and included only three events which represented 4.6 per cent of the sample. This result was close to 9 per cent for French MNCs in speculative grade published by the 2008 credit rating annual report of the French financial market authority, *Autorité des Marchés Financiers* (AMF).

In our study, rating changes were downgrades of one, two or three notches. For example, if the original rating was A+, the new rating was A for a downgrade of one notch and respectively A− and BBB+ for a downgrade of two and three notches. The sample included mainly one notch downgrades (86.2%), only 12.3 per cent of two notch downgrades and 1.5 per cent of three notch downgrades.

5.2.2   Effects of downgrades on stockholder value of MNCs

5.2.2.1   *Qualitative analysis of credit rating reports*

The objective in reading reports of rating agencies, using qualitative data process software, is to identify the main themes of analysts. Table 5.3 reports the 15 most frequently used words when justifying downgrades.

The results confirm the importance of arguments based on debt levels and cash (keywords 'debt' and 'cash'). The changes in these variables are due to external growth ('acquisitions') or lower operating incomes ('operating', 'sales' and 'earnings'). Difficult market conditions

Table 5.3   Keywords from credit rating reports

Keywords	Frequency	Keywords	Frequency	Keywords	Frequency
debt	236	operating	97	investment	44
cash	163	management	69	liquidity	32
market	138	sales	67	flexibility	26
acquisition	112	asset	63	profitability	24
business	100	earnings	48	capitalization	16

('market') are also often mentioned, as well as the competitive position ('company'). Finally, the key ratios of the financial analysis are the asset total, the levels of investment, the liquidity, the financial flexibility, the profitability and the capitalization.

The reports are divided into two categories which are approximately the same size. The first half of downgrades is due to an acquisition process. The second half of the reports shows a decrease in operating income and/or a difficult competitive position, due to a decline in the economic situation or increased competition.

5.2.2.2 Impacts of downgrades on stock prices

Following the calculations of event studies, our study removed events with extreme values (>40%) indicating a very sharp decrease in stock prices. These cases needed to undergo a complete individual analysis. The number of downgrades in our study was reduced from 65 to 60 events, because the goal was to avoid distorting the average results of small size sub-samples (number <30).

We then tested the effect of one of the two main reasons for 'acquisitions' and 'other reasons' downgrades. This category included declines in operating profits and/or negative changes in market conditions.

Table 5.4 shows an insignificant and average low change in stock prices over the period of (−1,+1) days surrounding a downgrade. Stock markets actually reacted negatively in half the cases (29 of 60). Table 5.5 then reveals the average negative results

Low or positive individual reactions can be justified on several grounds: an anticipation of the announcement by stockholders, the small impact on the debt cost or future cash flows, the wealth transfer from bondholders to stockholders. Indeed, a downgrade can be considered as good news for stockholders, because managers are likely to undertake more risky investments with higher future cash flows.

Table 5.4 Cumulated Average Abnormal Returns (CAARs) for downgrades

Downgrades	Total	Reasons for downgrades	
		Acquisitions	Other reasons
Number	60	30	30
−1	−0.02%	0.58%	−0.63%
0	−0.09%	0.10%	−0.28%
+1	−0.14%	−0.47%	0.18%
(−1,+1) days	−0.26%	0.21%	−0.73%

Table 5.5   CAARs from negative results for downgrades

Downgrades	Total	Reasons for downgrades	
		Acquisitions	Other Reasons
Number	29	13	16
−1	−0.86%	0.17%	−1.70%***
0	−2.01% **	−1.15%***	−2.71%*
+1	−2.26%*	−3.24%	−1.46%*
(−1,+1) days	−5.13%***	−4.22%**	−5.86%***

Note: *, **, ***: Results significantly different from zero at 10%, 5% and 1%, using Student T test.

Our results regarding MNCs which made an acquisition over the period of (−1,+1) days (0.21%), were similar to those of Goh and Ederington (1993) on the US stock market. They showed unanticipated and insignificant increases in close to zero stock prices.

In addition, our study (−0.73%) confirmed the conclusions of Goh and Ederington (1993) in the case of declines in operating income (−1.18%, significant result). Despite a difference of 0.94 per cent between the two sub-samples, we could not draw a conclusion concerning the distinction between reasons for downgrades. Indeed, our results were not significant.

Table 5.5 reports CAARs for downgrades which only lead to a decline in the stock price. It shows large and significant average changes on the day of the event (−2.01%), on the next day (−2.26%) and over the entire period (−1,+1) days (−5.13%). The reactions towards MNCs are higher when the event is not anticipated and when decreases in future cash flows are significant.

The average stockholder value was −5.13 per cent and included two categories: first, there was a decrease of −4.22 per cent for 13 MNCs downgraded following an acquisition; second, there was a fall of −5.86 per cent for 16 MNCs which recorded bad and/or disappointing operating performance. This confirms that the anticipation of the stock market is strong when downgrades are due to external growth. However, the difference between the two sub-samples was not sufficient to justify the level of reaction. Other criteria, notably reported by Lantin (2010), were more discriminating: rating class, number of notches, downgrades from a rating in class A to a rating in class BBB and from a rating in investment grade to speculative grade.

Table 5.6   Restructuring measures

Number	0–6 months (65)		0–1 year (65)		Companies threatened or downgraded in speculative grade (10)	
	Number of companies	Frequency	Number of companies	Frequency	0–6 months	0–1 year
Operational restructuring measures:	50	77%	54	83%	80%	80%
cost-cutting	33	51%	35	54%	70%	70%
layoffs	19	29%	21	32%	60%	60%
asset sell-offs	38	58%	41	63%	70%	70%
Additional information:						
refocusing	21	32%	24	37%	20%	20%
reduce capital expenditure	12	18%	13	20%	0%	0%
acquisitions/internal growth	24	37%	29	45%	0%	0%
Financial restructuring measures:	32	49%	39	60%	70%	70%
debt restructuring	25	38%	29	45%	60%	60%
equity issue	13	20%	14	21%	30%	30%
sale of shares to employees	5	8%	8	12%	0%	0%
Number of measures	2.1		2.3		2.9	2.9

5.2.3   Strategic changes following downgrades

5.2.3.1   *Restructuring actions undertaken by MNCs*

Based on the business press reports, Table 5.6 illustrates restructuring measures taken by MNCs during the year after their downgrade (0–1 year). We consider that a company takes operational measures if at least one of the three following actions is carried out:

- cost-cutting
- layoff
- and/or asset sell-off.

We used the same methodology to report the proportion of companies undertaking financial restructuring actions.

Table 5.7 reports the proportion of companies undertaking between zero and six restructuring actions (three operational events, three financial events) in the six months (0–6 months) and in the year (0–1 year) following their downgrade.

The results were consistent with those of Séverin and Dhennin (2003): a majority of MNCs undertake more than one restructuring action. On average, we measured two events in the six months following a downgrade (see Table 5.6). Restructuring actions are both operational and financial actions, even if there are more operational measures. Debt restructuring and share issuing are perhaps more difficult to initiate than cost-cutting or asset sell-offs: 58 per cent of companies in our study initiated divestitures in the six months following their downgrade; creditors may also require divestitures before renegotiating debt (see Box 5.3).

The results also provided some evidence that the measures were taken quickly, essentially during the six months following the downgrade. The end of this chapter will thus focus on this period of time. Companies can initiate restructuring as of the introduction of credit-watch. In addition, a downgrade to a rating in the speculative grade, or a threat (a rating change to BBB– with negative outlook), leads to massive restructuring plans with asset sell-offs (see Boxes 5.4 and 5.5).

Table 5.7   Frequency for restructuring actions

Number of events	0	1	2	3	4	5	6
0–6 months	14%	26%	20%	23%	15%	1%	0%
0–1 year	11%	18%	28%	23%	15%	5%	0%

Box 5.3   Vivendi Universal's debt restructuring

Faced with a liquidity crisis, Vivendi Universal had to sell assets very quickly in 2002. But this allowed it to negotiate a new credit line at a high cost. Then, top managers had time to define other assets to sell, in order to specialize under better conditions. In addition, the new credit line allowed Vivendi Universal to issue mandatory convertibles, in order to buy shares in the French company Cegetel, to consolidate its cash flows. Finally, the terms of the credit line could be renegotiated.

Source: *Les Echos*, 19 September 2002, p. 16; *Les Echos*, 18 November 2002, p. 20.

Box 5.4   Restructuring measures for Casino

'Last Friday, financial markets did not expect that Casino's stock price which had increased by 8.1 per cent the day before, would continue to gain 3.03 per cent at 57.75 Euros, still supported by the announcement of a 2 billion euro asset sell-offs plan. Casino made this major refocusing plan in order not to be downgraded to the speculative grade by Standard and Poor's. Stock analysts did not expect this reaction, especially from a company which was always reluctant to divest' (*Les Echos*, 20 March 2006, p. 31).

Box 5.5   Restructuring measures for Lafarge

Faced with the 2008 crisis, Lafarge carried out a 1.5 billion Euro capital increase whereas its market capitalization was 7 billion Euros and its financial debt 17 billion Euros. This capital increase was supported by a 600 million Euros cost reduction plan, 1 billion Euros asset sales and a drop by half the dividend that is to say 400 million euros. The company's aim was to avoid being downgraded to speculative grade. The funds allowed the company to repay the first two sections of the debt incurred to take control of Orascom in January 2008. It ruled out the financial covenant which scared financial market because the debt had to be paid if the value of the net debt ratio to Earnings Before Interest Taxes Depreciation and Amortization (EBITDA) exceeded 3.75.

Source: *Les Echos*, 23 February 2009, p. 21.

5.2.3.2 Impact of initial rating level on restructuring actions

We divided the sample of companies according to the initial rating class (see Table 5.8) and the two types of initial rating (see Table 5.9) in order to explain the influence of rating on restructuring measures.

The number of restructuring actions, essentially operational actions, increased even further the low initial rating. Only companies initially rated A, or higher, maintained strategic acquisitions and internal growth, even though they were downgraded. These observations suggest that there was an impact on the strategy of highly leveraged companies.

Table 5.8   Restructuring measures and initial rating class

	AA	A	BBB	BB
Number	15	23	24	3
Operational restructuring measures	60%	74%	87%	100%
cost-cutting	40%	39%	67%	67%
layoffs	13%	22%	37%	100%
asset sell-offs	40%	52%	71%	100%
Additional information				
refocusing	13%	39%	37%	33%
reducing capital expenditure	13%	17%	25%	0%
acquisitions/internal growth	53%	48%	21%	0%
Financial restructuring measures	53%	43%	46%	100%
debt restructuring	40%	35%	33%	100%
equity issue	20%	17%	17%	67%
sale of shares to employees	13%	0%	12%	0%
Number of measures	1.7	1.7	2.4	4.3

Table 5.9   Restructuring measures and initial rating

	AA to BBB+	BBB to BB−
Number	45	20
Operational restructuring measures	71%	90%
cost-cutting	42%	70%
layoffs	20%	50%
asset sell-offs	44%	90%
Additional information		
refocusing	24%	50%
reducing capital expenditure	16%	25%
acquisitions/internal growth	47%	15%
Financial restructuring measures	44%	60%
debt restructuring	33%	50%
equity issue	18%	25%
sale of shares to employees	7%	10%
Number of measures	1.6	3.0

Table 5.9 leads us to the conclusion that BBB seems to be the initial rating which increased the frequency of major restructuring plans. This corresponded to a downgrade from BBB rating to the BBB– lowest rating in the investment grade. MNCs, initially rated between AA and BBB+, undertook 1.6 actions over the 6 months period following their downgrade, compared with three actions for companies initially rated between BBB and BB–. The operational actions increased from 71 per cent to 90 per cent according to the two sub-samples. This was due to the increase in asset sell-offs as part of refocusing actions. Financial measures grew from 44 per cent to 60 per cent for MNCs rated between BBB and BB–, and half of them restructured their debt.

5.2.3.3   Influence of the reasons for downgrades

In addition to the initial rating level, the reasons for downgrades had an effect on the frequency and the type of measures taken by MNCs following their downgrade (see Table 5.10).

Table 5.10 reports many equity issues and/or debt renegotiation following an acquisition, in order to enhance the borrowing capacity for a future major investment. Operational measures were higher than financial measures: many companies wanted to reduce costs and to sell assets. The cost-cutting following the acquisition may be due to both downgrade and decline in outlook; indeed, agencies anticipated lower synergy gains than expected. In spite of divestitures in non-core business sales, MNCs maintained internal or external growth.

Table 5.10   Restructuring measures and reasons for downgrades

	Acquisition	Other reasons	Cases of liquidity crisis
Number	31	34	6
Operational restructuring measures	71%	82%	83%
cost-cutting	48%	53%	50%
layoffs	19%	38%	50%
asset sell-offs	52%	65%	83%
Additional information			
refocusing	29%	35%	33%
reducing capital expenditure	19%	18%	0%
acquisitions/internal growth	55%	21%	0%
Financial restructuring measures	42%	56%	100%
debt restructuring	32%	44%	83%
equity issue	16%	23%	67%
sale of shares to employees	13%	3%	0%
Number of measures	1.81	2.26	3.33

If the reasons for downgrades were different (unfavourable economic context and/or negative operating earnings), financial measures were more numerous than for downgrades following an acquisition. Massive financial plans were undertaken to avoid bankruptcy for MNCs facing a liquidity crisis. An increase of equity was often the only solution to save them.

5.3   Conclusion

This chapter contributes to a better understanding of stock market reactions to downgrades and of the type of strategic restructuring conducted by MNCs.

Reactions of stock prices for the downgraded MNCs in our study were not significantly different from zero on average. Indeed, the announcement may have already been expected by stock analysts and/or the impact on their debt cost and cash flows may have been low if the initial rating was high. However, this average result revealed different situations because only half of the downgrades destroyed stockholder value. The stock price reaction was more than –5 per cent over the period of (–1, +1) days around a downgrade. The reasons for the downgrade (acquisition or operating performance decline) seemed to have limited impact on stock market reactions.

In addition, we noticed many operational and financial changes in the six months following a downgrade. Divestiture was the main reaction for enhancing financial flexibility. The measures were all the more significant when the initial rating was low, in particular for non-core asset sales. Their frequency was higher when the initial rating was BBB (corresponding to a downgrade to the BBB– lowest rating in the investment grade). Finally, the reasons for downgrades had an effect on the type of restructuring: a downgrade in a difficult context involved a larger number of financial measures than a downgrade after an acquisition.

References

Batsch, L. (1999) *Finance et stratégie* (Paris: Economica).

Burgman, T. A. (1996) 'An Empirical Examination of Multinational Corporate Capital Structure', *Journal of International Business Studies*, 27 (3), 553–70.

Chkir, I. E. and Cosset, J.-C. (2001) 'Diversification Strategy and Capital Structure of Multinational Corporations', *Journal of Multinational Financial Management*, 11 (1), 17–37.

Eiteman, D. K., Stonehill, A. I. and Moffett, M. H. (2007) *Multinational Business Finance* (London: Addison Wesley, Pearson).

Faverjon, C. (2001) 'Les recentrages d'entreprises: motivations, caractéristiques et influence sur la valeur. Le cas des entreprises françaises cotées sur la période 1989–1998', unpublished doctoral thesis (Lyon: Jean Moulin Lyon 3 University).

Goh, J. C. and Ederington, L. H. (1993) 'Is a Bond Rating Downgrade Good News, Bad News, or No News to Stockholders?', *The Journal of Finance*, 48 (5), 2001–08.

Gray, S., Mirkovic, A. and Ragunathan, V. (2006) 'The Determinants of Credit Ratings: Australian Evidence', *Australian Journal of Management*, 31 (2), 333–54.

Hand, J., Holthausen, R. and Leftwich, R. (1992) 'The Effect of Bond Rating Agency Announcements on Bond and Stock Prices', *The Journal of Finance*, 67 (2), 733–52.

Holthausen, R. W. and Leftwich, R. W. (1986) 'The Effect of Bond Rating Changes on Common Stock Prices', *Journal of Financial Economics*, 17 (1), 57–89.

Iankova, E., Pochon, F. and Teïletche, J. (2009) 'L'impact des décisions des agences de notation sur le prix des actions: une comparaison du cas français avec les cas européen et américain', *Économie et prévision*, 2 (188), 1–21.

Lantin, F. (2010) *Impacts de la notation financière sur le prix des actions* (Saarbrücken: Editions Universitaires Européennes).

Lantin, F. and Roy, P. (2009) 'Le rôle du rating dans une stratégie de croissance externe', *Revue Française de Gestion*, 191, 15–32.

Lee, K. C. and Kwok, C. C. Y. (1988) 'Multinational Corporations vs. Domestic Corporations: International Environmental Factors and Determinants of Capital Structure', *Journal of International Business Studies*, 19 (2), 195–217.

Les Echos (2000) 'Analyse financière. Les valeurs de la semaine. Lafarge', 22 May.

Les Echos (2002a) 'Vivendi Universal desserre son étau financier au prix fort', 19 September.

Les Echos (2002b) 'Vivendi Universal a placé avec succès ses obligations remboursables en actions', 18 November.

Les Echos (2004) 'Analyse financière. Les valeurs de la semaine. Air Liquide', 8 March.

Les Echos (2006) 'Le groupe Casino revient en grâce sur les marchés', 20 March.

Les Echos (2009) 'Lafarge lance un plan de renflouement de 4,5 milliards d'euros', 23 February.

Les Echos (2010) 'GDF Suez nouveau numéro deux mondial de l'électricité', 11 August.

Low, P. Y. and Chen, K. H. (2004) 'Diversification and Capital Structure: Some International Evidence', *Review of Quantitative Finance and Accounting*, 23, 55–71.

Mansi, S. A. and Reeb, D. M. (2002) 'Corporate International Activity and Debt Financing', *Journal of International Business Studies*, 33 (1), 129–47.

Modigliani, F. and Miller, M. (1958) 'The Cost of Capital, Corporation Finance and the Theory of Investment', *American Economic Review*, 48 (3), 261–97.

Myers, S. C. (1977) 'Determinants of Corporate Borrowing', *Journal of Financial Economics*, 5, 147–75.

Norden, L. and Weber, M. (2004) 'Informational Efficiency of Credit Default Swap and Stock Markets: The Impact of Credit Rating Announcements', *Journal of Banking and Finance*, 28, 2813–43.

Paget-Blanc, E. (2003) 'Rating et probabilité de défaut des entreprises européennes: Détermination par un modèle de régression logistique ordonné', *Banque et Marchés*, 65, 38–47.

Palard, J.-E. (2007) 'Recentrage stratégique et politique de financement: le cas des firmes cotées en Europe (1987–2003)', *Finance Contrôle Stratégie*, 10 (3), 111–37.

Reuters (2005) 'Air Liquide – S&P relève sa perspective de négative à stable', 7 April.

Séverin, E. and Dhennin, S. (2003) 'Structure du capital et mesures de restructuration', *Finance Contrôle Stratégie*, 6 (1), 155–86.

Shapiro, A. C. (2003) *Multinational Financial Management* (London: Prentice Hall).

Zaima, J. K. and McCarthy, J. (1988) 'The Impact of Bond Rating Changes on Common Stocks and Bonds: Tests of the Wealth Redistribution Hypothesis', *The Financial Review*, 23 (4), 483–98.

Part II
The Complexity of Internal Management: Headquarters–Subsidiaries Relationships

6
Establishing Foreign Subsidiaries: The Accor Group

Ludivine Chalençon and Emna Moalla

In an unstable economic environment, multinational companies (MNCs) need to better manage their relationships with foreign subsidiaries. Xu and Shenkar (2002) argue that over one third of international trade takes place between MNCs' subsidiaries. According to UNCTAD (2010), foreign subsidiaries of MNCs have been less impacted by the 2008 economic crisis: the share of gross domestic product (GDP) gained by these subsidiaries reached the record level of 11 per cent. Foreign subsidiaries play an important role in the global economy, but headquarters' coordination seems rather complex. Therefore, companies need to adapt to local market specificities when they create and manage foreign subsidiaries. Several concepts have been defined in the specialized literature to describe these characteristics: country risk, cultural distance, institutions, and so on.

This chapter focuses on the multidimensional concept of distance in order to highlight the main areas of differences between headquarters and subsidiaries as a result of local market specificities. Distance may be identified through several dimensions. Ghemawat (2001) suggests four of them: cultural, administrative, geographic and economic. In the first section of this chapter, we will examine the importance of distance in a company's internationalization process. The second section will focus on the case of Accor and the key role played by different forms of distance in the establishment of foreign subsidiaries.

6.1 Distance: A multidimensional concept

Most MNCs manage a large number of subsidiaries all over the world. Faced with such diversity, they need to pay attention to cultural differences in order to take the right decisions and to efficiently manage their relationships with subsidiaries. Thus, many questions arise regarding the issues of choice and development process. How can companies manage such diversity? What are the dimensions that influence the decision of MNCs to enter foreign markets?

Specialized literature makes a distinction between companies with an incremental international development and born globals or international new ventures (Oviatt and McDougall, 1994). For several decades, increased importance has been given to the internationalization process of companies. The Uppsala model set up by the Scandinavian school in the 1970s remains one of the most well-known models in the field of international business.

Developed by Johanson and Wiedersheim-Paul (1975) and Johanson and Vahlne (1977), this model is based on the incremental and sequential character of the internationalization process. It relies on two main concepts, the learning effect and psychic distance. We will focus on the second concept defined by Johanson and Vahlne (2009, p. 1412) as 'factors that make it difficult to understand foreign environments'. These factors can be cultural, linguistic, educational, political, managerial or related to the level of a country's industrialization (Angué and Mayrhofer, 2010; Cheriet, 2010). This model correlated the internationalization process with psychic distance between domestic and foreign markets. Indeed, in order to reduce the risk and uncertainty related to a new environment, the company starts by developing its domestic market, and later expands its activities to other neighbouring markets with a low psychic distance. These markets have similar characteristics to the home country.

Recently, Johanson and Vahlne have reviewed their model based mainly on the network approach. They underline the importance of networking in the internationalization process, and assume that 'the internationalization process develops within a network' (Johanson and Vahlne, 2009, p. 1424) where relationships are characterized by specific levels of knowledge, commitment and trust. In the new model, psychic distance applies mainly to stakeholders within the network and not to markets.

According to the Uppsala model, the company takes into account psychic distance when moving from being a local enterprise to an MNC. Since the 1970s, and following the work of the Scandinavian school, the concept of distance has been the subject of several research papers. Many authors have confirmed the key role of psychic distance, but there is still an ongoing debate concerning its conceptualization and operationalization (Evans and Mavondo, 2002; Brewer, 2007).

Some studies have examined cultural and/or psychic distance, these two concepts being sometimes confused with one another in the literature. However, the concept of psychic distance is identified at the company's level and it develops according to the firm's learning process (Angué and Mayrhofer, 2010). Other distance dimensions are also important, and their impact on decision making and management may be significant.

In 2001, Ghemawat proposed a framework known as the 'CAGE (Cultural, Administrative, Geographic and Economic) distance framework'. The author's aim was to help managers assess the impact of distance on trading in foreign markets. Ghemawat (2001) defined four distance dimensions, but provided no information about their operationalization. Some studies have used this model as a framework for empirical research (Angué and Mayrhofer, 2010; Malhotra et al., 2009).

Cultural distance concerns the differences between two cultures. Culture is perceived as mental programming, a common reference system for a certain group of people. This reference system contains a set of standards and values which influence individuals' actions and decisions (Dupuis, 2004). Ghemawat (2001) defines cultural distance as a concept based on factors such as language, ethnicity, religious beliefs and social standards. In the international business literature, cultural distance is one of the most widely used concepts to explain internationalization factors, such as the location of foreign direct investments (FDI) or the choice of market entry modes. Most researchers have used the six cultural dimensions identified by Hofstede et al. (2010). Other cultural dimensions have been put forward, such as that by Schwartz (1992) or the GLOBE (Global Leadership and Organizational Behavior Effectiveness) study's dimensions (House et al., 2002).

Administrative or political distance is the least studied dimension in the specialized literature. It mainly derives from history, the institutional context and government policy. Indeed, history may refer, for instance, to the country's colonial past. Ghemawat (2001) argues that colonial ties reduce the administrative distance between countries. Government policy refers to the country's political stability. In the literature, particular attention is paid to the institutional dimension (Xu and Shenkar, 2002; Chao and Kumar, 2010). Institutional distance has been defined as the difference between countries' regulative, cognitive and normative institutions (Kostova, 1996). Xu and Shenkar (2002) highlight the importance of institutional distance for MNCs, which have to cope with several institutional environments.

Geographic distance is the most obvious dimension since it refers to the physical distance between countries. According to Angué and Mayrhofer (2010, p. 10), this dimension concerns 'the physical distance between countries or geographical areas in which partners operate. It results from a series of factors such as the absence of a common border, of transport (maritime, inland waterway, rail or road access) or communication infrastructures'. In the case of MNCs, geographic distance is the physical distance between the headquarters and its subsidiaries and partners. This distance may not only hinder headquarters–subsidiaries relationships, but also adversely affect the working relationship between partners. Several studies confirm the impact of geographic distance on the choice of location or market entry mode as well as on the management of diversity. Ragozzino (2009) shows, for instance, that US firms acquire more stakes in countries with low geographic distance. Similarly, Shenkar (2001) argues that geographical proximity reduces barriers and facilitates knowledge transfer. Ghemawat (2001) confirms that proximity allows effective information flows.

Economic distance is the difference in economic wealth between two countries, and particularly the difference in terms of quality and costs of natural, financial and human resources (Ghemawat, 2001). Consumers' income and purchasing power are important attributes for economic distance. Evans and Mavondo (2002) show that the economic environment is a key factor, and that it may affect foreign market attractiveness. Thus, the economic dimension appears to be particularly important and can influence MNCs' development choices and managerial practices.

In summary, distance is a multidimensional concept that has long been reduced to its cultural dimension. It should be noted that distance develops over time and depends on the company's experience, and general trends in the global environment. To demonstrate the impact of distance on the international expansion of MNCs, we will analyse the case of the French hotel company Accor.

6.2   The case of Accor

6.2.1   Presentation of the group

Founded in 1967 with the creation of Novotel-SIEH (Société d'Investissement et d'Exploitation Hôteliers, a hotel investment and operating company), the company launched its activities in France and later expanded internationally. In 1983, the group changed its name from Novotel-SIEH to Accor, and was listed on the Paris Stock

Exchange. Today, Accor is present in about 90 countries, with over 145,000 collaborators. Managing a large brand portfolio (see Figure 6.1), the company's focus remains on developing further its hotel offering. In 2009, the group turnover was estimated at 7.07 billion Euros, with 282 million Euros net income. Accor thus became the European market leader, and the fifth largest hotel group in the world. The company aims at becoming one of the three most competitive groups. In order to achieve this objective, it decided to adopt a specialization strategy focusing on its core business. Gilles Pélisson, Accor Chairman and Chief Executive Officer, stated, 'Today Accor holds a unique position in the industry thanks to its capacity to cover all key hotel segments.

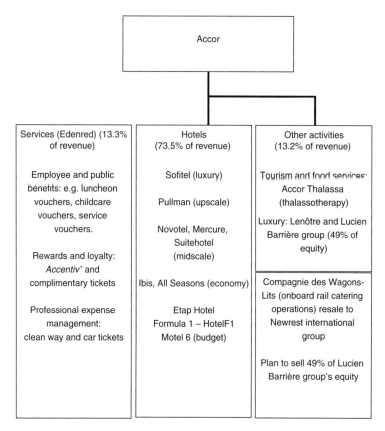

Figure 6.1   Organization of Accor
Source: Survey of Accor Group extracted from the database Xerfi, p. 39.

By becoming a pure player in the hotel sector, the group will be even more flexible and effective in its operation, in the use of shareholder capital and in its customer relationship management' (Accor, 2009, p. 85). Figure 6.1 presents the group's main activities.

In July 2010, Accor split its hotel operations from its other service activities (representing 13.3% of the group turnover in 2009), the latter of which are now grouped together in another distinct unit named Edenred, also listed on the Stock Exchange.

6.2.2   Accor's international expansion

Accor's international development shows the impact of distance on the choice of location. Indeed, the company took its first steps in France with a hotel in Lille, followed by several other hotels in large cities. It is only much later that the company's founders planned to expand internationally: 'without any real strategy and with limited resources, they boldly set out to explore and seek out new territories' (Accor, 2007, p. 31). They first targeted countries with low geographic distance and with similar economic and industrial structures. Indeed, the first international establishments were in Switzerland, Belgium and the UK. 'At the beginning, they naturally looked at neighboring countries where hotels were similar to those in France, that is to say, frankly outdated' (Accor, 2007, p. 31).

The first establishment outside France was in Geneva, with the creation of Novotel International. However, Accor experienced difficulties in developing these markets in spite of their geographic proximity. For example, in Belgium, the group had to face resistance by authorities as a result of ecological pressure.

International expansion continued and the group entered the Polish market in the early 1970s, thanks to Robert Molinari's meeting with the Polish Minister for Tourism – at that time, Robert Molinari was in charge of Accor's group development; this meeting imparted a new dynamic to Accor's expansion. Molinari's team suffered a real cultural shock: 'the team discovered another world: that of a country blocked in communist immobility' (Accor, 2007, p. 32). The political system and the culture were far removed from those existing in France, but also from those of other countries where the group had already established itself. Consequently, the team was forced to understand and adapt to a new operating system. Thanks to Robert Molinari's perseverance, 'the Polish government got involved in the construction of six 140-room Novotels, in accordance with state obligations' (Accor, 2007, p. 32). Cultural and administrative distance also influenced the management of the Polish subsidiary. In the face of this new context, the group chose to pursue a strategy of franchise contracts as a way of reducing diversity. Thus, Accor granted the Polish state the use of its brand name, but kept control over sales and service standards. This mode of entry enables the reduction of uncertainty, and respects cultural and political diversity.

> Moreover, the Polish government, as the franchisee, was in charge of management. Communist and bureaucratic management is characterized by the same large number of employees in each hotel, regardless of the number of customers. Despite this cultural shock with communist Poland, the Eastern European adventure really heartened the teams.
>
> (Accor, 2007, p. 33)

In another context, the group selected a different mode of entry. It chose to establish a partnership in the Netherlands to proceed with its expansion plans, and this partnership allowed Accor to become the country's leader. So Accor began to gain a wider international experience.

> In the 1990s, after the fall of the Berlin Wall, other successful 50–50 partnerships were formed in the Netherlands, as well as in Italy with the Agnelli group, in Brazil with the Brascon group and in Portugal with the Amorim group. Accor also took stakes in state-owned companies, for example, Pannonia in Hungary and Orbis in Poland.
>
> (Accor, 2007, p. 33)

The French group also invested in Africa, where it had to face different distance dimensions and other significant challenges, such as political instability, security, financing, organizational and recruitment issues.

> The key to these African success stories was a high degree of open-mindedness, a real taste for adventure, deep respect for others and their cultures, and a large measure of teams' autonomy which acted with full freedom.
>
> (Accor, 2007, p. 35)

Accor's first steps at the international level were difficult and fraught with obstacles. Indeed, several distance dimensions made this expansion complex. The international development of Accor seems to confirm the Uppsala model: companies develop initially in their domestic market before incrementally expanding into neighbouring markets with low psychic distance. To establish itself in more distant countries, Accor took into account different distance dimensions by adjusting its mode of entry, as in Poland.

6.2.3   Accor's current dynamic expansion

Accor's continued development includes increased hotel capacities, with plans for 200,000 new rooms by 2015, that is to say a 41 per cent increase compared with that in 2009. The first geographic area targeted is Europe, where the group plans to create 80,000 rooms, about 40 per cent of the projected total. The group also aims to consolidate its position in the Asia-Pacific region (29% of planned rooms) which registers rapid growth rates. This increase in hotel capacities mainly concerns the economy and budget segments.

Gilles Pélisson said, 'We wish to consolidate our strong base in Europe, the world's leading hotel market, with openings in key locations in selected countries. We also want to establish solid positions and strengthen our presence in high-growth regions like Asia (China and India), Latin America (Brazil), the Middle East, North Africa and Eastern Europe (Russia)' (Accor, 2009, p. 84).

To achieve its objectives, Accor has developed a project, entitled 'Ariane 2015', based on five strategic points: a strong brand portfolio, a dynamic commercial strategy, an active strategy related to accommodation capacities, an attractive management policy and an asset right policy. The aim of this project is to adapt ways of ownership to different hotel categories and various host countries, as well as to favour hotel management through franchises (in the short term, these contracts should represent about 40% of its hotel portfolio versus 21% at the time of writing) against whole ownership or fixed leases. Gilles Pélisson underlines the innovative nature of this reorganization: 'our business model is unique because our approach to ownership management – which we call our asset-right strategy – sets us apart from our competitors' (Accor, 2009, p. 84).

Having gained expertise at the international level, Accor favours contractual agreements to open new hotels throughout the world, applying its asset-right strategy: the choice of the type of contract depends on the market sector and the host country (see Box 6.1). This new strategy has been adopted to counteract the effects of the 2008 financial crisis. Accor has a wide range of management models unlike its rivals (whole ownership, fixed or variable lease, management and franchise contracts). The distribution of these different modes of management allows Accor to retain ownership through less capital-intensive forms.

Box 6.1   Type of contract by market segment

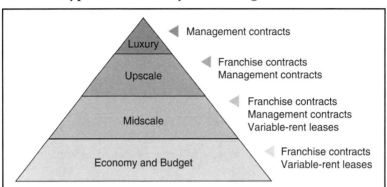

Management contracts: The group manages a hotel under one of its banners on behalf of the hotel's owner, who benefits from Accor's booking systems, marketing skills and hotel operating expertise for a fee. This operating structure is used mainly in the upscale and luxury segments and in emerging markets.

Franchise: Unlike a management contract hotel, a franchised hotel is operated by its owner, who uses one of the Accor brands, as well as its booking and distribution systems, in return for a fee. The hotel must also comply with the brand's standards.

Variable-rent leases: Accor rents the hotel from an investor and pays rents that may vary according to the hotel revenue. This solution is used extensively in the midscale and economy segments and in countries with stable economies.

Owned hotels: Accor owns the land and the hotel. This operating structure is used in the most economically stable regions.

Source: Accor, 2009, pp. 28–9.

'That's why, in recent years, the group refocused on hotel operations, divesting hotels and selling its know-how to franchisees' (Accor, 2009, p. 28). Its numerous sales – 157 'Formule 1' hotels were sold for 272 million Euros in October 2009 and 450 hotels are expected to be sold between 2010 and 2013 – enable the group to reduce the volatility of its income and to generate cash flow to finance its development.

To successfully carry out this ambitious expansion plan, we are going to work hand-in-hand with hotel investor partners, since

80 per cent of future openings will involve less capital-intensive operating structures.

(Accor, 2009, p. 84)

The asset right strategy underscores the importance of the host country's economic situation. Indeed, Accor first targets the most appropriate market segment for each planned foreign expansion. Depending on the result of its preliminary analyses, it opts for the most relevant entry mode. For instance, whole ownership is preferred in stable economic regions.

The impact of different aspects of distance has, therefore, changed during Accor's internationalization. During its initial international development, geographical distance was essential: the group began by opening new hotels in neighbouring countries. As expansion continued in more distant countries, administrative and cultural distances became more critical, in particular when entering the Polish market. Currently, the group takes into account other distance dimensions, for instance the economic dimension.

6.3   Conclusion

There are many challenges to the creation of foreign subsidiaries for MNCs, which have to take into consideration local market specificities. The management of the relationship between headquarters and subsidiaries is of necessity based on understanding diversity which can be analysed from the distance perspective. This chapter relies on the multidimensional approach of distance, proposed by Ghemawat (2001), to illustrate its role in complex relationships.

The analysis of the French group Accor allows the identification of the prevailing dimensions in terms of the location of its subsidiaries. Furthermore, the distance impact remains highly correlated with the experience effect identified in the Uppsala model. The influence of distance may be changing according to developments occurring in the global environment. Indeed, global transformations confront MNCs with a more complex environment while offering increasing growth opportunities. This chapter highlights the potential impact of distance in the establishment and development of foreign subsidiaries. Distance is frequently a challenge for MNCs. To meet this challenge, they must adapt their entry modes and managerial practices to the environment in which they wish to develop.

References

Accor (2007) *L'aventure du possible* (Paris: Accor).

Accor (2009) *Rapport annuel d'activités* (Paris: Accor).

Angué, K. and Mayrhofer, U. (2010) 'International R&D Cooperation: The Effects of Distance on the Choice of the Country of Partners', *M@n@gement*, 13 (1), 1–37.

Brewer, P. (2007) 'Psychic Distance and Australian Export Market Selection', *Australian Journal of Management*, 32 (1), 73–94.

Chao, M. C. H. and Kumar, V. (2010) 'The Impact of Institutional Distance of the International Diversity-Performance Relationship', *Journal of World Business*, 45 (1), 93–103.

Cheriet, F. (2010) 'Modèle d'Uppsala et implantation des firmes multinationales agroalimentaires: la présence de Danone en Algérie', *Revue Française de Gestion*, 36 (201), 45–64.

Dupuis, J.-P. (2004) 'Problème de cohérence théorique chez Philippe d'Iribarne: une voie de sortie', *Management International*, 8 (3), 21–9.

Evans, J. and Mavondo, F. T. (2002) 'Psychic Distance and Organizational Performance: An Empirical Examination of International Retailing Operations', *Journal of International Business Studies*, 33 (3), 515–32.

Ghemawat, P. (2001) 'Distance Still Matters: The Hard Reality of Global Expansion', *Harvard Business Review*, 79 (8), 137–47.

Hofstede, G., Hofstede, G. J. and Minkov, M. (2010) *Cultures et organizations* (Paris: Pearson).

House, R., Javidan, M., Hanges, P. and Dorfman, P. (2002) 'Understanding Cultures and Implicit Leadership Theories Across the Globe: An Introduction to Project GLOBE', *Journal of World Business*, 37 (1), 3–10.

Johanson, J. and Wiedersheim-Paul, F. (1975) 'The Internationalization of the Firm: Four Swedish Cases', *Journal of Management Studies*, 12 (3), 305–22.

Johanson, J. and Vahlne, J.-E. (1977) 'The Internationalization Process of the Firm: A Model of Knowledge Development and Increasing Foreign Market Commitments', *Journal of International Business Studies*, 8 (1), 23–32.

Johanson, J. and Vahlne, J.-E. (2009) 'The Uppsala Internationalization Process Model Revisited: From Liability of Foreignness to Liability of Outsidership', *Journal of International Business Studies*, 40 (9), 1411–31.

Kostova, T. (1996) 'Success of the Transnational Transfer of Organizational Practices within Multinational Companies', unpublished PhD thesis (Minneapolis: University of Minnesota).

Malhotra, S., Sivakumar, K. and Zhu, P. C. (2009) 'Distance Factors and Target Market Selection: The Moderating Effect of Market Potential', *International Marketing Review*, 26 (6), 651–73.

Oviatt, B. M. and McDougall, P. P. (1994) 'Toward a Theory of International New Ventures', *Journal of International Business Studies*, 25 (1), 45–64.

Ragozzino, R. (2009) 'The Effects of Geographic Distance on the Foreign Acquisition Activity of US Firms', *Management International Review*, 49 (4), 509–35.

Schwartz, S. H. (1992) 'Universals in the Content and Structure of Values: Theoretical Advances and Empirical Tests in 20 Countries' in M. P. Zanna (ed.), *Advances in Experimental Social Psychology*, 25, 1–66.

Shenkar, O. (2001) 'Cultural Distance Revisited: Towards a More Rigorous Conceptualization and Measurement of Cultural Differences', *Journal of International Business Studies*, 32 (3), 519–35.

UNCTAD (United Nations Conference on Trade and Development) (2010) *World Investment Report 2010* (New York/Geneva: United Nations Conference on Trade and Development).

Xu, D. and Shenkar, O. (2002) 'Institutional Distance and the Multinational Enterprise', *Academy of Management Review* (27) 4, 608–18.

7
The Legal Framework of the Relationship between Headquarters and Subsidiaries in MNCs

Jean-Baptiste Cartier and Christopher Melin

Legally, companies in a group are considered as legal entities that are independent from one another; economically, they are under the control of a strategic unit and subject to a joint policy. The central power which creates them defines the links that enable each subsidiary to contribute to the global project of the multinational company (MNC). The latter must therefore determine the activities and structures that will best foster the creation of wealth. However, the management of MNCs is complex (Colovic and Mayrhofer, 2011; Hennart, 2009), particularly since MNCs are spread across countries with different cultural, economic and institutional backgrounds. Studies of trends in company location and ownership strategies also show that decisions of managers are focused more specifically on the location of value chain activities (Porter, 1986), leading to geographical dispersion (Buckley and Ghauri, 2004).

The task of senior management in charge of structuring the relationships between headquarters and subsidiaries in MNCs is becoming critical (Birkinshaw and Pederson, 2009). Furthermore, the legal structures of subsidiaries are supposed to take the most effective forms considering, among other things, their relationship with headquarters (Cartier and Mayrhofer, 2007).

The banking sector has not been widely studied in the literature on headquarters–subsidiaries relationships, even though banking organizations are particularly willing to coordinate their activities (Lamarque, 2008). Bank supervision is dealing more and more with cost management, hierarchization and centralization of decision making. These supervision modes generate, in a changing environment, weak coordination, marked by individualism, fragmentation and low learning ability (Batac and Maymo, 2009). Many banks have recorded a series of financial losses resulting from risky decisions with no sound supervision procedure intended to detect slippages: the Crédit Agricole's 250 million US dollar trading loss by Richard Bierbaum in New York, in September 2007, echoes Société Générale's huge loss (nearly 4.9 billion Euros) in January 2008, in the Kerviel affair, where the trader Jérôme Kerviel engaged in very risky dealing, which resulted in significant losses for Société Générale. In any case, the explanation put forward was the headquarters' failure to supervise trading operations, which led to the implementation of a heavy reporting and control procedure at all levels, to assess the risks taken by the bank. It is in this particular context that we wish to study the links between the legal structure and the coordination and supervision mechanisms that structure headquarters–subsidiaries relationships of MNCs in the banking sector.

We will attempt, in the first section of this chapter, to define headquarters–subsidiaries relationships in MNCs, focusing on existing research; we will then present the legal dimension within headquarters–subsidiaries relationships. Finally, we will illustrate our analysis by an exploratory study of two French multinational corporations in the financial sector, Société Générale and Crédit Agricole.

7.1   Understanding headquarters–subsidiaries relationships through coordination and control mechanisms

The effort to coordinate all MNCs' activities is an issue that has often been studied in the specialized literature and it is still a popular research topic. In order to maintain their performance worldwide, MNCs must seek competitive advantages at all levels of the value chain; they may achieve them thanks to global configuration/coordination (Porter, 1986) and by overcoming organizational barriers while seeking to exploit them (Bartlett et al., 2004). The legal dimension is a means of achieving these competitive advantages, because it is possible to use, exploit or manipulate law in the interests of, or with the aim pursued by, actors (Masson, 2009): this will determine the implementation of more or less extensive coordination and control mechanisms.

7.1.1   Headquarters–subsidiaries relationships in MNCs

The United Nations Conference on Trade and Development (UNCTAD) lists the world's top 50 MNCs in the financial sector according to a dispersion index that takes into account the number of foreign subsidiaries and the number of host countries. On average, the first ten MNCs in the financial sector are located in around 50 countries (UNCTAD, 2010). For example, BNP Paribas (ranked second), is present in over 61 countries and accounts for a total of 596 foreign subsidiaries. Thus the challenge and complexity of organizing headquarters–subsidiaries relationships in MNCs is a critical topic, especially for multinational banks.

In the literature, headquarters–subsidiaries relationships are often studied within a classical framework: the dialectic of global integration/ local reactivity (Lawrence and Lorsch, 1967; Doz and Prahalad, 1984). This framework highlights various, and often conflicting, environmental pressures faced by MNCs in the world. Global integration refers to the 'centralized management of geographically dispersed activities on a continuous basis' (Doz and Prahalad, 1984, pp. 14–15). Local reactivity refers to 'resource commitment decisions taken autonomously by a subsidiary in response mainly to local requirements from competitors or customers' (ibid.).

To illustrate this, we conducted an exploratory study focused on the cases of Société Générale (see Box 7.1) and Crédit Agricole (see Box 7.2). We conducted interviews with a project manager at the Société Générale's headquarters, and with two members of the Executive Committee of Société Générale's subsidiary in Madagascar, supervising 40 branches. We also met two members of the Executive Committee of Crédit Agricole's Madagascan subsidiary, regrouping 27 local branches.

Box 7.1   Presentation of Société Générale

The activities developed by Société Générale are very broad, and cover retail banking (through networks of branches), specialized loans and insurance, private banking, asset management, services for investors, corporate and investment banking (CIB). Operating in 83 countries, its 157,000 employees (of which 62% are outside France) serve 32 million customers. In 2009, its Net Banking Income (NBI) amounted to 21.7 billion Euros and its net income to 678 million Euros (a decline of 66.7% compared with 2008, due to an outstanding event, the Kerviel affair).

In France, Société Générale has three complementary distribution channels in retail banking with different objectives: Société Générale, Crédit du Nord and Boursorama Bank. It has 10 million individual customers, nearly 40,000 employees and 3000 branches (2009 figures).

Retail banking abroad is present in 37 countries, with nearly 3800 branches and approximately 61,300 employees serving 13 million customers (individuals, companies, associations and institutions). It is particularly present in countries where the low maturity of the banking sector offers real opportunities for growth. The areas in which it operates are Eastern and Central Europe, the Mediterranean Basin, Sub-Saharan Africa and overseas territories.

The subsidiary of Société Générale in Madagascar is known as BFV-Société Générale (Banky Fampandrosoana ny Varotra – National Bank for Trade Development). Following the privatization programme undertaken by the Madagascan government in 1998, Société Générale bought a 70 per cent equity stake in BFV-Société Générale, leaving the remaining 30 per cent in public hands. BFV-Société Générale has 40 branches (22 in Antananarivo and 18 in the provinces) and accounts approximately for 20 per cent of the local market. This is a limited company with a capital of 5.5 million Euros. In 2007, it registered 8.7 million Euros net profit against 7 million Euros in 2006 (Mission économique de l'Ambassade de France à Madagascar, 2008).

Box 7.2   Presentation of Crédit Agricole

Involved in the agricultural sector, Crédit Agricole is based on mutual commitments. Its activity reached 2.7 billion Euros net income and generated 31.3 billion Euros Net Banking Income (NBI) in 2009. Its activities are organized around three business areas: retail banking in France and abroad, specialized financial areas (such as asset management, insurance, private banking, consumer credit, credit-leasing, factoring, and so on) and Corporate and Investment Banking (CIB).

A first player in the French banking sector (with 28% market share), a leader in retail banking in Europe (for earned income and number of branches), Crédit Agricole also operates in Africa with significant market positions. It has 11,500 branches in 70 countries in retail banking and employs over 160,000 staff to serve 59 million customers. Crédit Agricole's subsidiary in Madagascar is known as the BNI (Banky Nasioanaly ny Indostria – National Bank for Industry). This bank was the outcome of the merger between former Caisse de Crédit Agricole (established in 1930) and Crédit Foncier (established in 1920), during the French protectorate. It was a public bank after the independence of Madagascar and became part of Crédit

Lyonnais in 1991, following the first privatization in the country. Crédit Lyonnais holds 51 per cent of the shares of this joint stock company, the rest being owned by the Madagascan State (33%), the Company of Financing and Investment (10%) and others (6%). In 2006, after the purchase of Crédit Lyonnais by Crédit Agricole, BNI became a subsidiary of Crédit Agricole. BNI has 27 branches (15 in the provinces and 12 in Antananarivo) and controls about 25 per cent of the local market. In 2007, its net banking income amounted to 6.6 million Euros against 4.6 million Euros in 2006 (Mission économique de l'Ambassade de France à Madagascar, 2008).

In the international management literature, two concepts have been studied more specifically to describe headquarters–subsidiaries relationships: coordination and control mechanisms between MNCs' headquarters and subsidiaries.

7.1.2 Coordination and control mechanisms

We will present the typology of coordination mechanisms on the basis of a literature review (analysis of 85 research articles) from Martinez and Jarillo (1989). It is made up of two groups: 'formal' or 'bureaucratic' mechanisms and mechanisms known as 'informal or 'subtle'.

We can describe formal mechanisms according to the following features:

- centralization, which depend on the degree of centralization of decision making;
- formalization, which are implemented in the organization through rules, standards, job descriptions, standardized procedures, and so on;
- standard routines, which are established by all formalizing documents;
- planning, which are determined by the existence of mechanisms for strategic planning, budgeting, scheduling, and so on;
- outcome and behaviour control which are illustrated by performance monitoring, technical reports, sales and marketing data and staff supervision (direct supervision).

These formal mechanisms are often mentioned in research on headquarters–subsidiaries relationships. But there are other types of mechanisms called subtle, which develop a complementary aspect to the notion of coordination. The authors emphasize the complexity, the broad range and the difficulty of observing or measuring such coordination mechanisms in organizations.

Informal or subtle mechanisms are established through:

- horizontal relationships, which consist in the establishment of direct contacts between managers from different services in the vertical structure, seeking to solve a problem; they can also be temporary teams, working groups, committees, and so on;
- informal communication, which is the establishment of networks of personal and informal contacts different from lateral relations, given that such communication is not organized around a specific task: it takes place through participation in seminars, meetings, conferences, and so on;
- organizational culture, which aims at creating a system that specifies how to act and make decisions, defines the company's objectives and values through a process of individuals' socialization and takes the form of managers' transfers (expatriation), career management, measurement and reward system, and so on.

The concept of coordination is central in the literature about MNCs and the concept of control is, in a sense, complementary to it. In an empirical study on the integration of 57 subsidiaries of 34 American MNCs, Cray (1984) shows that control and coordination are the two preferred integration processes of MNCs. The author defines these key concepts as follows: 'the control is seen as a process that leads to adherence to a goal or target through the exercise of power or authority'; 'coordination is considered more as a process that helps develop the appropriate relationship between different business units within the same organization' (Cray, 1984, p. 86). In addition, Cray introduces the concept of centrifugal force. Indeed, headquarters seeking to limit powerful centrifugal force will tend to strongly integrate its subsidiaries, more often by using significant monitoring and coordinating tools.

Hennart (1993) suggests that MNCs' headquarters can adapt their control mode to the organization of subsidiaries. The author suggests a typology based on three possible control modes:

- bureaucratic, which can be exercised personally by a manager, or impersonally through rules and regulations;
- socialization, which refers to studies on expatriates; the presence of the headquarters' staff in the subsidiary is understood as a willing-ness to control the behaviour of the subsidiary's management staff;

- price, which is based on the result; some subsidiaries may, in this way, be assessed and controlled, despite a relative lack of transparency of their operation mode; in this case, the evaluation of employees is directly related to their individual results.

Thus the type of control set up by headquarters depends on their knowledge of the activities and behaviour of subsidiaries. The same headquarters may have different control modes according to their subsidiaries, even though different attitudes towards subsidiaries may cause problems of internal equity within a group. The control and coordination mechanisms would then have to be adapted to the situation.

Banking organizations are particularly willing to coordinate their activities (Lamarque, 2008). Despite the 'de-bureaucratization' observed in major industry players, interface problems persist between distribution channels (online banks and branches), between administrative and sales offices (transmission of information, compliance with procedures for products and services supply), and also between administrative services (duplication of tasks, control methods, information sharing). Control in banks is dealing more and more with cost management, prioritization and centralization of decision making. These control modes generate, in a changing environment, weak coordination marked by individualism, fragmentation and low learning ability (Batac and Maymo, 2009).

Finally, the more responsibilities and decentralized decision making processes subsidiaries have, the more difficult it is for headquarters to control their dispersed foreign activities. Indeed, managers of headquarters and subsidiaries may not share the same interests, and their differences seem even more acute in the context of MNCs (O'Donnell, 2000). If Société Générale is highly centralized (its headquarters drive the vast majority of projects and launch new products), this is not the case of Crédit Agricole. As the general secretary of the National Bank of Industry (BNI) puts it, 'we must make sure we adapt to the context and use local skills. Crédit Lyonnais had a highly centralized culture... Crédit Agricole has always had a relatively decentralized culture. ... It also gave less weight to expanding internationally and is still seeking itself in this area' (BNI General Secretary, interview 2010). Thus the image of Société Générale is made very visible in the branches of BFV-Société Générale, with posters promoting the values of the group displayed on the walls. The subsidiary both participates in the values of Société Générale and respects its rules. This is reinforced by a control mechanism related to expatriation; the subsidiary's president is also its general manager, and he is an expatriate from the headquarters ('control through socialization', Hennart, 1993). Indeed, the network director of BFV-Société Générale referred to the fact that his vision might be distorted, being himself an expatriate from Société Générale headquarters. We found this concept in their counterpart's speech calling Société Générale's headquarters 'mummy'. The Société Générale's subsidiary is particularly controlled for its credits and quality of risks. 'Internal audit' and 'audit risk' units are relocated from headquarters to subsidiaries. In terms of coordination, it has been underlined that a platform at the headquarters provides technical assistance to subsidiaries. According to the interviewee, this platform is considered to give subsidiaries 'controlled autonomy'. Société Générale developed a computer resource called normative bank, available to all subsidiaries; it is a compendium of best practices that have been used by Société Générale in its different networks and in various countries for many years. These best practices focus on several areas, such as organization, procedures, sales, human resources, and so on; and on the whole operational dimension in general.

We also find internal audit and risk units within the BNI of Crédit Agricole. According to the person interviewed in this branch, there is a 'close control' of headquarters on local decisions, thanks to consultations with units of the company's headquarters (the amount of delegation for the general manager of BNI is quite low, around 2 million Euros, against 50 to 100 million Euros for large subsidiaries). The managers of these units are not subordinated directly to the general manager of the subsidiary but hierarchically to the audit and risk structures of Crédit Agricole's headquarters in Paris, and are thus, in principle, independent of the local manager. There are also seminars between managers of the same professions in subsidiaries of the same geographic region. These are seminars to share best practices. They are mentioned as informal mechanisms of socialization in headquarters–subsidiaries relationships (Martinez and Jarillo, 1989). Within Crédit Agricole, seminars are held every two or three years to integrate all functional services of subsidiary managers. According to the interviewee, the role of the headquarters in relation to subsidiaries is limited to financial and risk control. The strategy of subsidiaries is based on strategic objectives set by the headquarters (this corresponds to a strategic planning of headquarters for subsidiaries, defined by Martinez and Jarillo, 1989, as a formal coordination mechanism called planning). The implementation of this strategy is local, without direct control over the way it is implemented. The subsidiary may take strategic initiatives based on its relationship to the client under the supervision of headquarters. If the headquarters do not wish a subsidiary to diversify a particular target, the subsidiary has to comply with these directives.

It is within this particular organizational context that we sought to approach the interactions between control mechanisms in headquarters–subsidiaries relationships of French banks and the legal structure of subsidiaries.

7.2 The legal dimension in headquarters–subsidiaries relationships

7.2.1 Law and management in headquarters–subsidiaries relationships

The question of foreign representation of MNCs is a recurring theme. The choice of the establishment mode depends on a strategic decision: according to it, the headquarters may more or less easily and freely develop their activities in the host country. Within the framework of headquarters–subsidiaries relationships, we notice a trend regarding law: it is not seen any longer as a constraint but as a tool. Law becomes an essential dimension and it fosters the group's development strategies (Snoussi, 2002; Buffaud and Imbert, 2005). In the banking sector, a distinction must be made between legal forms that are autonomous (subsidiary and affiliated bank) and those which are not autonomous from headquarters (branch, representative office) (see Box 7.3). As we wish to analyse the relationship between headquarters and subsidiaries (holding a majority of shares) as a whole, we shall focus only on the development of subsidiaries.

Box 7.3   Organization of legal activities

There are generally activities that have a 'legal structure' and those that are merely administrative segments or 'divisions' of headquarters.

The legal structure is a legal entity separating an organization from its environment. It involves the definition of a legal form of organization (in France, e.g., a limited company, a simplified joint stock company, a limited liability company, and so on), of a management structure, of a shareholder structure, of capital, but also of accounting obligations (balance sheet, income statement, appendices) for each entity. A subsidiary is an organization that has its own legal structure, a possibility of taking legal action, and therefore represents a legal entity.

By contrast, there are 'divisions' which are 'administrative' entities created by the organization from an economic point of view, to separate artificially varied existing activities inside the same legal structure. 'Business units', 'profit centres' and other 'cost centres' are administrative divisions of the organization which have no legal autonomy. The same applies to branches and representation offices. This form of organization is contrary to the development of subsidiaries for which legal separation is a central element and which involves other dimensions (ownership, management, legal form, balance sheet, subsidiary's profit and loss account, and so on).

The observation of MNCs since the 1990s highlights a significant change towards various organizations intending to promote the optimal organization of activities. Law plays its own part and contributes to this change. The trend requires adapted structures in headquarters–subsidiaries relationships. It heavily affects all MNCs. They have to design new formulas to take into account these adaptations and new characteristics, while maintaining the basis of headquarters–subsidiaries relationships. These new strategic and organizational formulas include the definition of specific legal forms, especially for subsidiaries. Nekhili and Boubacar (2007) emphasize that French banks chose the subsidiary and the branch as their two preferred organizational forms for foreign representations (however, with a different development over time); in less than ten years, between 1993 and 2001, the number of subsidiaries of French banks rose from 125 to 241, whereas the number of branches dropped from 125 to 97 during the same period.

In this context, the contractual dimension plays an important role. In fact, it is possible to influence relationships between different actors and their actions in the context of value creation. This adaptation has obvious consequences on the organization of Société Générale, and particularly on its requirements in terms of control, cooperation, research for increased efficiency as well as legal specificities. Lawyers are now seeking to adapt the organization to its environment as quickly and as efficiently as possible, knowing that it is also developing on its own. They are in charge of implementing changes, new forms allowing them to organize activities within a legal framework more suited to the needs expressed. Thus, the legal structure becomes a way for the organization to achieve its goals. In fact, it is usually through the choice of adapted rules that the organization will search to improve the coordination and control of diverse subsidiaries.

7.2.2 A formal legal framework that improves the integration of activities at Société Générale ...

The integration of activities within Société Générale includes regulatory measures that must be complied with. In general, they are binding for the parent company, who, in order to respect them, must de facto prescribe them to subsidiaries, when they are not directly subjected to these constraints. In the banking sector, they are known as the 'Basel agreements' (now 'Basel II'). They are part of a global attempt to regulate the banking industry. The aim is to prevent bankruptcy, through the establishment of a better balance between capital and risk. These prudential standards aim to limit banking risks such as credit or market risk (or counterparty risk) and especially operational risks, by playing on equity requirements. We define the operational risk as 'the risk of losses because of deficiency or failures due to procedures, people, systems or external events. The definition includes legal risks, but excludes strategic and reputational risks' (Basel Committee definition).

They limit the amount of loans granted, according to the amount of capital and the risk related to these loans. They came into the force on 1 January 2008, and have been part of a step by step process of improvement following Basel I, which did not take enough account of risk.

In general, the various criteria that affect the creation of the legal form play a central role in the way law is taken into account by the overall strategy of Société Générale. They are as follows:

- The choice of the level of responsibility (financial) that the headquarters are ready to take in case of difficulties concerning the subsidiary. This means choosing a legal form for the subsidiary with a limited (capital) or unlimited responsibility. In general, the parent company has a limited responsibility for its shareholders' contributions, to avoid too heavy losses or unintentional slippages from the subsidiary that could not be borne by the headquarters, or would affect the entire group. Thus, in Madagascar, Crédit Agricole and Société Générale have developed subsidiaries in the form of limited companies, where their responsibilities are limited to their contribution.
- The choice of the entity that manages the subsidiary. This may be a body similar to the board of directors (concentration of powers), or a dual power between executive and supervisory boards. In the first case, which is the most common, the board represents various

shareholders of the company, but it is also composed of the most important managers. It serves as a place of exchange and discussion prior to making decisions. Its members, elected in the general meeting, are collectively responsible for the organization's strategic choices and for their implementation, while respecting the shareholders' expectations concerning the subsidiary (social object). The chair of the board plays a major role in implementing these choices. They are assisted by a general manager, although it is common to combine both functions in France. In the second case, the supervisory board is composed exclusively of shareholder representatives. It is in charge of planning major strategic orientations and monitors the executive board. It does not deal with the daily management of the company's current affairs. By contrast, the executive board is composed entirely of the company's operational managers and is responsible for carrying out strategic decisions of the supervisory board. It is responsible to the company for its management. Société Générale faced a structural change due to the Kerviel affair; before this, Daniel Button was President and General Manager. He had to step down and give up his function as a general manager, to remain 'only' President of the Board, Frédéric Oudéa, becoming General Manager and taking over the operational management of Société Generale.

- The choice of the type of structure. This depends on the number of shareholders and their size: in other words, it may be a partnership, where the *intuitu personae* is strong, and where the number of partners is limited (which means that the overall size of the company is limited); or a joint stock company, where a large amount of capital may be provided (for a more significant development in the future) through the participation of a large number of shareholders. In this case, anonymity is the rule, and freedom to buy or sell stocks becomes central. Subsidiaries may then have a larger social capital (through a larger number of players holding shares), but the control over who's holding the stocks is not a major dimension of this legal form. The form adopted by the two Madagascan branches (limited companies) confirms the preference for joint stock companies to partnerships with a limited number of shareholders (which does not exclude having a limited number of shareholders).
- The choice of the subsidiary's control level by the parent company. In other words, do the headquarters wish to hold only a simple majority in the subsidiary, or would they rather have a 'large majority' through control over decisions of extraordinary general meetings? In the first case, the operational supervision of the subsidiary may be performed

through a simple majority (of voting rights), that is to say 50 per cent plus one vote. They may then appoint executives, manage the subsidiary (with respect to the interests of all shareholders), seek accounts approval, establish agreements between the parent-company and the subsidiary. In the second case, the headquarters must hold two thirds of voting rights. This allows them to freely decide to change corporate objectives, status, capital amount, and so on. Indeed, 51 per cent of Crédit Agricole's subsidiary in Madagascar is held by its headquarters, compared with 70 per cent for Société Générale. In the first case, the subsidiary is simply controlled, whereas in the second case, the level of participation gives the headquarters more freedom to control the subsidiary.

- The choice of the appointment of subsidiary managers. They represent shareholders and assume responsibility for achieving the objectives set by the board of directors, and thus by the main shareholders. For BNI, there are two managers: the general manager (also administrator) who is appointed by Crédit Agricole, and the president, who is chosen by the Madagascan government. In contrast, in BFV-Société Générale, the parent company appoints the president who is also the general manager. The Madagascan government is not involved in this choice.
- The choice to list or not the subsidiary on the stock market. In the case of a listed subsidiary, it is necessary to have a specific legal form such as a limited company; a limited liability company cannot be listed in France. In Madagascar, although the two branches have the status of a limited company, they are not listed, because there are still no financial markets in the country.
- The choice of the governance system. It must be effective enough to anticipate and solve conflicts between the subsidiary's managers and the group as a majority shareholder. Even if law generally determines the balance of power and individual rights, it is quite possible to come across a dictatorial president or a tyrannical shareholder. An adapted governance system does not rule out any divergence of interest or conflict, it only contributes to the emergence of solutions. The study of the board and managers of each subsidiary is interesting: for historical reasons, BNI, the first privatized bank in 1991, is a limited company, still owned by the Madagascan government, which holds nearly 33 per cent of voting rights, while Crédit Agricole holds only 51 per cent of voting rights. This relatively important participation is reflected in the role of each board member: the board is made up of seven members, four of whom are appointed by Crédit Agricole and

three by the Madagascan government. Crédit Agricole may not adopt decisions in the extraordinary general meeting without the approval of the Madagascan State. This explains why Madagascar appoints the president of the board of directors, who is not a member of the executive committee, while Crédit Agricole appoints the general manager. By contrast, Société Générale owns 70 per cent of BFV-Société Générale's voting rights (BFV-Société Générale is also a limited company), compared with only 28 per cent owned by the Madagascan government. Société Générale can freely make decisions in both ordinary and extraordinary general meetings. Also, the distribution of functions within the board is different: six functions for Société Générale against only three for the State. Société Générale appoints the general manager who is the local representative of the headquarters. He has all powers and, although he is formally accountable to the board, he really reports only to the headquarters. As the director of the BFV-Société Générale network summarizes it, 'the Madagascan government, as a shareholder, has a say in the board of directors. It asks questions, makes remarks, but the operational management remains in the hands of Société Générale. Our board of directors is not a convenience board. It asks real questions. Indeed, the board of directors discusses strategic points that will in any case be implemented'.

(Director BFV-Société Générale, interview 2010)

Thanks to these different dimensions, one can establish the required legal structure, which will best promote headquarters–subsidiaries relationships by reinforcing the integration of activities. The most common form, especially in international relationships, is the limited company, as it allows a 'classic' organization which can be found in almost all countries with similar characteristics (responsibility limited to contribution, appointments of executives, organization), including a board of directors and a general meeting, and so on) and some specificities (setting-up of the board, the possibility to remove directors, and so on).

7.2.3   ... while promoting the search for local responsiveness

Boards of directors serve as a place of exchange and discussion prior to making decisions, as well as an intermediary maintaining interactive information between headquarters and subsidiaries. It is important that its composition (and therefore its representations) be plural: plurality of shareholders' viewpoints, plurality of internal actors, plurality of local external partners who can provide both external expertise and knowledge of the economic environment in which the company operates.

The legal form should be considered as a means of achieving business performance and improving efficiency (Vauplane, 2008; Du Manoir de Juaye, 2004). The organization of power may take many forms, depending on several criteria, the most important being the concentration of decision rights and useful information. The subsidiary's management develops according to the group's conceptions, and therefore its room for manoeuvre is dependent on this. For example, the group may need to control or, on the contrary, decentralize decision making in its different subsidiaries, it may need to have a cohesive decision-making unit or leave room for initiatives. In order to organize subsidiaries within the group, the parent company has several solutions insofar as allocating executive powers within the subsidiary is concerned.

If specific information is concentrated in the hands of the executive committee, the headquarters may, first of all, grant very limited powers to deal with the management of certain tasks, or with specific functions within the subsidiary. The subsidiary is then considered to be a simple organizational and practical component of the parent company, without any particular characteristics. In this case and for efficiency's sake, the concentration of decision-making powers in the parent company (through its representative) is the most appropriate scenario since it holds the most important source of specific information. Management is concentrated in the hands of the president of the board of directors who is also a general manager and representative of the parent company. The board of directors of the subsidiary plays only a theoretical role in the decision-making process and endorses decisions made elsewhere. The subsidiary has only a very limited legal autonomy compared with the group, and its managers are mere executers of the decisions made by the group. We find an illustration of this in the words of BNI's General Secretary: 'concerning credit allocation, the decision is made by the risk managers in Paris, even though it formally rests with the board; de facto, if Paris gives its agreement, the allocation may go ahead. The board only endorses the decision' (Interview, 2010).

If specific information is concentrated in the hands of other actors, the parent company may grant more power to the president and other managers of the subsidiary. The autonomy of the subsidiary and its managers will then be significant in operational and even strategic management. There is no parent company's decision-making unit in this case, because the subsidiary is best suited to generate value. The role of the board is essentially to strengthen local expertise. Decentralized decision making at the subsidiary level is the most effective scenario. The functions of the board will have to be clarified: its collegiality, its powers, its composition and operational rules. In this case, the information may derive from several actors that ought to be brought together in order to create optimal value for the subsidiary.

If specific information is scattered across various actors throughout the chain of command, the parent company may finally define an intermediate situation, where the agreement of the parent company on certain issues or certain expenses, its prior approval for certain procedures or in some cases a double signature are required, but which leaves the subsidiary with a large autonomy. Managers have therefore a certain leeway in carrying out the group's decisions. Rights will be distributed as follows: the subsidiary's management requires the separation of the functions of the president (representing the parent company) and the general manager, who enjoys a large autonomy in terms of daily operations, as well as a high degree of freedom in terms of organization and action. This should minimize existing asymmetrical information. The operational and effective management of the group's internal branches should improve and become clearer. This is particularly helpful when developing diverse internal operations in autonomous structures, delegating the management of operations while keeping control over activities and their development. Thus, BNI's General Secretary states that 'the general manager's signature is unmistakable. I've known five or six of them since my arrival, each one left his own personal mark on BNI's development. Some played the game of the parent company, in other words, were the parent company's good little soldiers; others promoted the autonomy of their local subsidiary. Let's say that our distinction is to remain a small company within the group, so their motto often was, "To live happily, we have to hide away". We do our best to do honestly and effectively everything that the parent company requires from us. We are aware of major general policies, but we also have to ensure we adapt to the environment and use local skills' (Interview, 2010).

The board of directors serves as a channel for conveying information between headquarters and subsidiaries. It may simply record this information, or be an actual forum of exchange and cooperation between managers of the subsidiary and the parent company. The setting-up of the board must be adapted in order to obtain the highest possible value. Its specificities and the search for local responsiveness play a major role in its composition; thus, among the six BFV-Société Générale members appointed by Société Générale, three really represent the headquarters and three are local expatriates, which enables the group to better adjust to market supply. The Network Director of BFV-Société Générale summarizes the situation as follows: 'local strategy is possible, I think we even have enough autonomy, but we are also under the supervision of our board' (Interview, 2010). Similarly, three out of four representatives of Crédit Agricole, are local expatriates. Thus, BNI's banking products portfolio is made up of Madagascan products, whereas the products of BFV-Société Générale are those of Société Générale which have been adapted to the Madagascan market.

Finally, the local reactivity may again be illustrated by the establishment at BFV-Société Générale of an almost unique system of phone banking in Société Générale's subsidiaries (which is not available to French customers of Société Générale). It offers the opportunity to pay various expenses via one's phone at merchants or in administrations, thanks to the purchase of phone credits. According to the statement of the General Secretary of BFV-Société Générale, 'this idea arose from a reflection process (conducted locally) on the local needs of customers and from a partnership with a major mobile operator in the Madagascan market' (Interview, 2010); it is therefore based on a significant contractual dimension. Similarly, BFV-Société Générale is present in 'real' time on its entire network, 'a BFV-Société Générale customer is not only a client of the branch, he is a client of BFV-Société Générale; that is to say, that he can carry out a transaction anywhere, as if he were in his branch. Today, at Société Générale in France, we work on yesterday's deposit. Here, we work on your deposit the second you make it. As an example, if I deposit money right now, I know that my account will be credited the second the computerized transaction is made' (BFV-Société Générale, General Secretary, interview 2010).

Thus, the legal dimension is a variable that should not be underestimated. It enhances and promotes the overall integration of subsidiaries by parent companies, while developing local reactivity, in order to meet customer needs, seize opportunities, and so on. It offers the flexibility needed to adapt the structure to business reality, to local constraints and requirements, to requirements of headquarters and the diverse personalities of managers; but also to give formal direction to the subsidiary, meaning to its action and objectives while performing *a posteriori* control on the reality of these elements.

7.3 Conclusion

The literature highlights multiple relationships between headquarters and subsidiaries. Within these relationships, aspects related to global integration and local responsiveness are critical. They progress in parallel and MNCs can develop only by taking them into account.

The legal dimensions of these relationships should not be overlooked: they guide the selection of a legal form, favour one type of relationship over another and act on the control and coordination dimensions. Similarly, headquarters influence the setting-up of the legal structure and the distribution of power between different actors (the parent company, local partners and shareholders); for example, through the board of directors of the subsidiary, or the separation of the functions of the president and the general manager. Organizations or companies that require specific features choose specific organizational forms or legal structures (Lamoreaux and Rosenthal, 2006; Allouche and Huault, 1998; Amann and Couret, 1992). The creativity and adaptability of these structures, thanks to legal dimensions, are important sources of competitive advantage and value creation for Société Générale, since they enable the group to meet multiple needs expressed by headquarters and subsidiaries, but especially by stakeholders. The legal dimension can offer significant opportunities to the company both operationally and strategically. According to their finance, coordination, control and internal power organization requirements, parent companies will seek to take advantage of opportunities offered by various legal structures. Some regulations created new opportunities for MNCs. In France, the development of subsidiaries will be primarily (or exclusively) achieved through a Société par Actions Simplifiée (SAS), a simplified joint stock company (Cartier, 2008), which means that they have a very high degree of flexibility through the introduction of considerable contractual freedom.

The study on the banking sector also highlights legal constraints that weigh heavily on this sector through the provisions of Basel II. They apply only to European banks which have to impose their requirements on foreign subsidiaries in order to control their level of risk. This affects directly, and significantly, headquarters–subsidiaries relationships, and requires the strengthening of global integration, through the implementation of more control and, particularly, more sophisticated risk and audit controls. Despite this sophisticated formal framework, headquarters–subsidiaries relationships manage to keep a high degree of local responsiveness, particularly to meet specific customer needs. This is especially true for developing countries that do not have the same availability of banking facilities, or the same expectations from a bank as in the country of origin of the MNC.

References

Allouche, J. and Huault, I. (1998) 'Contrôle, coordination et régulation: les nouvelles formes organisationnelles', *Finance, Contrôle, Stratégie*, 1 (2), 5–31.

Amann, B. and Couret, A. (1992) 'Les relations actionnaires-dirigeants suivant le type de structure', *Revue Française de Gestion*, 87, 93–102.

Bartlett, C. A., Ghoshal, S. and Birkinshaw, J. (2004) 'Developing Coordination and Control: The Organizational Challenge' in C. A. Bartlett, S. Ghoshal and J. Birkinshaw (eds), *Transnational Management: Text, Cases, and Readings in Cross-Border Management*, 4th edn (Boston: McGraw Hill), pp. 339–55.

Batac, J. and Maymo, V. (2009) 'Les nouveaux outils de pilotage dans les banques', *Revue Française de Gestion*, 191, 153–66.

Birkinshaw, J. M. and Pederson, T. (2009) 'Strategy and Management in MNE Subsidiaries' in A. M. Rugman and T. Brewer (eds), *Oxford Handbook of International Business*, 2nd edn (Oxford: Oxford University Press), pp. 380–401.

Buckley, P. J. and Ghauri, P. (2004) 'Globalisation, Economic Geography and the Strategy of Multinational Enterprises', *Journal of International Business Studies*, 35 (2), 81–98.

Buffaud, F. and Imbert, A. (2005) 'Les dangers courus par une société-mère responsable des actes de sa filiale', *Option Finance*, 835, 31–3.

Cartier, J. B. (2008) 'Coopération et contrôle des parties–prenantes à travers le rôle du conseil d'administration des filiales de groupes: quels effets sur le développement des SAS (société par actions simplifiée)?', *19ème Congrès du réseau des Instituts d'Administration des Entreprises (IAE)*, Lille, 10–12 September.

Cartier, J. B. and Mayrhofer, U. (2007) 'Gestion de l'incertitude, cadrage juridique des filiales et SAS', *Revue Sciences de Gestion*, 62, 21–43.

Colovic, A. and Mayrhofer, U. (2011) 'Optimising the Location of R&D and Production Activities: Trends in the Automotive Industry', *European Planning Studies*, 19 (8), 1481–98.

Cray, D. (1984) 'Control and Coordination in Multinational Corporations', *Journal of International Business Studies*, 15 (2), 85–97.

Doz, Y. L. and Prahalad, C. K. (1984) 'Patterns of Strategic Control within Multinational Corporations', *Journal of International Business Studies*, 15 (2), 55–72.

Du Manoir de Juaye, T. (2004) *Le droit pour dynamiser votre business: stratégie judiciaire, stratégie de la protection du patrimoine, stratégie d'alliances et de pouvoir* (Paris: Editions d'Organisation).

Hennart, J.-F. (1993) 'Explaining the Swollen Middle: Why Most Transactions are a Mix of Market and Hierarchy', *Organization Science*, 4 (4), 529–47.

Hennart, J.-F. (2009) 'Down with MNE-Centric Theories! Market Entry and Expansion as the Bundling of MNE and Local Assets', *Journal of International Business Studies*, 40 (9), 1432–54.

Lamarque, E. (2008) *Management de la banque: Risques, relation client, organisation* (Paris: Pearson Education).

Lamoreaux, N. R. and Rosenthal, J. L. (2006) 'Entity Shielding and the Development of Business Forms: A Comparative Perspective', *Harvard Law Review Forum*, 119 (6), 238–45.

Lawrence, P. R. and Lorsch, J. W. (1967) 'The Integrator: A New Management Job', *Academy of Management Review*, 5, 211–17.

Martinez, J. I. and Jarillo, C. J. (1989) 'The Evolution of Research on Coordination Mechanisms in Multinational Corporations', *Journal of International Business Studies*, 20 (3), 489–515.

Masson, A. (ed.) (2009) *Les stratégies juridiques de l'entreprise* (Brussels: Larcier).

Mission économique de l'Ambassade de France à Madagascar (2008) *Le marché bancaire à Madagascar* (Antananarivo).

Nekhili, M. and Boubacar, H. (2007) 'Les déterminants du choix de la forme d'implantation bancaire à l'étranger: une analyse théorique', *La Revue des Sciences de Gestion, Direction et Gestion*, 224–25, 167–76.

O'Donnell, S. W. (2000) 'Managing Foreign Subsidiaries: Agents of Headquarters, or an Interdependent Network?', *Strategic Management Journal*, 21 (5), 525–48.

Porter, M. E. (1986) 'Changing Patterns of International Competition', *California Management Review*, 28 (2), 9–40.

Snoussi, M. (2002) 'Les stratégies juridiques des multinationales: l'exemple des prix de transfert', *Revue internationale de droit économique*, 3, 443–69.

Vauplane, H. D. (2008) 'Le rôle du juriste: gardien du temple ou facilitateur de business?', *Banque Magazine*, 704, 84–6.

8
Innovation Processes in MNCs: The Case of Groupe SEB

Lusine Arzumanyan and Christopher Melin

Multinational companies (MNCs) play an important role in the process of the creation and diffusion of innovations. More than 95 per cent of 700 companies investing in research and development (R&D) across the world are multinationals, and they account for half of the total invested amount (Castellani and Zanfei, 2006). Moreover, one-third of the 100 largest companies are involved in the high-tech industry, in sectors such as electronics, pharmaceuticals or chemicals. MNCs are therefore critical to the development of a country's technological capital. The economies of industrialized countries rely increasingly on R&D activities to provide companies with competitive advantages (CAS, 2007).

Today's challenge for MNCs is to identify consumption trends in emerging countries, relate them to new technologies and develop new products or services to be rapidly promoted worldwide (Bartlett and Beamish, 2010). This chapter aims to understand the innovation process in one particular MNC, the French Groupe SEB. In the first section, we will focus on the conceptual framework of the innovation process in MNCs. In the second section, we will highlight the activities of Groupe SEB, the world leader in small household appliances. Finally, we will examine the innovation process within this group.

8.1 Understanding innovation in MNCs

In a knowledge-based economy, innovation can be considered as a growth driver, a means to create added value and competitiveness, as well as a strategic aspect for the development of companies. In the last few decades, many multinationals had to relocate their production and research and development (R&D) facilities in order to optimize their global value-chain (Colovic and Mayrhofer, 2011). In the past, these functions were centralized in the companies' headquarters. Today, we witness a marked tendency to a wider geographic dispersion that may take different forms such as cooperative alliances with foreign partners, acquisitions of foreign companies, the off-shoring of R&D activities, and so on.

8.1.1   R&D: A strategic priority

The 2010 European Commission study on investments in industrial R&D provided information about 1400 major MNCs (400 of which were located in the European Union) and ranked them according to the amount they invested in R&D (see Table 8.1).

In 2009 and for the second consecutive year, the Japanese car manufacturer Toyota was the world leader for investments in R&D, with 6.8 billion Euros. Three European companies also appear in the ranking: Volkswagen, the European leader with an R&D investment of 5.8 billion Euros, Nokia and Sanofi-Aventis. If we compare the R&D/total sales ratio for 2008 with that for 2009, we notice that the investment in R&D remains a strategic priority for companies, despite a difficult economic environment.

However, as for production activities, the innovation process is gradually moving to emerging countries, such as China and India, as these countries are developing technological awareness. For example, between 1995 and 2002, China doubled its spending on R&D, which increased from 0.6 per cent to 1.2 per cent of its Gross Domestic Product (GDP). Today, more than 400 R&D centres in China and 77 in India have been established by foreign companies. In 2008, China ranked third worldwide in terms of GDP with 4222 billion US dollars, behind the US (14,330 billion US dollars) and Japan (4844 US billion dollars) (Chen and Nivoix, 2009).

According to a study commissioned by the French government in 2008, entitled 'France 2025', the US, Europe and Japan will remain among the world leaders in R&D. Nevertheless, their relative investment share in R&D might drop sharply in favour of Asia. Thus, China and India might represent around 20 per cent of the world investment in R&D, that is to say more than double the amount of their spending at the time of writing.

8.1.2   Innovation processes

The concept of innovation has been defined by many researchers and specialists. Considering the complexity of innovation activities, it seems difficult to agree on a universal definition. According to Schumpeter

Table 8.1 Top ten world investors in R&D (2009)

Rank	Company	Industry	Country of headquarters	Investment in R&D in billion €	Variation investment in R&D 09/08 in %	Variation investment in R&D 08/07 in %	R&D/total sales in % 2009	R&D/total sales in % 2008
1	Toyota	automobile	Japan	6,768.46	−5.7	7.6	4.4	3.6
2	Roche	pharmaceuticals	Switzerland	6,401.86	9.1	5	19.4	19.1
3	Microsoft	software	USA	6,073.20	−3.3	10.4	13.9	15.4
4	Volkswagen	automobile	Germany	5,790.00	−2.3	20.4	5.7	5.3
5	Pfizer	pharmaceuticals	USA	5,404.13	−2.4	−1.8	15.5	16.5
6	Novartis	pharmaceuticals	Switzerland	5,156.02	2.5	12.6	16.7	17.4
7	Nokia	telecommunications	Finland	4,997.00	−6.1	0.8	12.2	10.5
8	Johnson & Johnson	pharmaceuticals	USA	4,868.87	−7.8	−1.3	11.3	11.9
9	Sanofi-Aventis	pharmaceuticals	France	4,569.00	0.2	0.9	15.3	16.5
10	Samsung Electronics	electronics	South Korea	4,282.00	1.9	10.8	5.4	5.8

Source: European Commission (2010).

(1935), the invention and its corresponding innovation are completely different concepts from an economic or sociological point of view. In this regard, Alter (2002) defines invention as the creation of a new technical or organizational product, service or device, whereas innovation is the social and economic process that leads to an invention being used or not. Innovation refers both to the process of innovation and its result (new product).

At this point, it seems interesting to emphasize the difference between innovation as a process and its result (new product). Innovation is an action that requires a set of intellectual and material resources without guarantee of success or acceptance by the user. Unlike the process, the result depends on the evaluation by the stakeholder, hence its subjectivity. The difference between process and result is therefore critical to our study, as we will focus mainly on the process of innovation.

Traditionally, the innovation strategies of companies are either 'centre-for-global' or 'local-for-local'. These strategies show the conflict which could stem from the headquarters' wish to centralize R&D and innovation (global integration of activities) and the need to recognize the diversity of local markets (local reactivity of activities). In the first case, innovation is created at the headquarter level, in order to be promoted on the domestic market before being marketed worldwide. The role of subsidiaries then is to introduce the innovation to the local market. In the second case, the focus is on the specificities of local markets and the need to adapt to them. Thus, subsidiaries create innovations with their own resources and competencies for their local market.

The question of centralization or decentralization of activities in MNCs has been explored in the specialized literature and, more specifically, in studies dealing with relationships between headquarters and subsidiaries. This dimension is addressed through the analytical grid 'global integration/local reactivity' (Doz and Prahalad, 1984). This grid shows different, and often contradictory, external signals that companies have to face. In the authors' opinion, global integration is 'a methodically centralized management of geographically dispersed activities' whereas local reactivity concerns 'the autonomous decisions of subsidiaries on the resource allocation following the market demand or competitive pressure' (Doz and Prahalad, 1984, pp. 14–15).

Bartlett et al. (2003) emphasize that in order to maintain their performance worldwide, MNCs must look for competitive advantages at all stages of the value-chain. To achieve the objective of coordinating geographically dispersed activities, companies have to overcome organizational obstacles.

In this chapter, we will aim to understand the general process of innovation in MNCs. We will review the case of Groupe SEB which formalized its innovation process management. Our empirical study is based on the analysis of secondary data (annual reports, internal documents, and so on), completed by several interviews with managers involved in the innovation process.

8.2 Presentation of Groupe SEB

Groupe SEB can be regarded as a reference in the small household appliance industry where the globalization of markets requires the involvement of teams in all stages of the innovation process. In the cookware sector, as in small household appliances, Groupe SEB has always stressed the importance of innovation, technological excellence and industrial know-how. In 2010, Groupe SEB was awarded the Prize for Best Strategy in the 'group' category, by the French Ministry of Economy and Employment. The group was rewarded for its internationalization strategy which significantly accelerated in the past 15 years.

8.2.1 Strategic business units and brand portfolio of Groupe SEB

Groupe SEB, which has its headquarters in Lyon, is the world leader for small household appliances. In 2009, its turnover amounted to 3.17 billion Euros. The group runs two activities which can be considered as complementary:

1. small household appliances, in which the group holds 10 per cent of the world market share;
2. cookware, in which the group holds a 16 per cent market share.

Groupe SEB is competing with numerous companies, most of which are large and small household appliance manufacturers (Bosch and Siemens Home Appliances [BSH], Electrolux, Fagor, and so on), multispecialists having a good brand image and an extended distribution network (Jarden, Philips, and so on), companies specializing in small household appliances (De Longhi, and so on) and/or cookware (Hamilton Beach, and so on) (Xerfi Entreprises, 2010).

Groupe SEB markets its products in more than 150 countries via 60 production and sales units in the world. The internationalization of its activities was achieved through acquisitions which took place over the last 40 years. Today, Groupe SEB has a portfolio of 20 well-known brands (Rowenta, All-Clad, Lagostina, Supor, and so on). In 2009,

Table 8.2   Global brands of Groupe SEB

Acquisition date	Brand	Activity
1968	Tefal	cookware (French company)
1988	Rowenta	small household appliances (American company)
2001–2	Moulinex/Krups	small household appliances (French company)
2004	All-Clad	premium cookware (American company)
2005	Lagostina	premium cookware (Italian company)
2007	Supor	cooking equipment (Chinese company)

Source: Groupe SEB (2010).

Table 8.3   Sales breakdown by geographic region of Groupe SEB in % (2009)

Country/geographic region	Total sales (%)
France	22
Other countries of the European Union	23
Asia-Pacific	19
Central and Eastern Europe, Commonwealth of Independent States and other countries	17
North America	11
Latin America	8
Total	100

Source: Groupe SEB (2010).

the total value of its brands amounted to 297 billion Euros. Six out of 20 brands are marketed internationally (see Table 8.2).

8.2.2   Differentiated innovation strategies: mature *versus* emerging countries

During the last few years, Groupe SEB strongly developed in regions where the market for small household appliances was growing, such as Asia, Latin America and Western Europe. Table 8.3 shows the total sales per region.

Groupe SEB developed differentiated strategies for mature and emerging countries. In developed countries, the group based its development strategy on major technological advances (e.g., Actifry, a frier using 'almost no oil'), due to the fact that demand in mature markets grows continuously and rapidly. Conversely, in emerging markets, Groupe SEB adopted a different strategy.

> Innovation is not the priority objective in emerging countries. In these countries, the markets develop thanks to basic products. Our growth will therefore rely on a reinforced presence, for example, in South-East Asia where we will establish subsidiaries, as the market is developing fast and we need to provide adapted products.
> (R&D Methods Process Manager, interview 2010)

The acquisition of the Chinese company Supor is a relevant example of Groupe SEB's strategy in emerging countries (see Box 8.1).

Box 8.1   Supor, a new development opportunity on the Chinese market

Following a takeover bid, Groupe SEB took control of the Chinese company Supor in December 2007, with the acquisition of 52.74 per cent of its shares. By acquiring China's number one in cookware and the number two in small household appliances, Groupe SEB showed its ambition to expand in China and South-East Asia. For Groupe SEB, the Chinese company represents several strategic advantages: an excellent brand image on the local market, a good knowledge of market mechanisms and an extended distribution network.

To facilitate the integration of Supor, Groupe SEB opened a campus in Hangzhou and developed several educational programmes within the company university. According to the marketing director, who is in charge of marketing projects for transversal products, Groupe SEB carries out 'education for a better understanding between the Europeans and the Chinese. The Chinese campus should provide more than a simple cultural approach' (Marketing Director, interview 2010).

In 2008, Supor created and launched the first long-lasting stainless steel anticorrosion wok without coating. The internal audit director of Groupe SEB pointed out that 'in Asia, people steam a lot of rice in big woks, hence our large choice of rice cookers, a segment from which SEB was absent, but now we have a market share' (Internal Audit Director, interview 2010).

In 2009, the Chinese company contributed around 348 billion Euros to the Groupe SEB's sales turnover. Supor holds a strong position in the cookware business (52% of sales) with an extended offer covering frying pans, woks, saucepans, pressure cookers, and so on.

8.3   The innovation process in Groupe SEB

8.3.1   Innovation: A key success factor

Despite economic fluctuations and market changes over the past few years, Groupe SEB has maintained its worldwide leadership in all strategic business units thanks to its competitiveness. Innovation is the key success factor that allows the company to maintain its competitive advantage. The current innovation strategy targets the creation of better products, allowing the company to sell them with a stronger added-value and at a higher price. 'We don't know how to manufacture cheap goods. We have a business model where the turnover is boosted by innovation, not only for branded products but for basic products too. Therefore, the innovation process is absolutely necessary and critical, it is basic to survival' (Internal Audit Director, interview 2010).

The resulting profit allows Groupe SEB to invest in R&D and communication in order to further boost sales according to a virtuous circle (see Figure 8.1).

> One of our key factors of performance is making our business model work from an economic point of view, that is to say, have innovative products and sell them at a sufficiently high price to be able to afford an advertising campaign that will allow to sell even more.
>
> (Director of Marketing Projects for Transversal Products,
> interview 2010)

Therefore, the group invests around 2 per cent of its turnover in R&D (that is, 64 billion Euros) and launches about 200 new products per year. In 2009, it was the 18th most important patent applicant in France, far ahead of other large French MNCs.

Figure 8.1   Virtuous circle of innovation in Groupe SEB
Source: Groupe SEB (2010).

8.3.2 Different stages in the innovation process

The process of innovation management is one of the key components of Groupe SEB's strategy. 'The innovation process of Groupe SEB is clearly defined. This process is unique and must be applied everywhere and by everyone' (Internal Audit Director, interview 2010).

The innovation process is composed of three stages (see Table 8.4):

1. exploration;
2. demonstration;
3. implementation.

During the exploration stage, new ideas are generated. Once the marketing department considers that there may be a market for an idea, and the technical service can propose adapted solutions, the demonstration stage begins. During this stage, the marketing department studies the market *via* consumer groups, while the technical service carries out feasibility studies to elaborate a technical solution or a prototype. Finally, the implementation phase can start. This last stage is made up of several steps:

- defining the design, the aesthetic value and technical features of the product;
- studying in detail product manufacturing, the commercial launch as well as the packaging;
- preparing the introduction on the market, which involves the marketing department.

Table 8.4 Innovation process in Groupe SEB

Exploration	Demonstration	Implementation
Generate ideas for the future and test their potential	Demonstrate the feasibility of a product	Invest to create a new product or improve an existing one
Open environment	Uncertain, but oriented environment	Concrete actions
• for ideas • for governance	• focus on result • main steps of the process	• precise objectives • defined processes

Source: Groupe SEB (2010).

It is worth noting that less than 5 per cent of the resources are used for the exploration phase, 20 per cent for the demonstration phase and 75 per cent for the implementation phase.

It seems important to note that the terms used in the description of each stages, such as 'focus on result', 'defined processes' and 'main steps of the process', are detailed further in the documentation of Groupe SEB. This innovation process, called product offer creation, not only belongs to the R&D department, but it may also be used throughout the group.

8.3.3 The coordination of innovation activities between headquarters and sales subsidiaries

A sales subsidiary, which is responsible for the "product offer creation", is in direct contact with distributors and end-users, and can get the necessary information ("insights") for business units.

(Director of Marketing Projects for Transversal Products,
interview 2010)

Concerning the organization of the innovation process, the R&D and marketing departments cooperate on a regular basis. These departments are structured by divisions according to three groups of products: cookware, small household appliances and home and personal care products. Each department is composed of three teams in charge of innovation: marketing, technical support and design (see Figure 8.2).

In the divisions, teams work and take decisions together. In order to manage communication and avoid conflicts, product and innovation committees have been established. These committees are also

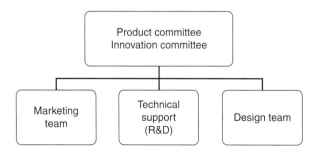

Figure 8.2   Groupe SEB's divisional structure
Source: Interviews within Groupe SEB (2010).

responsible for validating innovation proposals. All divisions are located in France; the participation of sales subsidiaries in the innovation process is therefore limited.

> In the innovation process, subsidiaries can play a warning role at the beginning of the process, but they mainly contribute to product launching, which remains a very important stage.
>
> (Director of Marketing Projects for Transversal Products, interview 2010)

Groupe SEB is an MNC specializing in manufacturing consumer goods which are very different from one country to another. For example, cooking habits are different in China, the US or Brazil, and therefore it is important that the perception of the local market can be transmitted to central departments. Products, colours and, more generally, needs, are particularly subject to difference. For example, in Asia, people often eat rice. It is therefore important to offer a large choice of rice cookers, a segment from which the group had been absent for a long period.

Marketing departments, managed centrally at the level of strategic business units, are the driving force of the process: they are project integrators. In fact, the marketing department has the final say in the determination of the selling potential. Research is also centralized, but most of its development can be performed by specialized subsidiaries located overseas, in Brazil, China, Italy or the US.

The conducted analysis demonstrates that the standardization of the process is the key coordination mechanism of innovation within Groupe SEB.

8.4   Conclusion

In this chapter, we have tried to understand the innovation process in an MNC by focusing on the French Groupe SEB. The collected data show that the operation and the management of the innovation process are centralized within the group, while the participation of subsidiaries remains limited. Groupe SEB has chosen to standardize its innovation process, in order to provide all participants with a common work environment. However, considering the specificities of emerging countries, the company now seeks to implement a system that allows the increasing involvement of local subsidiaries in the innovation process.

References

Alter, N. (2002) *Les logiques d'innovation: Approche pluridisciplinaire* (Paris: La Découverte).

Bartlett, C. A., Ghoshal, S. and Birkinshaw, J. (2003) *Transnational Management: Text, Cases, and Readings in Cross-Border Management*, 4th edn (New York: McGraw-Hill Irwin).

Bartlett, C. A. and Beamish, P. W. (2010) *Transnational Management: Text, Cases, and Readings in Cross-Border Management*, 6th edn (New York: McGraw-Hill Irwin).

CAS (Centre d'analyse stratégique) (2007) *Internationalisation de la R&D des entreprises et attractivité de la France*, Report for the French government (Paris: CAS).

Castellani, D. and Zanfei, A. (2006) *Multinational Firms, Innovation and Productivity* (Cheltenham: Edward Elgar).

Chen, M. and Nivoix, S. (2009) 'L'impact de la crise en quatre tableaux. En réponse à la crise: la Chine en quête d'un nouveau modèle', *Forum of Atlas/AFMI – Association Francophone de Management International* (Paris: Cnam and ESCP Europe).

Colovic, A. and Mayrhofer, U. (2011) 'Optimising the Location of R&D and Production Activities: Trends in the Automotive Industry', *European Planning Studies*, 19 (8), 1481–98.

Doz, Y. L. and Prahalad, C. K. (1984) 'Patterns of Strategic Control within Multinational Corporations', *Journal of International Business Studies*, 15 (2), 55–72.

European Commission (2010) *Rapport sur les investissements en R&D industrielle* (Brussels: European Commission).

Groupe SEB (2008) *Rapport d'activité et de développement durable* (Ecully: Groupe SEB).

Groupe SEB (2009) *Rapport d'activité et de développement durable* (Ecully: Groupe SEB).

Schumpeter, J. A. (1935) *Théorie de l'évolution économique* (Paris: Dalloz).

Xerfi Entreprises (2010) *Le Groupe SEB* (Paris: Xerfi).

9
Creating an Observatory of International Managerial Professions

Jérôme Rive and Paul Marc Collin

Management in an international context is performed by managers who consider their jobs to have characteristics in terms of knowledge, know-how and skills that go beyond purely functional features. The international dimension provides important specificities to the context of analysing managerial professions. These particularly varied managerial positions are subjected to numerous changes and their development and dynamics can be analysed through creating an observatory of international professions, in particular in multinational companies (MNCs). The aim of such an observatory is to better understand the expectations of internationalized companies, particularly those which are globalized and anticipate changes in international trade. The prospective job forecast approach (Boyer and Scouarnec, 2009) serves as a theoretical framework for the creation of this observatory.

9.1 Job forecast: A theoretical approach

9.1.1 The prospective approach and the concept of profession

The definitions of job forecast are numerous. For Hatem and Préel (1995), job forecast has several features: it is primarily a comprehensive, cross- and multidisciplinary approach; it is also a long-term approach, with a broad perspective, which enables disruptions to emerge, and allows a higher degree of flexibility. Job forecast also entails a rational approach, using proven tools and operating with clarity and transparency. It is a participative approach, and finally, it is an approach that enables an action plan to be formulated.

The common feature to different definitions of the term 'profession' is the concept of individual predominantly technical skills. The profession consists of acquired knowledge and skills applied to product processing or services. The ROME directory (*Répertoire Opérationnel des Métiers et des Emplois*, or operational directory of professions and jobs) suggests the following approach: occupational categories result from combining the social status of the manager with the professional environment. Professional fields include skills related to a position, a technology or a business sector, so illustrating that the managerial profession is a group of closely related jobs.

Companies have used the concept of profession particularly for specialization strategies. In this context, it relates to skills the coordination of which allows operating on one or more strategic segments. According to Martinet (1983), the managerial profession is comparable to a global know-how that can satisfy demand by means of a suitable offer. The profession may be acquired, strengthened and developed over time. It can also be transferred. At the sectoral level, the profession encompasses a broad set of tasks and functions related to a specific sector; for example, health, telecommunications, the automotive industry or tourism.

9.1.2   The job forecast

Employment, qualifications and training have been subject to many prospective studies, but confidence has gradually eroded to the point that these studies have been questioned. The sectoral job analysis and forecast approach is the most common one, as the demand for this type of survey is very high. Due to forecasting errors and labour shortages, the demand for this type of survey is permanent. Reports on job perspectives in the upcoming years tend to focus on recruitment difficulties, labour shortages and pressures on labour markets, and usually examine occupational areas in terms of labour demand and supply. Thus, they provide an overview of major trends in the employment market. However, in our opinion, these macroeconomic approaches to national labour markets appear to lack both perspective and openness to current developments and transformations in the international environment.

Any job forecast approach implies taking into account the passage of time and certain definitions and perceptions of time. Depending on time direction (towards either the past or the future) and time nature (time for knowledge or time for action), Boyer and Scouarnec (2009) advocate a different relationship to time in human resource management (HRM). They list four possible attitudes towards time: reaction, pro-action, hindsight and forecast. Of these, only forecast is future-oriented, and relates to time for knowledge.

In HRM, job planning approaches deal with the issue of anticipation. The objective of these approaches is to maintain an appropriate balance between organizational needs and human resources, projecting it to support future corporate strategy. Theoretically, imbalances due to deviations and both quantitative and qualitative overstaffing or under-staffing have to be reduced by adjusting career development, training or recruitment policies. However, all these human resource planning approaches and methods are part of a day-to-day management approach and focus on the short term. They are much more oriented towards time for action, and finally towards a reactive response. In line with Boyer and Scouarnec's work, we would like to go beyond conventional HRM planning methods to reflect the human perception of time and 'its heterogeneity, systemics, comprehensiveness and past/present/future linkage' (op. cit., p. 102).

9.1.3 Observing jobs

Observation is a prerequisite of forecasting. A central objective of job forecasting is to pave the way for the creation of an observatory of jobs and professions, dedicated to analysing work situations and projecting them to the future. The methods used are numerous. Among them are literature reviews, semi-structured interviews, questionnaires, participant observation and action research. Boyer and Scouarnec (2005) used semi-structured interviews and questionnaires to identify environmental professions; and other occupations have been studied such as emergency assistance services, sales occupations, information and communication technologies (ICT) professions and automotive design professions. Our aim is to extend this methodology to the field of international management and to develop an observatory of international business professions, particularly in MNCs.

With regard to business practices, it should be noted that job observatories allow the carrying out of strategic functions, such as helping in human resource planning (utilized by companies such as Areva, Carrefour, Rhodia, Thales, *Société Française de Radiotéléphonie* [SFR], Generali, PSA Peugeot Citroën, ST Microelectronics and Cap Gemini), developing a structured outlook on trends in the professions supporting day-to-day human resource management (as in Thales Company, where the annual performance interview is an opportunity to discuss positions over the course of the next two or three years, the manager and the collaborator having a guide of possible pathways in different professions) and promoting social dialogue.

It is interesting to take a look at industry practices. The observatory of insurance professions helps to identify changes and checks in particular the relevance of job classification criteria. For the observatory of pharmaceutical industries, it is also a way of advertising activities and professions and the skills associated with them.

The profession forecast is a way of anticipating alternative futures in terms of skills, activities, responsibilities for a given profession. It thus makes it possible to imagine knowledge and qualifications, expertise and professional skills, behaviour and social skills which tomorrow will be best adapted to serve the individual and the organization. That is why it requires from the actors/experts a co-construction of the analysed professions, as well as a valuation of the same professions. It includes a reflection on individual jobs and work organization (Boyer and Scouarnec, 2005).

To sum up, we can argue that job forecast is underpinned by five motives:

1. a broader concept of human resource management in terms of space and time;
2. the break from a tradition of mechanical foresight;
3. a focus on what is possible (logics of evolution scenarios);
4. a co-construction by the actors-experts;
5. a valuation of the concept of profession.

Two approaches, then, can be distinguished and developed: an inter-organizational approach and an intra-organizational approach.

9.2   Towards an international application

In this section, we will demonstrate the benefits of applying the profession forecast approach in the international context, and more precisely to MNCs. This framework might prove very useful in such a context, as it is characterized by the necessity of supporting the development of MNCs with competent and autonomous teams. The goal of an optimized management system of talents is to recruit and train individuals to be ready to offer a direct contribution to the internationalization process of the company, but also to coach ambitious local staff in order to give their career a genuine international dimension.

9.2.1   A turbulent environment calling for analyses and discussions

Market globalization and recent transformations in the international environment lead a growing proportion of companies to develop international activities, because they have to follow customers or find growth potential abroad. It is then essential to find talented human resources with diverse professional profiles. Obviously, functional characteristics are important, but others are complementary and discriminative too, such as transversal, autonomous and risk-conscious dimensions. Survival of companies in international markets, regardless of their size, is a paramount challenge (Faibis, 2011). Just as profession forecast is important to all companies, it might prove particularly critical for MNCs, especially in the context of headquarters–subsidiaries coordination in key management dimensions.

We can witness the emergence and development of numerous MNCs, aiming at reaching a critical size in the world market (Dunning and Lundan, 2008). To maintain their competitive advantage, these companies have established subsidiaries in the fields of marketing, production and even research and development (R&D) beyond their national boundaries, moving further away from their home region (Rugman, 2005). Globalization of markets, as well as recent transformations in the international environment, have led to the emergence of new players, notably in emerging markets, challenging the strategy of traditional Western MNCs (Faibis, 2011) which have to deal with these new competitors (Milliot and Tournois, 2010).

9.2.2 Definition of the reach of the observatory and the skills to be observed

Global MNCs may be considered as network-integrated structures, thanks to their international teams (Roberts et al., 1998; Govindarajan and Gupta, 2001) or thanks to their virtual international teams (Duarte and Snyder, 2001). The priority of teams is to meet the needs of clients in an immediate, flexible and non-controversial way (Montoya-Weiss et al., 2001). Moreover, competition is now related to inter-organizational cooperation on an international scale in very precisely defined fields, as well as to other generally accepted competitive relationships. This requires mutual adaptation of processes and organizational systems, but also a great openness on the part of teams, especially when adapting to the diversity of organizational cultures.

Beyond classical and common internationalization strategies such as ethnocentric, polycentric, regiocentric and geocentric strategies, developed by Heenan and Perlmutter (1979) (see Chapter 1), Scholz's (2000) typology quoted by Stein (2008), appears more relevant to our project, as it associates cultural and decision-making strategies. The so-called mono-cultural, multicultural and intercultural strategies are then associated with centralized, decentralized and federal decision-making strategies and international human resource management strategies. Job design and purposes might probably be impacted, and therefore we have to take this dimension into account in our project.

The objective of establishing a profession observatory and a mapping of international jobs is to offer a global and general presentation of key professions in this business sector from an anticipatory perspective. Our project will focus mainly on activities that are international, or developed in an international context. We propose studying all MNCs, regardless of their organization models. The contingent job descriptions specific to certain companies will not be included in our research. The description of professions is by nature generic and extensive: it is related to business activities and their associated key competences. Professions will be described with their essential characteristics and then aggregated into groups and sub-groups of professions. The result will be a consistent and structured presentation of professions which offers a trans-disciplinary overview of existing professions; it will also offer the opportunity of easily identifying major trends in the development of managerial professions in the field of international management.

9.2.3 From international professions and skills to a mapping of international professions

Regarding competences, it appears logical to identify two families of activities: activities developed within the framework of international mobility, that is to say outside the local context of origin; and activities developed locally, but connected to international ones.

In the context of international mobility, there is a high level of diversity in the competences mobilized by international managers, combining strategic, environmental, managerial, relational and inter-personal dimensions (see Chapter 10). Descriptions of competences frequently refer to the approach described by Fink et al. (2005), making a distinction between knowledge of the local market, competences regarding the management of a profit centre, competences in management, network-related competences and individual competences. Moreover, it is common to consider that job characteristics are related to job profiles, the duration of the contract, the length of communication and the type of international mission (Waxin, 2008). In addition, as mentioned by Black et al. (1992), the degree of interpersonal interaction with local staff, which is inherent to the function and role of an international manager, plays an important part.

More globally, as underlined by Barmeyer and Mayrhofer (2002), the necessary skills in international management are related to professional and technical competences, frequently connected with the profession itself, but also to foreign language skills, knowledge about social, organizational and economic environments, as well as to intercultural skills. Let us consider for a moment this 'inter' dimension in relation to a national or a cultural element. The notion of intercultural competence, which has achieved some success in the field of HRM in North America and in Germany, is still not yet often considered in France (Demorgon and Lipianski, 1999). Defined as 'a set of analytical and strategic abilities which broaden an individual's spectrum of interpretations and actions in his/her inter-individual interactions with members of other cultures' (Barmeyer, 2008, p. 212), the notion of intercultural competence is fundamental to the search for a description of international competences, especially regarding the education of the benefits of differences, perceived as complementary and facilitating consistent and efficient interactions.

International professions are multiple and multidimensional, from the export manager to the director of international activities, the international key account manager, the international product manager, the international project manager, the international after-sales services manager, the international risks manager, the management controller of a foreign subsidiary, the corporate credit manager and the coordinator of international affairs; and the list is not exhaustive. To make the observatory operational, we have decided to use a mapping developed by the French *Conseillers du Commerce Extérieur de la France* (CCEF, the foreign trade advisers association of France). This reference document is used to observe international junior or senior managers in different markets. In their files, we can find data such as objectives of the position, hierarchical interface, responsibilities, potential career developments, expected professional competences, required qualities and performance criteria. Each position is visualized through a graph, allowing a comparison between jobs along six dimensions, independence, customer relationships, communication skills, conceptual thinking, creativity and innovation, transversality. Each dimension is then evaluated according to a four-level scale. We consider this tool, developed by practitioners, to be a dynamic heuristic instrument, which encapsulates the complexity and diversity of the activities observed.

9.3 Conclusion

Prospective planning is central making MNCs more competitive, combining the logic of knowledge with the logic of action, the academic with pragmatic dimensions. The project is ambitious and needs to involve practitioners. The observatory's purpose is to analyse international professions, especially in MNCs, beyond the international mobility of individuals. Such an approach is necessary because international activities have become an essential part of companies. MNCs will be analysed as well as other types of organizations, small and medium-sized enterprises for example. We believe that the human factor is at the core of the international development of companies. This work will be undertaken with the active participation of experts in international professions. The job forecast approach is fundamental and it is a source of continuous trans-disciplinary learning for MNCs. In this chapter, we have introduced the foundations of the observatory, and the time has come to develop this instrument.

References

Barmeyer, C. (2008) 'Le développement des compétences interculturelles' in M.-F. Waxin and C. Barmeyer (eds) *Gestion des ressources humaines internationales* (Rueil-Malmaison: Edition Liaisons) pp. 209–47.
Barmeyer, C. and Mayrhofer, U. (2002) 'Le management interculturel: facteur de réussite des fusions-acquisitions internationales?', *Gérer et Comprendre*, 70, 24–33.
Black, J. S., Gregersen, H. B. and Mendenhall, M. E. (1992) 'Toward a Theoretical Framework of Repatriation Adjustment', *Journal of International Business Studies*, 23 (4), 737–60.
Boyer, L. and Scouarnec, A. (2005) *L'observatoire des métiers* (Cormelles-le-Royal: Editions Management & Société).
Boyer, L. and Scouarnec, A. (2009) *La prospective des métiers* (Cormelles-le-Royal: Editions Management & Société).
Demorgon, J. and Lipianski, E. M. (eds) (1999) *Guide de l'interculturel en formation* (Paris: Retz).
Duarte, D. L. and Snyder, N. T. (2001) *Mastering Virtual Teams: Strategies, Tools and Techniques that Succed*, 2nd edn (San Francisco: Jossey-Bass).
Dunning, J. H. and Lundan, S. M. (2008) *Multinational Enterprises and the Global Economy*, 2nd edn (Cheltenham: Edward Elgar Publishing).
Faibis, L. (ed.) (2011) *La France et ses multinationales – Stratégie globale et intérêt national* (Paris: Xerfi).
Fink, G., Meierwert, S. and Rohr, U. (2005) 'The Use of Repatriate Knowledge in Organizations', *Human Resources Planning*, 28 (4), 30–6.
Govindarajan, V. and Gupta, A. K. (2001) 'Building an Effective Global Business Team', *Sloan Management Review*, 42 (4), 63–71.
Hatem, F. and Préel, B. (1995) *Pour une prospective participative* (Issy-les-Moulineaux: BIPE-Conseil).
Heenan, D. A. and Perlmutter, H. V. (1979) *Multinational Organization Development* (Reading, MA: Addison-Wesley).
Martinet, A.-C. (1983) *Stratégie* (Paris: Vuibert).

Milliot, E. and Tournois, N. (eds) (2010) *The Paradoxes of Globalisation* (Basingstoke: Palgrave Macmillan).

Montoya-Weiss, M. M., Massey, A. P. and Song, M. (2001) 'Getting it Together: Temporal Coordination and Conflict Management in Global Virtual Teams', *Academy of Management Journal*, 44 (6), 1251–62.

Roberts, K., Kossek, E. E. and Ozeki, C. (1998) 'Managing the Global Workforce: Challenges and Strategies', *Academy of Management Executive*, 12 (4), 93–106.

Rugman, A. M. (2005) *The Regional Multinationals* (Cambridge: Cambridge University Press).

Scholz, C. (2000) *Personalmanagement: Informationsorientierte und verhaltenstheoretische Grundlagen* (Munich: Vahlen).

Stein, V. (2008) 'Le contexte de l'internationalisation de la GRH' in M.-F. Waxin and C. Barmeyer (eds) *Gestion des ressources humaines internationales* (Rueil-Malmaison: Editions Liaisons) pp. 25–55.

Waxin, M.-F. (2008) 'Le recrutement et la sélection à l'international' in M.-F. Waxin and C. Barmeyer (eds) *Gestion des ressources humaines internationals* (Rueil-Malmaison: Editions Liaisons) pp. 151–208.

10
International Mobility: An Opportunity for Managers to Acquire and Transfer Competencies

Pascale Berthier and Alain Roger

As companies globalize, 'human capital' tends to become a strategic asset; hence, the increasing number of studies focusing on the international mobility of managers. When companies decide to grow internationally, managerial and organizational factors play a key role, together with strategic, financial and commercial factors. The corporate culture, the international experience of managers, knowledge networks, competencies and the control and coordination of subsidiaries must be taken into account, since organizational structures of multinational companies (MNCs) have become more complex (Meier and Schier, 2005). Managerial and organizational factors influence the way companies make decisions concerning the international mobility of managers and the way expatriates or 'international managers' acquire the competencies they need (Pierre, 2008).

Mayrhofer (2005) outlines three main forms of international development: exportation; contractual agreements, such as franchises and licences; and foreign direct investments (FDI). According to Mayrhofer, inter-firm linkages, especially cooperative alliances, joint ventures and mergers and acquisitions, have increased significantly since the 1980s. This type of development influences the expatriation policy which must be adjusted to the relationships established between headquarters and subsidiaries, or between partner companies in joint ventures. International mobility entails preparing and managing expatriates throughout their international mobility period, including repatriation. The development and transfer of competencies gained by expatriates provide a unique opportunity to create a global mindset within the company, by preparing future expatriates and employees who interact with colleagues abroad.

When cultural awareness is high, cultural diversity is enhanced and international competencies acquired by expatriates are dealt with and transferred throughout the company. Cultural diversity is a key factor in Perlmutter's typology (1969) (see Chapter 1): it ranges from the less sensitive (ethnocentric) to the more sensitive type (geocentric). Ethnocentric companies are culturally self-centred and less sensitive to cultural differences; polycentric and regiocentric companies acknowledge cultural diversity in their foreign subsidiaries, but allow them a certain degree of autonomy and do not deal with competencies transfer between subsidiaries and headquarters; geocentric companies are culturally sensitive and foster intercultural competencies. Considering the globalization context and the growing attention paid to knowledge management, knowledge assets have become strategic assets and international know-how gained by companies is a competitive advantage (Bonache et al., 2001).

International mobility can benefit both managers who acquire new competencies and the company to which these competencies are transferred (Le Pargneux, 2009). However, studies show that knowledge transfer does not always take place (Adler, 1981) and that turning individual learning into organizational learning is not an easy task. This lack of transfer may be frustrating both for expatriates, who would like to use and share their international experience, and for companies, which do not get the 'return on investment' they expected.

A study published by APEC (Association Pour l'Emploi des Cadres, the French association for the employment of managers) (2004), analysed 20 European companies and showed that, for their international expansion, French companies mainly send expatriates during the setting up phase, and that local managers are recruited thereafter. Of course, this can vary according to the international commitment and maturity of each company. Franko (1973) describes the development cycle as a U-curve, because the company needs expatriates at the beginning and at the end of its internationalization phase. The number of expatriates is high at the beginning, when the company exports or engages in a partnership, and at the end, when it establishes subsidiaries and transfers knowledge back home. During the intermediary phase, the company recruits local managers and employees, so that the number of expatriates tends to decrease. Thus, it is mainly during the first and the third phases that companies deal with the development and transfer of competencies of expatriates.

In this chapter, we will first describe the competencies expatriates acquire abroad, then we will summarize the results of a field study which was conducted with 40 top managers in three French MNCs. The study enabled us to identify the factors which facilitate or inhibit knowledge transfer, both on the company and on the expatriate side.

10.1   Expatriation as an accelerating learning period

The literature describes the different phases of international mobility as follows:

- Phase 1, selection and preparation;
- Phase 2, foreign assignment and opportunities for competency development;
- Phase 3, repatriation – or new foreign assignments – and the opportunity to use or transfer newly acquired competencies.

The preparation phase is an opportunity to clarify motives of international assignments, which may be to transfer competencies to a foreign subsidiary, to control and coordinate activities or to develop individual potentials. Whereas the first two motives are demand driven, focused on organizational needs, the third one is learning driven, focused on learning and development. This third motive refers to a two-way competency transfer, from headquarters to subsidiaries and from subsidiaries to headquarters (Lazarova and Tarique, 2005). The expatriate's willingness to transfer competencies might vary according to the motives of expatriation: if the expatriate holds a management position, the propensity to transfer will be higher. If the expatriate's mission is to transfer technical expertise, the ability to transfer competencies back home is lower and can even result in a loss of competencies (Roussillon,1984).

During the foreign assignment phase, the expatriates have to achieve organizational objectives; by doing this, they can also enhance existing competencies or develop new ones. This period may be qualified as a 'fast learning' period if the adjustment phase is positive. Black (1988) makes a distinction between three types of adjustment: adjustment to living conditions; adjustment to interaction with local people; and adjustment to the work environment. Numerous factors influence adjustment, among which are the support the expatriates get from their family and issues related to environmental characteristics.

During the repatriation phase, the retention of expatriates is seen as a major company issue. When defining the key success factors of expatriation, Yan et al. (2002) add the use and transfer of newly acquired competencies to the notion of retention. More recently, Le Pargneux

(2009) identified knowledge acquisition as an individual success factor and knowledge transfer as an organizational success factor.

If companies wish to build on opportunities of knowledge transfer offered by expatriation processes, they have to identify transferable competencies and define the factors that will facilitate or prevent knowledge transfer. Some authors (Berthoin Antal, 2001; Fink et al., 2005) have designed typologies that describe competencies gained by expatriates. Others looked at the characteristics of competencies: are they specific or generic (Penmartin, 2005), tacit or explicit (Polanyi, 1996)? The first ones refer to the competencies themselves, the second ones deal with their transferability.

10.1.1   Typologies of competencies

Berthoin Antal's typology (2000) divides knowledge into five categories:

1. Declarative knowledge is theoretical, factual and is generally named expertise (the 'what'). It is explicit, concrete and easy to transfer (Anderson, 1983).
2. Procedural knowledge concerns processes that lead to action and is described as know-how (the 'how'). It has a lot to do with learning by doing, and is considered by Cohen and Bacdayan (1996) as less explicit and less transferable in new circumstances.
3. Conditional knowledge deals with the 'when', the conditions enabling individuals to use their declarative and procedural knowledge (Paris et al., 1983). Tardiff (1992) considers conditional knowledge as a key asset in the knowledge transfer process, because it enables individuals to choose the appropriate conditions and timing for transfer (Berthoin Antal, 2000).
4. Axiomatic knowledge deals with the 'why'. It mainly concerns the learning process and enables individuals to understand the causes of each action (Sackmann, 1992).
5. Relational knowledge deals with the personal network (the 'who') and can play a major role in competency transfer, which generally implies interaction between individuals.

Beyond this typology, Fink et al. (2005) offer a concrete description of competencies; they draw a distinction between those related to the market (knowledge of local environment), to profit centre management, to management as a whole (to manage a project or a team, to manage communication), to network management (in both home and host countries) and to personal competencies (open-mindedness, self confidence). This typology stresses the diversity of strategic, environmental, managerial and personal competencies acquired by expatriates. Fink et al. observe that general management competencies acquired abroad are seldom used upon return home, because of the lack of general management positions at headquarters. This creates frustration among the expatriates concerned.

10.1.2   Characteristics of competencies

Competencies may be more or less easy to transfer. Polanyi's (1996) typology is often referred to by many authors (Bonache et al., 2001; Subramaniam and Venkatraman, 2001; Wang et al., 2004). It draws a distinction between explicit and tacit knowledge. Explicit knowledge refers to knowledge that can be expressed by words, drawings or metaphors. Tacit knowledge concerns knowledge, such as a craftsman's skills, that is difficult to express, whatever the language form, and which needs a translation into explicit knowledge before it can be transferred. The translation of tacit knowledge of expatriates into explicit knowledge is a condition for knowledge transfer (Nonaka and Takeuchi, 1995; Selmer, 2002).

Bonache et al. (2001) describe tacit knowledge as knowledge that cannot be codified or described in operating manuals, and that can be observed only when it is applied. This knowledge is difficult to copy and becomes a strategic resource for companies. Individuals themselves might not be conscious of having such knowledge. Its tacit nature makes it difficult to express and transfer, and many expatriates consider tacit knowledge as being non transferable (Adler, 1981).

Penmartin (2005) makes a distinction between specific competencies and generic ones. Specific competencies are more technical and may be transferred when a given expertise is needed. These are often key competencies for the company and their value is intrinsic (Bonache and Brewster, 2001). To develop such competencies, the company may have to use appropriate transfer tools, such as internal memos, procedures, emails and sometimes oral communication (Prax, 2003). As far as international mobility is concerned, local competencies acquired within a subsidiary and concerning cultural, political, economic and legal aspects are considered as key competencies, and must be transferred to the parent company by repatriates (Downes and Thomas, 2000).

Michel (2003) studied the issue of knowledge transferability within or outside the company and refers to the notion of 'specific human asset'. This means that the specific or semi-specific character of some competencies, or mix of competencies, might result in a lack of transferability. In some situations, a company or a work unit may be the only one to require a competency. The author calls this the 'not perfectible transferable human asset'.

Generic competencies are transversal, easily transferable, whatever the context. They concern the ability to anticipate and pilot projects, to conclude, to communicate, to manage and to influence. They are very valuable to individuals.

Different types of careers might lead to the development of different types of competencies. A traditional organizational career within the same company might lead to the development of specific competencies, whereas a career 'without borders' might lead individuals to develop generic competencies that serve their career goals. Tung (1998) noticed that this second type of career has become the norm for international managers who want to develop their generic competencies for career purposes. This might go against the company's interest, which is to benefit from the specific competencies of its managers (Sullivan, 1995).

Ignoring the specific/generic distinction, Argote et al. (2003) confirm that companies learn more from their own experience than from the experience of others, hence the importance of internally developed competencies. As far as competencies of expatriates are concerned, the typologies discussed above are essential to the comprehension of transformation and transfer mechanisms. Tacit knowledge transfer implies interaction, whereas explicit knowledge can be transferred via manuals or procedures. Tacit or specific competencies are high value competencies for organizations, while generic or relational skills are highly valued by individuals. This situation may result in conflicts of interest. Considering that expatriates acquire competencies during their period abroad, and that companies want to acquire these competencies, we conducted a field study and interviewed a sample of repatriated managers, in order to better understand the transfer process.

10.2   Competency transfer from individuals to organizations

Observing learning and transfer processes among repatriates has enabled us to highlight facilitating and inhibiting factors for the company as well as for the individual. Our study dealt with three French MNCs, which all have a strong technological dimension. Their total sales range from 10 to 60 billion Euros, and their staff is over 60,000. We interviewed 39 expatriated managers who had returned to their home country (France) for less than two years. This time span enabled them to recall their expatriation experience with a certain degree of reliability (Stahl and Cerdin, 2004). Our sample was of 34 men and 5 women; the youngest was 32 and the eldest 57; the average age was 45; the majority of them held a master's degree; 74 per cent of them were engineers and the others graduated from business schools (15%) or universities. Expatriation motives were rather similar to the ones mentioned in the literature: to manage and control activities in subsidiaries, to transfer expertise or to develop individual potentials (in this case, individuals were generally considered as future managers).

Semi-directive interviews were conducted and fully transcribed, so allowing a comprehensive analysis. We could identify the competencies acquired by expatriates, as well as both the facilitating and inhibiting factors of their transfer, related to the organization or to individuals. The types of competences acquired by expatriates are presented in Table 10.1. They correspond to Fink et al.'s (2005) typology, which encompasses intercultural/environmental, personal, managerial and relational/political competencies.

10.2.1   Intercultural competencies

Intercultural – or international – competencies depend on people's sensitivity to cultural differences and ability to think differently. 'My know-how is international awareness, I don't think French anymore' (MNC engineering manager in Germany, interview 2010). 'Learn first that people don't think the way we do' (MNC vice-president strategy in Asia, interview 2010). 'It means to see what's going on in other people's

Table 10.1   Competencies acquired by expatriates

Type of competencies	Number of quotations in interviews
Intercultural	26
Personal (open-mindedness, ability to step back, self-knowledge)	14
Managerial	10
Political	10
Profit centre management	7
Network/relational	3

heads. Expatriation allows you to X-ray people, and this experience is really specific. People who haven't been exposed to it can't do this' (MNC general manager in China, interview 2010). 'To bring together people from different cultures and build up a team' (MNC general manager in Tunisia, interview 2010). 'It's not so different to manage abroad; the only point is to be aware of cultural differences. My interaction with people is certainly different from that of someone who only worked in France' (MNC regional manager in Asia, interview 2010).

Expatriates who have been sent to English speaking countries argue that their command of the language is a key asset when they return home. They also insist upon multicultural awareness as a key success factor for them and their company (see Table 10.2). But these intercultural skills are contingent on contexts and people (Dupuis, 2005); they enable someone to begin to understand people from other cultural backgrounds and to build hypotheses that will be confirmed or

Table 10.2 Examples of cultural representations of expatriates

Geographical zone/country	Cultural representations
USA/Canada/Australia	Importance of contract: 'Americans adopt a dispassionate approach to work'. Different management style: 'no passion, motivation of employees deeply concerned with employability'. Conviviality at work (coffee breaks, barbecues): 'one of us always managed to bring lots of smarties'.
England	Self-confidence: 'everybody can express his opinion'; 'the role of management is to help people grow'. Result-orientation, teamwork
Germany/Belgium	Pragmatism: 'Compared to the French, Belgians are very pragmatic... work is not so intellectual'. Organizing skills
Asia/China	Respect for others: 'I had the feeling that we went one step further when we went to Asia, that we discovered a way of life, respect'. Information seeking through various channels: 'encirclement technique', 'I enjoyed using Chinese techniques'.

Source: Interviews with expatriates of French MNCs, 2010.

disproved according to their interactions in a foreign country. Irrmann (2008a) compares intercultural competency with automobile driving: 'consulting maps (comparing intercultural dimensions) may be useful to find your way, but the moment of truth is when you enter the intercultural vehicle and you drive it. Only thus will you realize that it is more difficult to interact than to compare yourself to others' (p. 159). The ability to communicate and the ability to interact help people cope with an intercultural situation. Both dimensions are clearly identified by our respondents as being critical.

This intercultural competency often involves taking some distance from one's home country when observing how foreigners work: 'understand that we have a way of thinking and of working that is not necessarily the same abroad' (MNC subsidiary manager in Asia, interview 2010). However, there may be a risk of developing stereotypes of different cultures as presented in Table 10.2. Stereotyping leads to the categorizing of people without taking into account the diversity within each population. Another type of stereotyping takes place when members of the home organization consider expatriates as being part of a specific category and are reluctant to integrate them when they return home.

10.2.2   Personal competencies

Personal competencies often mentioned by the expatriates of our sample are open-mindedness, self-confidence and self-awareness.

- Open-mindedness: expatriation 'develops adaptation skills, open-mindedness, the ability to see problems in a different way', and it leads to better listening, better understanding. 'You accept differences, you try to better understand them', '[you] understand, listen to the way the other person speaks'. It develops 'the ability to listen, to broaden a little your field of reflection, and to enhance your solutions when you work on a problem'; 'I learned that you can often act differently from people around you' (MNC process engineer in Germany, interview 2010).
- Self-confidence: 'take much distance, ask yourself, "What did this person really mean?"'; 'experience in Egypt was for me like an exile as I was confronted with a totally different reality' (MNC manager in Egypt, interview 2010). 'It gave me more confidence because in a British environment, everybody is entitled to give his opinion'; 'finally, we are less uptight, less afraid to fail, I would say. I think it makes you more flexible,' (MNC manager of mergers and acquisitions in Great Britain, interview 2010).

- Self-awareness: 'a better knowledge of my own limitations, and therefore of myself'; 'it's incredible, because you go abroad without really knowing where you are going, why you went there; and you come back a few years later ... and yes, you know very well what you want and what you are good at' (MNC subsidiary manager in Mexico, interview 2010).

10.2.3 Managerial competencies

Managerial competencies include competencies in team and profit centre management.

- Team management is perceived as being more complex for expatriates: 'team management is actually always the most demanding, the most complex task and, when you do not have the same habits of mind ... it makes the exercise more difficult' (MNC sales manager in Africa, interview 2010). Motivating people takes different forms in each country, mainly when employees are not strongly attached to the company (in the US, Great Britain or Australia, for example). This can influence the type of management: 'for me, the most efficient way of changing things, and mainly people, is to be a source of inspiration' (MNC manager of mergers and acquisitions in Great Britain, interview 2010); 'coming into contact with other cultures necessarily helps you approach management, relationships and communication' (MNC sales manager in Africa, interview 2010). 'I learned a completely different way of managing in Great Britain' (MNC financial manager in Great Britain, interview 2010). Then, people also learn how to delegate, because they cannot control everything: 'I signed many papers without really knowing how to delegate' (MNC office manager in China, interview 2010); 'it gave me a much broader experience on how to make people from different cultures work together' (MNC operations manager in Canada, interview 2010); it helps with 'managing people who don't belong to my culture and who have to work together' (MNC subsidiary manager in Africa, interview 2010). 'The rule is always to manage people: Indians, French, etc.' (MNC regional manager in China, interview 2010). Some expatriates also learn how to work in project mode: 'you learn how to organize a building site, to define clear responsibilities, a manager, a deadline' (MNC project manager in Laos, interview 2010).
- Competencies in profit centre management develop along with responsibilities: 'expatriation is also the opportunity to be your own boss'; managing a subsidiary is perceived as 'an excellent training

in profit centre management', 'you work in operational structures which are actually small or medium sized enterprises' (MNC subsidiary manager in Africa, interview 2010). 'It allowed me to be closer to clients and to have a better understanding of the environment' (MNC project manager in Scandinavia, interview 2010). 'My job also included human resource management, which I was not familiar with: I had to manage 80 employees. Then, you really have the feeling you are piloting a company, and it is exciting' (MNC joint venture manager in Africa, interview 2010).

10.2.4 Political and networking competencies

Political and networking competencies are first described by expatriates as ways to manage high level political relationships: 'the point of projects is to actually work at a high level when you discuss with governments, with bankers' (MNC project manager in Asia, interview 2010). 'It not only involves managing a company, it also means representing your group, and meeting local authorities at all levels' (MNC subsidiary manager of Europe and Middle East, interview 2010). 'I have never worked in a context with so many different trends, so many different stakes and so much lobbying' (MNC project manager in Asia, interview 2010). 'Political and social relationships also play an important part' (MNC subsidiary manager in Asia, interview 2010). 'I also learned diplomacy; I learned how to make concessions' (MNC office manager in China, interview 2010).

Network competencies develop along with the creation of one's own network: 'now, I am more aware of the importance of networks, of having your own network, of taking the time to monitor what is going on in terms of organization' (MNC finance manager in Germany, interview 2010); 'you really have to do it yourself, to create your network and to keep it alive' (MNC joint venture manager in Africa, interview 2010); or people develop a network that will be useful to the company: 'many things happen through us just because we are French; hence, the creation of a network of people who know you; this gives you a knowledge that will be very important for the company' (MNC subsidiary manager in Great Britain, interview 2010). 'Obtaining the contract was a significant help for us because when you are there, you create a local network of political, financial and industrial supports which then allows you to reach win-win solutions' (MNC subsidiary manager in Africa, interview 2010).

Other competencies relate to gaining an expertise; for example, in finance: 'I learned everything about finance, let us say the financial management of a company, cash flow planning, and so on' (MNC subsidiary manager in Africa, interview 2010); in the field of international negotiation: 'the main contribution is negotiation ... but it is quite different in an international context', (MNC subsidiary manager in Asia, interview 2010); or in the field of law or logistics: 'drawing up reports on disputes right at the beginning of procedures' (MNC project manager in Scandinavia, interview 2010).

In these three technical-oriented MNCs, we would expect that the learning of technical competencies would be critical, but it represents only a small part of the competencies already discussed. This can be explained by two main factors: first, our sample included high-level managers in charge of managing subsidiaries, units or projects; and second, the transfer of expertise in these companies mainly takes place from the headquarters to the subsidiaries and not the reverse.

It is important to understand how these competencies gained by expatriates during an experience of international mobility are transferred upon their return home.

10.3 Facilitating and inhibiting factors of competence transfer

The factors facilitating or limiting this transfer can be related to the organization or to the expatriate.

10.3.1 Organizational factors

Organizational culture, human resource management processes and reactions of colleagues at work may favour the transfer of competences gained abroad, or, on the contrary, hinder it. A 'learning' organizational culture favours the transfer of competencies. Expatriates explain how they learnt from the past: sometimes, companies organize exchange sessions in order to build on experience. The presence in the company of a large number of employees with international experience also facilitates the transfer, because they are more open to expatriates. Conversely, however, an ethnocentric culture can be a limitation and may lead to the NIH ('Not Invented Here') syndrome described by Berthoin Antal (2000).

Well-adapted human resource processes, like the help provided to expatriates to facilitate their return home, the position they hold and the way competencies are managed, can improve the transfer of competencies. Helping expatriates when they return to their home country mainly means preparing and anticipating this return and providing a logistical and social support. The absence of these factors was often mentioned by the expatriates of our sample as being unsatisfactory. After benefiting from substantial support when they went abroad, they regretted the absence of support when they came back. One of them compared their departure with the departure of a space shuttle: everybody is there to watch it go, but its return 'does not interest anybody'. Expatriates consider that their return should be anticipated six months in advance and that they should be prepared for this unexpected 'cultural counter-shock'. They expected logistical support for them and their families (a list of administrative procedures, housing, schools, spouse's work, and so on). They realize that returning is actually like a new departure, a rupture they did not anticipate.

Positions expatriates hold when they return home is one of the key success factors: according to them, the ideal position is one with responsibilities, related to their position abroad and including the management of a team, thus facilitating the transfer, because it corresponds to their role abroad. Expatriates insist on the continuity of their career path and on the importance of their profession as such: because of career paths designed by human resource services, some expatriates had to quit what they consider as their profession. Owing to the lack of support, they tend to manage their career themselves, and some of them find their position when they return home through their social network within the company. Yet, they expect the organization to manage competencies. Questioned on the type of knowledge or competencies they gained during their expatriation period, the subjects of the study appear to have difficulties identifying them. They consider that companies could help them more identify, formalize and transfer competencies, but they observe that they do not encourage them and that their processes are not adapted.

The behaviour of the other members of the organization can be encouraging, by being eager to learn; or, conversely, they may reject somebody who 'abandoned' them and who has become 'big-headed'. In the first case, when expatriates feel that others are interested in their competencies, they are ready to make the effort to transfer them. Conversely, if others are not interested or even show a xenophobic attitude (Adler, 1981) based on negative stereotypes towards expatriates, the transfer is limited. Table 10.3 presents a summary of the main facilitating or inhibiting factors.

10.3.2   Individual factors

Even if organizational conditions are favourable, expatriates are not always ready to use or share competencies they acquired during their

Table 10.3 Facilitating and inhibiting organizational factors

Facilitating factors	Inhibiting factors
Corporate culture/values	
Learning organization Motives for expatriation: business, management Number of employees with international experience	Motives for expatriation: transfer of technical expertise Ethnocentrism
Human resource processes	
Position upon return home linked with position abroad, higher responsibilities, team management Competence management: Identification (of new competencies), formalization (feedback on experience), transmission (internal university)	Technical job abroad Position upon return home not linked with experience abroad, lack of continuity in the career path Management of return: lack of help or support Competency management: lack of identification and formalization of competencies, no request, no capitalization
Behaviour of company members	
Useful competencies: meet organizational needs Readiness of colleagues to absorb new competencies	Competencies not useful for people Not open or receptive colleagues Stereotypes towards expatriates

period abroad. They do not always have the skills or the motivation to do this, which is often linked to their satisfaction with the welcoming conditions on their return home.

The ability for expatriates to transfer their new competencies is particularly limited when the competencies are tacit, and therefore difficult to transfer. Tacit knowledge requires two main conditions to be transferred: expatriates must be able to manage interactions and be able to translate tacit knowledge into explicit knowledge. They may have developed these capacities during their experience abroad, thus enabling them to transfer their know-how or promote the company's values. Therefore, they may act as a role model, use their network or the power linked to their status within the company upon their return.

The motivation of expatriates to transfer depends on the signals they receive from the company (organizational and social support), but also on their values with regard to solidarity, exchange and sharing competence. If their mission abroad included learning and potential development, they may be motivated to transfer competencies as a gift exchange. Conversely, if they consider that the experience they gained cannot be transmitted or is useless for others because their competencies are too contextual or obsolete, they will not be motivated to transfer them. If the objectives of expatriation were transfer of expertise or concerned supervising functions, expatriates will also be more reluctant to transfer.

Satisfaction upon return is closely linked to the type of position expatriates hold after their return home, and also to the organizational or social support they received. Our results indicate that the level of satisfaction did not influence the amount of transfer: 82 per cent of the expatriates of our sample transferred some of the competencies they developed, even if they expressed some dissatisfaction.

However, satisfaction seems to have an impact on the scope of the transfer: satisfied expatriates are more often requested to transfer, and they transfer to a larger number of people through conferences, presentations or training sessions. Those who are satisfied with their position, but dissatisfied with the support they received, transfer to their close environment (their team) because they consider that it is part of their role as a manager. Dissatisfied expatriates transfer only to younger managers whom they consider to be more receptive than others. Table 10.4 presents a summary of these individual factors.

10.4   Conclusion

When expatriates are questioned about their competencies, they spontaneously mention their 'experience', whereas human resource managers refer to the competency tools they developed to define evaluation guides or grids. It is difficult for both parties to agree because they seldom clarify their expectations. Some managers consider that transferring competencies is part of their role. Then, expatriates are willing to meet organizational expectations if their position allows it and if they are requested to do so.

One of the limitations of our study is that it is based on the perception of expatriates who hold important positions in high technology companies. Further research would be necessary to generalize it to other types of companies. Results show that expatriates are generally able to transfer some of the competencies they developed during their period abroad, and that they are more often motivated to transfer them when

Table 10.4 Individual factors facilitating and inhibiting transfer

Facilitating factors	Inhibiting factors
Skills	
Type of knowledge and competencies: conditional (when?), relational (who?), rare, specific Know-how in terms of transfer Expatriate's capacity to promote change, use of network, role models and power	Type of competencies: tacit – linked to experience, obsolete Difficulty for the expatriate to transfer: feeling that experience cannot be transferred Lack of time Attitude upon return: conformity/change
Motivation	
Personal values Expectations from others: recognition and receptivity of colleagues	Lack of initiative from the expatriate
Satisfaction after return	
Satisfaction upon return linked to the new position Wide scope for transfer	Dissatisfaction after return because of lack of organizational support Limited scope for transfer

they feel committed to the organization, either because they are altruistic, or because they consider that transfer is part of their new position. An important limitation to this transfer is the fact that other members of the organization may not be ready to receive the competencies that expatriates could transfer to them. Expatriates mention a gap between the company's official stance – international competencies being a strategic asset, internationalization of practices – and the reality on the ground characterized by a lack of organizational support and a lack of help upon return home, after having received a strong support when they left. They are appalled at the ethnocentric attitudes and xenophobic behaviours of some of their colleagues. There are formalizing processes mainly for technical competences considered as critical by the company.

We have also shown that the level of satisfaction does not directly influence transfer, but that it has an impact on the scope for transfer, which is wider and progressively increases when the expatriate is more satisfied. Organizational support – mainly through adequate organizational processes – is often considered as a missing factor; therefore, improving support significantly when expatriates return home would allow broadening the scope for transfer, and a larger number of employees could benefit from the experience of expatriates.

Black and Gregersen (1999) already pointed out that competencies developed by expatriates were considered as 'strategic assets', but that the return on investment of international mobility was still weak. Berthoin Antal (2000) underlines that when transfer takes place it is mainly on the expatriate's initiative, or by chance in the wake of a specific event. Without any initiative from the company, the transfer seldom takes place, and its scope is limited. The feeling of being strongly supported when they go abroad, and very weakly when they come back, often creates a feeling of dissatisfaction in the employees and a lack of motivation in sharing the competences they have developed. Human resource managers should therefore pay special attention to human resource processes when expatriates return home after international mobility and to the capitalization of competences acquired abroad. This would encourage transfer and help moving towards a learning organization, where the international experience of expatriates benefits the largest number of employees and contributes to individual enrichment as well as corporate development.

If the internationalization of companies was often achieved through international acquisitions and by sending expatriates from headquarters to subsidiaries, the challenge is now to 'learn how to learn' by integrating and using knowledge existing worldwide. Moving from an international company to an MNC mainly entails developing a global learning culture. Intercultural management therefore becomes a norm and one of the important factors of a company's international development (Irrmann, 2008b).

References

Adler, N. (1981) 'Re-Entry: Managing Cross-Cultural Transitions', *Group and Organizational Studies*, 6 (3), 341–56.

Adler, N. (1991) *International Dimensions of Organizational Behaviour*, 2nd edn (Boston, MA: PWS Kent Publishing).

Anderson, J. R. (1983) *The Architecture of Cognition* (Cambridge, MA: Harvard University Press).

APEC (Association Pour l'Emploi des Cadres) (2004) *Mondialisation: quels impacts pour l'emploi cadre?* (Paris: Association Pour l'Emploi des Cadres).

Argote, L., McEvily, B. and Reagans, R. (2003) 'Managing Knowledge in organizations: An Integrative Framework and Review of Emerging Themes', *Management Science*, 49 (4), 571–82.

Berthoin Antal, A. (2000) 'Types of Knowledge Gained by Expatriate Managers', *Journal of General Management*, 26 (2), 32–51.

Berthoin Antal, A. (2001) 'Expatriate's Contribution to Organizational Learning', *Journal of General Management*, 26 (4), 62–84.

Black, J. S. (1988) 'Work Role Transition: A Study of American Expatriate Managers in Japan', *Journal of International Business Studies*, 19 (2), 277–94.

Black, J. S. and Gregersen, H. B. (1999) 'The Right Way to Manage Expats', *Harvard Business Review*, 77 (2), 52–61.

Bonache, J. and Brewster, C. (2001) 'Knowledge Transfer and the Management of Expatriation', *Thunderbird International Business Review*, 43 (1), 145–68.

Bonache, J., Brewster, C. and Suutari, V. (2001) 'Expatriation: A Developing Research Agenda', *Thunderbird International Business Review*, 43 (1), 1–11.

Cohen, M. D. and Bacdayan, P. (1996) 'Organizational Routines are Stored as Procedural Memory: Evidence from a Laboratory Study' in M. D. Cohen and L. S. Sproull (eds) *Organizational Learning* (London: Sage Publications), pp. 403–29.

Downes, M. and Thomas, A. S. (2000) 'Knowledge Transfer through Expatriation: The U-Curve Approach to Overseas Staffing', *Journal of Management Issues*, 12 (2), 131–51.

Dupuis, J. P. (2005) 'Décloisonner les approches classiques' in E. Davel, J.-P. Dupuis and J.-F. Chanlat (eds) *Gestion en contexte interculturel* (Québec: Les Presses de l'Université de Laval), pp. 73–118.

Fink, G., Meierwert, S. and Rohr, U. (2005) 'The Use of Repatriate Knowledge in Organizations', *Human Resources Planning*, 28 (4), 30–6.

Franko, L. G. (1973) 'Who Manages Multinational Enterprises?', *Columbia Journal of World Business*, 8 (2), 30–42.

Irrmann O. (2008a) 'Culture, organisation et stratégie' in E. Davel, J.-P. Dupuis and J.-F. Chanlat (eds), *Gestion en contexte interculturel* (Québec: Les Presses de l'Université de Laval), pp. 165–205.

Irrmann O. (2008b) 'Une approche interactionniste' in E. Davel, J.-P. Dupuis and J.-F. Chanlat (eds), *Gestion en contexte interculturel* (Québec: Les Presses de l'Université de Laval), pp. 119–62.

Lazarova, M. and Tarique, I. (2005) 'Knowledge Transfer upon Repatriation', *Journal of World Business*, 40 (4), 361–73.

Le Pargneux, M. (2009) 'La réussite de la mobilité internationale, perspective individuelle et organisationnelle', unpublished doctoral thesis (Corte: Université de Corse).

Mayrhofer, U. (2005) 'Les rapprochements, forme d'internationalisation privilégiée par les entreprises?', *Gestion – Revue Internationale de Gestion*, 29 (4), 15–22.

Meier, O. and Schier, G. (2005) *Entreprises multinationales: stratégie, restructuration, gouvernance* (Paris: Dunod).

Michel, S. (2003) 'La gestion des actifs spécifiques humains – les hommes clé comme archétype' in J. Allouche (ed.) *Encyclopédie des Ressources Humaines* (Paris: Vuibert), pp. 10–18.

Nonaka, I. and Takeuchi, H. (1995) *The Knowledge-Creating Company: How Japanese Companies Create the Dynamics of Innovation* (Oxford: Oxford University Press).

Paris, S. G., Lipson, M. Y. and Wixson, K. K. (1983) 'Becoming a Strategic Reader', *Contemporary Educational Psychology*, 8, 293–316.

Penmartin, D. (2005) *La compétence au coeur de la GRH* (Cormelles-le-Royal: Editions Management et Société).

Perlmutter, H. (1969) 'The Tortuous Evolution of the Multinational Corporation', *Columbia Journal of World Business*, 4 (1), 9–19.

Pierre, P. (2008) 'Le gestionnaire international' in E. Davel, J.-P. Dupuis and J.-F. Chanlat (eds) *Gestion en contexte interculturel* (Québec: Les Presses de l'Université de Laval) pp. 207–51.

Polanyi, M. (1996) *The Tacit Dimension* (London: Routledge).

Prax, J. Y. (2003) *Le Manuel du Knowledge Management, une approche de deuxième génération* (Paris: Dunod).

Roussillon, S. (1984) *Attentes et projets professionnels des cadres expatriés*, conference proceedings, École Supérieure des Sciences Économiques et Commerciales (Paris: ESSEC).

Sackmann, S. A. (1992) 'Culture and Subcultures: An Analysis of Organizational Knowledge', *Administrative Science Quarterly*, 37 (1), 140–61.

Selmer, J. (2002) 'To Train or Not to Train? European Expatriate Managers in China', *International Journal of Cross Cultural Management*, 2 (1), 37–51.

Stahl, G. K. and Cerdin, J. L. (2004) 'Global Careers in French and German Multinational Corporations', *The Journal of Management Development*, 23 (9), 885–902.

Subramanian, M. and Venkatraman, N. (2001) 'Determinants of Transnational New Product Development Capability: Testing the Influence of Transferring and Deploying Tacit Overseas Knowledge', *Strategic Management Journal*, 22 (4), 359–78.

Sullivan, S. E. (1999) 'The Changing Nature of Careers: A Review and Research Agenda', *Journal of Management*, 25 (3), 457–84.

Tardiff, J. (1992) *Pour un enseignement stratégique* (Montreal: Editions Logiques).

Tung, R. (1998) 'American Expatriates Abroad: From Neophytes to Cosmopolitans', *Journal of World Business*, 33 (2), 125–45.

Wang, P., Tong, T. W. and Koh, C. P. (2004) 'An Integrated Model of Knowledge Transfer from MNC Parent to China Subsidiary', *Journal of World Business*, 39 (2), 168–82.

Yan, A., Zhu, G. and Hall, D. T. (2002) 'International Assignments for Career Building: A Model of Agency Relationships and Psychological Contracts', *Academy of Management Review*, 27 (3), 373–91.

Part III
Management of Multiple Partnerships Formed by Multinational Companies

11
How do MNCs Manage Successful Partnerships?

Emna Moalla and Dora Triki

Economic globalization has led to the establishment of an increasing number of partnerships between companies. The success of partnerships is an important topic of interest in the international business literature. Many multinational companies (MNCs) frequently use cooperative strategies to enter new markets. The reasons for creating partnerships include accessing resources, reducing uncertainty and increasing legitimacy (Forgues et al., 2006). However, cooperative strategies are often considered to be unstable, and their performance variable (Brulhart, 2005).

This chapter examines how the performance of partnerships can be assessed. We will analyse major success factors that have been identified in the specialized literature and present an exploratory study conducted in an MNC which operates in the event management sector and is located in Lyon: GL events.

11.1 Partnerships in MNCs

11.1.1 Characteristics and typology

Studies of inter-firm cooperation are subject to increased attention from researchers and managers (Arino and Ring, 2010), which can be explained by the remarkable growth of this organizational form since the 1980s. Several terms are used in the literature to define these relationships between companies: partnerships, inter-firm collaboration, cooperative agreements, inter-firm linkages. Companies engaged in such agreements choose to preserve their independence and to share part or all of their resources in order to reach a common goal (Mayrhofer, 2001). Agreements are based on a relational contract between companies, thus following an economic as well as a social logic (Forgues et al., 2006).

There are several forms of partnerships:

- a joint venture is a partnership that involves the creation of a new, independent, legal entity by two or several partners;
- a minority equity investment refers to the acquisition of a minority, or cross equity stake in another company;
- contractual partnerships, such as licences, franchises and research and development (R&D) agreements are partnerships formalized by a contract.

Based on research conducted by Angué (2006) and Mayrhofer (2001), the typology, presented in Table 11.1 focuses on two main criteria, equity relationship and legal structure.

International partnerships associate companies from different countries. They can serve many interests. The most obvious one is internationalization and new market entry. In this context, environmental uncertainty and the degree of risk are relatively high. A partnership with a local company can allow the reduction of uncertainty and share the risk by providing the necessary skills to adapt to the local market. In this case, the local partner benefits from a new product that could complement an already existing range of products.

However, the goal of partnerships cannot be restricted to the development of new geographic markets (Blanchot, 2006).

Table 11.1   Typology of inter-firm partnerships

Equity partnerships		Contractual partnerships	
Agreement with the creation of a new legal structure	Joint venture (equal, unequal)	Agreement without creation of a legal structure	Contractual agreements R&D contracts Consortium Licensing Franchising Subcontracting
Agreement without creation of a legal structure	Minority equity investment (cross or unilateral)		Others

Source: Angué (2006); Mayrhofer (2001).

- Companies might develop R&D partnerships, especially in the high technology industry, where they mainly seek new resources and skills to be able to innovate.
- Partnerships can minimize transaction costs; for example, by reducing the negotiation costs of export contracts.
- Companies can benefit from new resources from partner companies, which facilitate the development of new skills.
- Partnerships can improve a company's competitive position, or help gain market share. In this case, companies may look for strategic complementarities with some of their competitors. These complementarities can include resources as well as skills. Therefore, the acquisition and sharing of resources between partners allow the transfer of skills and knowledge, so creating a learning effect.
- The interaction between individuals develops the production of new organizational knowledge. Hence, partnerships enable companies to better understand know-how and to improve learning.

Partnerships entail benefits not only in terms of risk sharing or learning and gaining knowledge, but also as a way of improving the performance of the partners. In this chapter, we will focus more specifically on equity relationships.

11.1.2 Partnership performance

The concept of performance has been extensively studied in the field of international business. It has also been attracting the attention of managers and companies (Bener and Glaister, 2010). However, there is still no consensus on an appropriate definition of this multidimensional concept. As international business activities continue to grow, many organizations establish partnerships with companies from other countries. These collaborations have become an important element of internationalization strategies. They are considered as a strategic tool necessary to compete on domestic and international markets.

Nonetheless, reported failure rates of partnerships appear to be high, ranging from 30 to 70 per cent (Reuer, 2004). Indeed, cooperative strategies are often characterized by instability, low performance and high costs. In international partnerships, MNCs have to deal with a new environment and have to cooperate with companies shaped by different organizational and national cultures (Brulhart, 2005). Measuring performance in this context is a difficult task. Is it preferable to consider the performance of the cooperative structure, or the performance of parent companies? Is performance synonymous with success or failure?

Franko (1971) was the first to examine how parent control could impact the performance of international joint ventures (IJV). Since this seminal work, other researchers have focused on the topic without reaching a consensus. According to Garrette and Dussauge (1995), it is not easy to anticipate the success or the failure of partnerships. The termination of an alliance is not synonymous with failure. In some cases, partners may have achieved their objectives and do not seek to extend their collaboration. *A contrario*, an alliance may survive, not because of its performance, but because the partners do not know how to separate; in such a case, maintaining the partnership seems to be the less risky option. Indeed, if for some reason the partnership stops prematurely, for example, before launching a joint product, it means that the partnership has failed. There is still no consensus on appropriate performance criteria.

According to the international business literature (see Table 11.2), performance can be assessed by both objective and subjective measures (Child et al., 2005). Objective measures include longevity, survival, stability and quantitative indicators. Studies using quantitative measures rely on various criteria such as financial ratios; for example, return on investment (ROI), return on sales (ROS), stock market reaction and growth of sales. However, these measures have several limitations. They are not always appropriate for reflecting long-term objectives of alliances; they only explain past performance and are considered as an 'autopsy' by Boualem and Taghzouti (2009). Finally, survival and longevity are the most widely used criteria in the literature. Some authors argue that a relationship is maintained because partners expect the potential of value-creation to be higher than in other development modes (Boualem and Taghzouti, 2009).

Subjective measures refer to the assessment of performance by opinions expressed by managers of the partner companies, or by managers

Table 11.2 Performance measurement in partnerships

Type of measure	Performance criteria
Objective	Longevity
	Survival
	Stability
	Quantitative indicators (profitability, sales, and so on)
Subjective	Partner satisfaction
	Knowledge transfer
	Goal achievement

of the cooperative relationship. They concern the global satisfaction of partners, learning processes and the achievement of objectives. Satisfaction is considered as a perceptual measurement, differing according to respondents and to strategic intentions of partner companies. Learning has been considered as an important issue of partnerships. Child et al. (2005) argue that 'strategic alliances, including joint ventures, are basically all about organizational learning and should be structured towards this end' (p. 6). From a knowledge-based perspective, learning refers to the capacity to integrate external knowledge and to transform it into routines (Jaouen, 2006). The establishment of a partnership can be justified by the company's ability to identify useful resources or competences possessed by potential partners. Alliances are relationships where partners contribute different resources and enhance learning opportunities. However, in a 'Trojan horse' joint venture, companies attempt to learn quickly in order to rapidly integrate certain competences held by the partner before dissolving the joint venture. The achievement of common goals is considered as a relevant performance criteria. Nevertheless, the goals of alliance partners may evolve over time.

A study by Chandler and Hanks (1993) shows a strong correlation between subjective and objective performance measures. However, we have highlighted that each of these measures has strengths and weaknesses. Meschi (2009) recommends the application of both objective and subjective measures to ensure maximum consistency.

11.2   Success factors of partnerships

Despite the abundant literature about partnerships, researchers seem to agree on the identification of two categories of factors influencing the success of partnerships (see Table 11.3): internal factors and external factors (Robson et al., 2002).

11.2.1   Internal factors

Internal factors can influence the performance and the stability of a cooperative relationship. These factors are related to partner companies, the operation and the specificities of the partnership.

11.2.1.1   Factors related to partners

Among the internal factors influencing performance and stability are those related to the partner companies involved.

- Experience: previous studies have analysed the impact of experience on performance. These studies expect partners to develop specific know-how in the management of alliances. Delios and Beamish (2004) find that experience is significantly related to survival. Specialists make a distinction between cooperation experience with partner companies (Brulhart, 2005) and international experience linked to host countries (Luo, 2007). Results of the impact of experience on performance remain inconclusive.
- Partner asymmetries: asymmetric partners are companies with a different strategic position concerning the control of resources, financial capacities, and so on. In an international context, partnerships evolve in differing economic environments (Assens and Cherbib, 2010). Academics define partner asymmetry in terms of size, bargaining power, ownership structure, differences in national and organizational cultures, and so on. This asymmetry may cause disagreement between partners. Some empirical studies show that asymmetry can help stabilize the relationship, while others consider that it leads to an anticipated termination of the cooperation (Cheriet, 2009).
- Number of partners: studies on alliance performance indicate that the number of partners appears to be a key factor. It is recognized that multi-party partnerships are efficient because transaction costs and the probability of opportunism are reduced in such contexts. Nevertheless, Gong et al. (2007) demonstrate that these partnerships are difficult to manage. In fact, a large number of partner companies means more resources to be pooled, thus increasing both coordination difficulties and potential conflicts.
- Direct competition: according to Garrette and Dussauge (1995), alliances among competing companies are considered as a paradox because, instead of competing, these companies are engaged in partnerships. When partners are competitors, they will attempt to integrate the competencies of partners, while they may pursue different goals, so leading to disagreements. However, relationships between competing partners are not necessarily doomed to fail. In the case of complementary alliances, the collaboration may be successful.
- Goal compatibility and strategic fit: these factors refer to the extent to which partners have similar objectives. In this regard, goal compatibility reduces uncertainty, opportunistic behaviour and consequently enhances the success of partnerships.
- Path homology of managers: according to Blanchot (2006), this is an antecedent of trust. Successful relationships can be built when alliance managers share the same ambitions.

11.2.1.2   Factors related to the operation of the partnership

Other internal factors influencing performance and stability are those related to the operation of the partnership.

- Commitment: several authors demonstrate that commitment reduces the likelihood of opportunistic behaviour of partner companies. Many studies focus on the effect of commitment on alliance performance (Brouthers and Nakos, 2004). A lack of commitment from partner companies may have a negative effect on the cooperative relationship. It is necessary for partners to have the same interest in terms of value creation in order to guarantee an efficient partnership.
- Trust: Barmeyer et al. (2009) highlight that trust plays a crucial role in cooperative relationships. It contributes to a better understanding of interactions between the partners and to explain their performance. If the relationship is based on trust, there will be a higher level of communication. However, trust remains a sensitive issue because partnerships are formed between independent companies that can also be competitors. Indeed, there is a high risk of opportunism, and partners may less likely commit their resources.
- Differences in corporate culture: this factor refers to corporate culture (e.g., management practices) shared between partners. When companies differ in their business practices, conflicting behaviours and misunderstandings may occur, possibly inducing high costs. Blanchot (2006) emphasizes the importance of investing time and energy in the development of routines to facilitate interaction; however, this may hinder the achievement of the objectives defined by the partners.

11.2.1.3   Factors related to specificities of partnerships

Another category of factors influencing performance and stability is that related to the specificities of the partnership.

- Diversification: some studies demonstrate that partnerships are better strategies than acquisitions. Bleeke and Ernst (1992) found that, for diversification strategies, cooperation is more successful than any other form of strategic development.
- Ownership structure: this factor is considered as a significant determinant of performance. Several studies point out the necessity to thoroughly examine the relationship between control and performance, especially for equity partnerships; for example, international joint ventures. According to Mjoen and Tallman (1997), 'equity

positions often determine the composition of the board of directors, and the board usually appoints high level executives; the partner with a dominant equity position has the ability to exercise more control' (p. 259). Some studies show that joint ventures where foreign partners hold a majority ownership tend to achieve low performance (Beamish, 1984), while others demonstrate that shared control makes international joint ventures more stable (Blodgett, 1992).

- Governance structure: this factor is related to control mechanisms. Partner companies should focus their control on joint activities perceived as critical and strategically important such as marketing, R&D, production, and so on. In order to control these activities, partners usually set up formal standard procedures and reporting (Nguyen, 2009). The establishment of formal control is considered as a first step towards enhancing trust.

11.2.2   External factors

External factors that can influence the performance and the stability of a cooperative relationship mainly concern the environment of the host country and industry characteristics.

11.2.2.1   *Factors related to the host country environment*

Various aspects of the environment of the host country can have an important effect on a partnership's performance.

- Culture distance: this refers to differences in values and standards between two countries. Empirical studies emphasize the effect of partner similarities on international cooperation. Cultural differences can lead to communication problems, causing managerial conflicts, due to misunderstandings. Indeed, working in an international context may increase opportunistic behaviour which can negatively impact the reputation of the partners. Nevertheless, some researchers suggest that differences in national cultures may be beneficial. For example, it might be a source of innovation.
- Country risk: several studies show that the stability of partnerships is correlated to country-level variables, particularly in the context of developing countries. In this regard, Yan (1998) notes that 'for international joint ventures formed in developing or transition economies, the turbulent political and economic environment, together with intercultural and inter-organizational dynamics make the management of cooperative relationships particularly challenging' (p. 773) According to Meschi and Riccio (2008), country risk may be viewed

as a determinant of the termination of an international joint venture. By contrast, Barkema and Vermeulen (1997) observe that this variable has no impact on the stability of alliances. Empirical studies dealing with the relationship between country risk and performance thus lead to inconclusive results.

- Host country regulations: governments put into place regulations, usually in order to attract foreign direct investments (FDI). Political and economic certainty within a host country also influence the performance of partnerships.

11.2.2.2 *Factors related to industry characteristics*

The dynamics of the industry may be a condition of success for the involved partnerships. The factors that have an influence on a partnership's performance and stability are growth, profitability and structure.

- Growth: the industry life cycle (nascent, growing, mature and declining) is strategic information that enables partners to predict the evolution of the sector, and thus ensure its growth and profitability.
- Profitability: the profitability of an industry can influence the performance of an alliance.

Table 11.3 Major success factors of partnerships

	Success factors	Indicators
Internal factors	Factors related to partners	Experience
		Partner asymmetry
		Number of partners
		Direct competition
		Goal compatibility and strategic fit
		Path homology of managers
	Factors related to the operation	Commitment
		Trust
		Differences in corporate culture
	Factors related to specificities of partnerships	Diversification
		Ownership structure
		Governance structure
External factors	Host country environment	Cultural distance
		Country risk
		Host country regulations
	Industry characteristics	Industry growth
		Industry profitability
		Industry structure

- Structure: this may vary from country to country, shaped by industrial concentration, consumer behaviour, market demand or the existence of market entry barriers.

Initial conditions of an alliance refer to the specific characteristics and objectives of partner companies, and several authors add this variable to the factors mentioned in Table 11.3 (Blanchot, 2006).

Several empirical studies confirm that partnerships are more stable and therefore more efficient than wholly owned subsidiaries, particularly in the context of developing countries. Conversely, other researchers show that subsidiaries allow the achievement of higher performance (Yiu and Makino, 2002).

11.3   Successful partnerships of MNCs: the case of GL events

Our empirical study was based on an MNC specializing in event solutions and services, GL events. The company chose to grow mainly through partnerships. In order to identify the success factors of partnerships formed by this company, we analysed both primary data (interviews with the Director of International Development and an international project manager of the group) and secondary data (annual reports, internal documents and press reviews).

11.3.1   Presentation of GL events

GL events is a French company established in 1989 as a result of the merger between Polygone Group (number one in France for exhibitions and event facilities) and Cré-Rossi (rental of trade fair furniture, accessories and surfaces). The group operates in three market segments: trade fairs and exhibitions for professionals and the general public; congresses, conventions, seminars and incentive events; and corporate, institutional, cultural and sports events (see Box 11.1).

Box 11.1   Key figures of GL events (2010)

- Total sales: 727.2 million Euros
- Net income: 26.4 million Euros
- 35 convention centres, exhibition halls, concert halls and reception areas
- 91 offices in France and worldwide
- 3435 employees

Initially, GL events chose to grow in the French market through acquisitions. Indeed, between 1990 and 1997, the group acquired companies in the event organization sector in order to strengthen its global solution strategy. Since 1998, the year of its initial listing on the Second Market of the Paris Stock Exchange, GL events has conducted a strategy of international growth based mainly on partnerships.

> There were several opportunistic attempts in the 1980s in Spain, Morocco, and Germany. However, it was not an organized and structured growth strategy ... The international department has really been operational in a structured way from the year 1998. We have been able to actually develop international activities from 1998.
> (GL events Director of International Development, interview 2010)

This international expansion strategy is based mainly on the opportunities offered by host countries. The attractiveness of destinations is measured by the degree of importance of the events that are organized. For instance, in the case of Brazil, GL events secured a contract to organize the Pan-American Games in 2007 and signed a 50-year management concession for the Curitiba Convention Centre. Both opportunities justified the group's establishment in Brazil and enabled it to enjoy a strong position there. The company has benefited from these excellent conditions, having signed a contract to organize the World Cup in 2014 and the Olympic Games in Rio de Janeiro in 2016.

To develop activities on foreign markets, GL events has established privileged partnerships, mainly joint ventures. This organizational form offers several advantages: market access, risk reduction and sharing, skill combination, access to resources, economies of scale among others. The local partners of GL events provide both market knowledge and the resources to organize events. For example, in 2010, the group signed a contract to organize the Commonwealth Games in India. It established a joint venture with a local company named Litmus. GL events plans to pursue its international partnership strategy and to strengthen its position in order to organize other events like those in Brazil.

11.3.2 Success factors of partnerships formed by GL events

Performance factors of partnerships can be related to partner companies, to the operation of the partnerships and to specificities of partnerships, but also to the environment and the industry. In the case of GL events, the Director of International Development highlights the importance of the integration of new entities into the group. Indeed, integration in this case is polysemous because it combines several performance factors.

> What matters is the quality of the entity's integration in the group because, eventually, that will determine – after the first or the second year, which are always euphoric – whether the entity is going to operate as a subsidiary or as a classical partner.
> (GL events Director of International Development, interview 2010)

For its establishment in new markets, a company can experience difficulties in understanding certain cultural characteristics of the host country and the managerial practices of local partners. Because of the difficulty of controlling these factors, GL events decided to associate with local partners to reach its goal. The Director of International Development of the company gives the example of India stating various local constraints the company has to cope with.

> Do we know how to understand local constraints? Will we know how to adapt to these key local contacts?'
> (GL events International Project Manager, interview 2010)

The success of partnerships also depends on factors related to the industry. Indeed, the stage in the industry life cycle differs from one market to another. For example, GL events organized the Olympic Games in Sydney in 2000. At the end of the project, the French personnel from GL events had to return home because the events industry in Australia was already mature and had limited development prospects. By contrast, GL events is optimistic about the profitability of the sector in Brazil and in India. The company estimates that the industry is growing in Brazil and is nascent in India.

> If I take the example of Sydney, we went home after the Olympic Games. Why? Because ... the industry was already very mature without attractive prices – they were rather low – and actors had already determined roles; so there was not a lot of potential for growth.
> (GL events Director of International Development, interview 2010)

To succeed cooperative relationships it is important that partner companies agree on objectives and follow the same strategic direction. This success factor is highly dependent on stakeholders and the compatibility of their goals. GL events underlines the importance of the adaptation of the partner and its understanding of the expectations of the group and vice versa.

GL events has a particular ownership structure regarding joint ventures. Indeed, the company chooses to hold majority ownership. To organize the World Cup in 2010 in South Africa, GL events created a joint venture with a local company, Oasys Innovation, in which it held a majority equity stake.

Moreover, successful partnerships are based on trust. Trust remains an important factor in order to develop close relationships and to improve communication.

> Trust is fundamental. You will not be able to audit or control every five minutes! Physically, it is impossible, even if you have local people.
> (GL events International Project Manager, interview 2010)

The characteristics and the degree of understanding between the managers of partnerships are also factors that can enhance communication. Figure 11.1 indicates the key success factors of partnerships established by GL events.

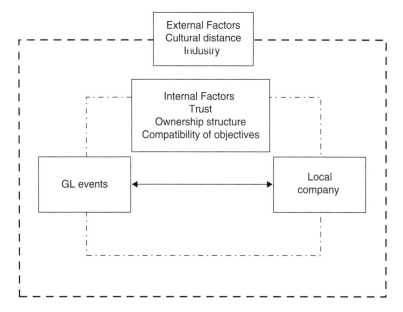

Figure 11.1   Success factors of partnerships at GL events

Our study has identified the characteristics of partnerships in the service industry. It shows that the achievement of objectives is one of the most important criteria for assessing the performance of partnerships. In fact, in the events sector, companies are required to achieve their goals towards event organizers, such as FIFA (Fédération Internationale de Football Association) for the World Cup. Moreover, the budget may be an important factor in this industry and can be considered as a financial performance criteria.

The case of GL events also shows that, in a new and uncertain environment, trust is a fundamental factor for the performance of partnerships. In fact, the company does not control the local environment and must develop trust in order to ensure the stability and success of partnerships. Other factors relating to the external environment are also important such as national culture, industry growth and profitability.

11.4   Conclusion

The proliferation of partnerships has resulted in the interest taken in this topic by both researchers and managers. However, the success of partnerships is not always obvious: it is a challenge that partners have to take up every day. The challenge is even more difficult to face if the relationship involves partners of different nationalities. Then, several factors determine the success of partnerships.

In this chapter, we have focused on performance measurement criteria and success factors. An analysis of research conducted in this field enabled us to construct a grid comprising major performance indicators. These indicators are probably not exhaustive, but they seem to be the most commonly used factors in empirical studies. We built mainly on Blanchot's research (2006) and we chose to adopt a global approach by integrating different types of factors, in order to explain the performance of partnerships. The analysis of international partnerships formed by GL events emphasizes that the performance of alliance strategies can be explained by both internal and external factors.

References

Angué, K. (2006) 'Les partenaires de coopération en recherche et développement dans les sciences du vivant', unpublished doctoral dissertation (Nice: Université de Nice Sophia-Antipolis).

Arino, A. and Ring, P. S. (2010) 'The Role of Fairness in Alliance Formation', *Strategic Management Journal*, 31 (10), 1054–87.

Assens, C. and Cherbib, J. (2010) 'L'Alliance asymétrique: une stratégie durable?', *La Revue des Sciences de Gestion, Direction et Gestion*, 243–44, 111–20.

Barkema, H. and Vermuelen, F. (1997) 'What Differences in the Cross Cultural Backgrounds of Partners are Detrimental for International Joint Ventures?', *Journal of International Business Studies*, 28 (4), 845–64.

Barmeyer, C., Mayrhofer, U. and Mothe, C. (2009) 'Le rôle de la confiance dans le management des rapprochements franco-allemands' in M. Kalika (ed.) *Les hommes et le management: des réponses à la crise. Mélanges en l'honneur de Sabine Urban* (Paris: Economica), pp. 281–97.

Beamish, P. W. (1984) 'Joint Venture Performance in Developing Countries', unpublished doctoral dissertation (London, Ontario: University of Western Ontario).

Bener, M. and Glaister, K. W. (2010) 'Determinants of Performance in International Joint Ventures', *Journal of Strategy and Management*, 3 (3), 188–214.

Blanchot, F. (2006) 'Alliances et performances: un essai de synthèse', working paper CREPA-DRM (Centre de Recherche en Management et Organisation – Dauphine Recherches en Management), 2006.1.

Bleeke, J. and Ernst, D. (1992) 'Réussir une Alliance Transfrontalière', *Harvard-L'Expansion*, 65, 66–77.

Blodgett, L. L. (1992) 'Factors in the Instability of International Joint Ventures: An Event History Analysis', *Strategic Management Journal*, 13 (3), 475–81.

Boualem, A. and Taghzouti, A. (2009) *Vers un pilotage des alliances stratégiques par des méthodes perceptives de la valeur: l'influence de la 'performance perçue' sur la propension des managers à nouer et maintenir des alliances*, Conference of the Association Internationale de Management Stratégique (AIMS), Grenoble, 3–5 June.

Brouthers, K. D. and Nakos, G. (2004) 'SME Entry Mode Choice and Performance: A Transaction Cost Perspective', *Entrepreneurship Theory and Practice* (28) 3, 229–47.

Brulhart, F. (2005) 'Expérience du partenariat, expérience du partenaire, connivence interpersonnelle: quel impact sur la réussite du partenariat vertical?', *M@n@gement*, 8 (4), 167–91.

Chandler, G. N. and Hanks, S. H. (1993) 'Measuring the Performance of Emerging Businesses: A Validation Study', *Journal of Business Venturing*, 8 (5), 391–408.

Cheriet, F. (2009) 'L'instabilité des alliances stratégiques asymétriques: cas des relations entre les firmes multinationales et les entreprises locales agroalimentaires en Méditerranée', unpublished doctoral thesis (Montpellier: Université Montpellier 1).

Child, J., Faulkner, D. and Tallman, P. B. (2005) *Cooperative Strategy: Managing Alliances Networks and Joint Ventures* (Oxford: Oxford University Press).

Delios, A. and Beamish, P.W. (2004) 'Joint Venture Performance Revisited: Japanese Foreign Subsidiaries Worldwide', *Management International Review*, 44 (1), 69–91.

Forgues, B., Frechet, M. and Josserand, E. (2006) 'Relations interorganisationnelles. Conceptualisation, résultats et voies de recherche', *Revue Française de Gestion*, 5 (164), 17–33.

Franko, L. G. (1971) 'Joint Venture Divorce in the Multinational Company', *Columbia Journal of World Business*, 6 (3), 13–22.

Garrette, B. and Dussauge, P. (1995) *Les stratégies d'alliance* (Paris: Les Editions d'Organisation).

Gong, Y., Shenkar, O., Luo, Y. and Nyaw, M.-K. (2007) 'Do Multiple Parents Help or Hinder International Joint Venture Performance? The Mediating Roles of Contract Completeness and Partner Cooperation', *Strategic Management Journal*, 28 (10), 1021–34.

Jaouen, A. (2006) 'La question centrale des ressources dans les alliances straté-giques', *Revue de l'Economie Méridionale*, 214, 107–24.

Luo, Y. (2007) 'The Independent and Interactive Roles of Procedural, Distributive, and Interactional Justice in Strategic Alliances', *Academy of Management Journal*, 50 (3), 644–64.

Mayrhofer, U. (2001) *Les rapprochements d'entreprises, une nouvelle logique straté-gique? Une analyse des entreprises françaises et allemandes* (Berne: Peter Lang).

Meschi, P.-X. (2009) 'Les alliances entre grandes entreprises: le cas des joint ventures' in O. Meier (ed.) *Stratégies de croissance. Fusions-acquisitions, alliances stratégiques, développement interne* (Paris: Dunod) pp. 109–25.

Meschi, P.-X. and Riccio, E. (2008) 'Country Risk, National Cultural Differences between Partners and Survival of International Joint Ventures in Brazil', *International Business Review*, 17 (3), 250–66.

Mjoen, H. and Tallman, S. (1997) 'Control and Performance of International Joint Ventures', *Organization Science*, 8 (3), 257–74.

Nguyen, H. L. (2009) 'Foreign Parent Control and International Joint Venture Performance: Evidence of Finnish Multinational Firms', unpublished doctoral dissertation (Vaasa: University of Vaasa).

Reuer, J. J. (2004) 'Introduction-Strategic Alliance Research: Progress and Prospects' in J. J. Reuer (ed.) *Strategic Alliances: Theory and Evidence* (Oxford: Oxford University Press), pp. 1–16.

Robson, M. J., Leonidou, L. C. and Katsikeas, C. S. (2002) 'Factors Influencing Joint Venture Performance: Theoretical Perspectives, Assessment, and Future Directions', *Management International Review*, 42 (4), 385–418.

Yan, A. (1998) 'Structural Stability and Reconfiguration of International Joint Ventures', *Journal of International Business Studies*, 29 (4), 773–95.

Yiu, D. and Makino, S. (2002) 'The Choice between Joint Venture and Wholly Owned Subsidiary: An Institutional Perspective', *Organization Science*, 13 (6), 667–83.

12
Managing Alliances of MNCs: Does National Culture Matter?

Yves-Frédéric Livian

The management of multinational companies (MNCs) raises the question about the conflict between the standardization of methods and persistent local specificities. Some authors analyse the development of MNCs by highlighting their similarities in a context of generalized globalization and widespread financial capitalism. Others insist on the necessity for MNCs to cope with different individuals, methods and values, which sometimes resist convergence.

One part of the debate consists of dealing with the question of cultures, and more specifically of national cultures. Do they contrast, sometimes in a hidden way, with the control and coordination efforts made by management boards? Are MNCs not the proper site of differences and multicultural conflicts? Are organizational cultures powerful enough to obliterate national differences (Barmeyer and Davoine, 2006)?

12.1 The debate on the impact of national culture

No book on this question fails to mention the culturalist issue, generally starting by paying tribute to Hofstede's survey (1982; Hofstede et al., 2010). According to some authors, the more globalization develops, the more local characteristics continue to differ (D'Iribarne, 1998, 2008).

However, the way the question is addressed is not satisfactory. It is not worth reopening the debate between 'culturalists' and 'institutionalists' which took place in France in the years 1992–3 (Chevrier, 2003). But do corporate strategies, major restructuring decisions and organization modes really take into account cultural differences? While such differences cannot be denied, do they really play such a critical role in decisions taken by MNCs?

Some authors have tried to demonstrate the influence of national values on strategic decisions (Carr and Harris, 2004) but these studies are rare. It seems that culturalists analyse the impact of national cultures on social interactions (communication, time management, type of leadership, and so on) and, at the top level, the globalized economic game developed in parallel. The culturalist literature, when it deals with MNCs, rarely deals with executive decisions, which are difficult to analyse from an anthropological point of view. It is as if the intercultural analysis was achieved outside the economic and financial environment.

The ongoing debate between homogeneity and differences can be ended if we consider that the two movements are equally present in MNCs, but at different levels. The anthropological view can provide a rich analysis, but it is not sufficient to understand the strategies and organizational decisions of companies. The debate between homogeneity and differences suffers from a decoupling of both aspects.

Cultural differences and adjustments take place at a local level and 'humanistic' solutions suggested by the intercultural management literature concern this level: foreign language learning, inter-comprehension development, open-mindedness, and so on. These recommendations may seem rather naïve in the context of strategic decisions made in globalized capitalism where financial criteria are dominant.

Concepts taken from contemporary French pragmatist sociology provide some interesting insights. One essential idea from this theoretical framework seems particularly relevant: the logics of plurality of action. To move on from the holistic–individualistic debate, French sociologists insist, in diverse ways, on the plurality of actors and of their actions; and they lead us to study the plurality of action in MNCs at both the global and at the local level. Dubet (1994) puts the emphasis on the actor who must manage different logics. De Singly (1993) shows a multi-dimensional individual in search of a mix of identities. More specifically, the 'pragmatist sociology' programme initiated by Boltanski and Chiappello (1999) emphasizes the permanent adaptation to situations (Nachi, 2006). Thévenot (2006) entitles his book *Plural Action* and analyses the plural ways adopted by individuals that engage in practical situations. One can consider that individuals and groups do not have to choose between accepting imposed homogeneous management methods and maintaining local specificities. They can either combine both, or choose successively one or another, depending on the situation.

This analysis gets rid of adverse theories which either stress the inevitable domination of the homogenization of international management

Table 12.1 The seven worlds

Worlds	Common principle	What is appreciated	What is depreciated	Test
Inspiration	inspiration	newness, originality, passion	routine, conformism	flash of genius
Domestic	hierarchy, tradition, personal relationships	honour, family, personal circles	no respect for habits, customs	ceremony, rite
Opinion	opinion of others	reputation, recognition	being unknown	communication
Civic	collective	official, formal	illegality, individualism	law, rule, public action
Market	competition	value, interest, price	loss, decline	business, contract
Industrial	efficiency, performance	performing, functional	inefficient	plan, programme
Connectionist	network, links	rapidity, flexibility	stability, closure	beginning and end of project

Source: Adapted from Boltanski and Chiappello (1999); Thévenot (2006).

models (an opinion often found among economists), or the generalization of irredentism, homogeneity being only apparent and resistance to these models systematic (an opinion that anthropologists like to share).

Today, the question of justified agreement is central. Conflicts and debates are continuously present, and parties must justify their positions. What principles are these justifications based on? Boltanski and Chiappello (1999) and Thévenot (2006) have developed a global analysis of different values which actors can rely on (Amblard et al., 2005; Livian, 2010). Situations must be understood according to the representations and justifications provided by the actors themselves. These justifications belong to different 'worlds' which guide the actions of actors. These worlds are made up of individuals, values and objects, having some consistency and providing a framework in which conflicts will be dealt with and compromise will be found. Boltanski and Chiappello (1999) and Thévenot (2006) list seven 'common worlds' (see Table 12.1):

1. the inspiration world (innovation),
2. the domestic world (personal relations),

3. the opinion world (reputation),
4. the civic world (collective, general interest),
5. the market world (price),
6. the industrial world (performance, efficiency),
7. the connectionist world (network).

For each one, a 'test' represents the 'moment of truth' which determines the world in which the actors actually are. For example, launching a new product refers to the market world; an election refers to the civic world; media recognition refers to the opinion world, and so on.

On the one hand, companies, like other organizations, combine several worlds, and different justifications are put forward for this; for example, the advertiser operates in the inspiration world, the union shop steward may be in the civic world, the salesman in the market world, and so on. But ultimately, compromises are found in order to move beyond criticisms that each world may make to another. These compromises are not determined in advance and depend on the situation.

On the other hand, the same person may successively apply different principles, for example, by getting involved in a commercial transaction, then by enhancing a personal relation based on trust, and then by making a cold hard calculation, and so on. Such an absence of global determination, underlined by the pragmatist movement, seems well adapted to the study of behaviours in an international environment: everyone can put forward several principles (tradition, innovation, economic choice, and so on) and yet may feel they belong to several groups (family, company, profession, country, and so on). Therefore, it is crucial to know, in some key situations, what principle(s) have been used and what balance may have been struck between different justifications (or which one has managed to prevail over the others).

Table 12.2   Presentation of the four companies (2009)

Company	Sector	Total sales (in billion Euros)	Staff	Number of countries covered	Law
Alcatel-Lucent	communication, telephone	15.2	77,000	130	French
EADS	aircrafts, helicopters	42.8	119,500	46	Dutch
Renault Nissan	automotive	33.7	121,400	118	French
Danone	dairy products, water, etc.	14.9	80,900	100	French

In this chapter (see Table 12.2), four MNCs will be analysed by using these concepts in order to find out what justifications have been put forward, and on what principles agreements have been set up in relation to the different possible worlds.

12.2 Four cases of international cooperation

12.2.1 Alcatel-Lucent: A Franco-American Group, but above all a giant in crisis

Alcatel-Lucent is a Franco-American group operating in 130 countries. It was established following a merger of two very old groups, which have roots in the industrial history of both countries: on the American side, Western Electric, established in 1869, and American Bell Telephone, in 1880; on the French side, Compagnie Générale d'Electricité (CGE), established in 1898. The analysis of professional and national cultures may be illuminating, but the configuration of both partners is the result of a series of sales and buyouts; and the events which took place since its establishment in 2006 highlight the rigorous financial logic which dominated the industry's complete technological restructuring (telecommunication equipment).

The general common principles were clear from the beginning: industrial and research and development (R&D) synergy, based on the convergence of the Internet, fixed and mobile phones, and commercial complementariness (Alcatel was not very present in North America). The industrial world and the market world references were both important. The civic world reference was also present at the beginning, because some national balance was struck in the first executive chart as five divisional managers came from Alcatel, four from Lucent, the Chief Executive Officer (CEO) was American and the chairman was French.

But the results of financial tests were soon obvious: significant losses and disappointing synergy; shares lost 50 per cent of their value on the stock exchange. The bi-national executive committee was cumbersome and inefficient and restructuring plans followed one another: in 2006, company executives announced 4000 redundancies over two years. The market test led to a new executive committee made up of seven people (five former Alcatel and two former Lucent members), the number of divisions was reduced, the financial director was dismissed.

International training programmes were launched in order to improve communication. Fluent English was required. But the point was, what other strategic choice could be made in such a fast moving sector? Of course, the two founding companies had different images, which ran contrary to national stereotypes: Lucent was seen as being rigid, and Alcatel was considered to be more decentralized and innovative. The marketing division was more important on the French side. Had the 'arrogant' engineering culture, so often criticized in French companies, switched to the American side?

In fact, that was not the point: shareholders were disappointed by the results and two executives had been fired (with a comfortable severance package) and replaced by a bi-national couple. The new president was Philippe Camus, former co-president of European Aeronautic Defence and Space Company (EADS) (see section 12.2.2) and former senior director of an American business bank.

The justifications essentially concerned the market world. The financial strategy was maintained: cost reduction by selling the computer division to Hewlett Packard, sale of the electric engines division, and so on. The industrial world test consisted of a new offer with technological innovation; for example, in September 2009, an offer was made in a more relaxed atmosphere since the company had become profitable again in the second term of 2009.

The objective of the group was to become a profitable MNC, adapted to its market and in line with international standards. There is no doubt that the political cultures in France and the US are different (D'Iribarne 2008) and that day-to-day working methods are not the same. Language and communication modes may also create obstacles. But what impact did these differences have on the development of the group? It is doubtful that they played a major role. Isomorphic pressures – to use the institutionalist sociology vocabulary (Powell and Di Maggio, 1991) – were very strong: governance standards, pressures from financial markets, mimetism of technological strategies, and so on.

The market world and the industrial world were dominant and performance criteria belonged to a well-known and accepted register: profitability, growth, debt reduction, and so on. Inside these worlds, decision justifications were clear and respected; there was no real dispute (e.g., cultural) over these criteria. There may have been tensions and differences of opinion, but these were within a legitimately recognized framework.

12.2.2   EADS: A European group experiencing a conflict of power

EADS, born in 2000 and baptized by France, Germany and Spain, brought together aeronautics and defence activities, thanks to Aerospatiale-Matra, Construcciones Aeronáuticas Sociedad Anónima (CASA) and Deutsche Aerospace AG (DASA) (AG meaning *Aktiengesellschaft* or limited company). It was necessary to find a balanced distribution of executive jobs among the three countries and to locate the headquarters in a neutral place (Amsterdam) (Barmeyer and Mayrhofer, 2004). But the industrial project was clear: to meet the demand of the world market, using the synergy between the composing units. The first two CEOs, Thomas Enders and Noël Forgeard, initially could not get along, and their age and training were different, but tensions subsided after a while.

The civic world was important: there were general rules, national laws and state authority, in particular on the French side. But if controversies had remained at this level, compromises would have been very difficult to find. The test which decided the organization's fate was the delay of the A380 project, in 2005. This industrial failure had an immediate impact on the company's value, since its share value collapsed on the stock exchange in 2006. This test was all the more crucial in that the A380 project was the flagship product of the new unified organization. A transnational organization was set up, with 6500 engineers from different nationalities working in several sites.

The production of such an aircraft, distributed across 16 sites, with different computer systems and running parallel to other projects (the A400M in particular) proved to be a headache, and an international consultant was called in to assist. National culture aspects were significant: everybody had to work in English, and their methods had to be coordinated. One study highlights the different perceptions of employees across the three countries (Meier, 2006) but the results were very conventional, close to stereotypes: the French were seen as giving priority to hierarchy, the Germans had a more collective approach, the British were pragmatic and emphasized short-term results, and so on. However, a high percentage of employees demonstrated their willingness to stress similarities rather than differences.

The most striking event belonged to the market world: 17 EADS executives suddenly sold their shares before the share price dropped, raising suspicion of insider dealing. This infringement on morality took place when EADS put forward its ethical code, which was formalized in an international agreement. In 2004, EADS published a social responsibility policy, with 'transparency and reliability' being the watchwords, according to Thomas Müller, the prestigious chief financial officer of the space division. Public opinion was important for a company like EADS, but not essential.

A large MNC such as EADS may attempt to use civic justifications (social responsibility, the slogan 'many cultures, one dream', support of civic initiatives, and so on), but these justifications are not vital. Factories, products, technologies, financial flows are essential items and the crucial test lies in the commercial launching of an aircraft in accordance with signed agreements. The market world brought together different nationalities in a commercial project where differences would level out. Power was at stake, as shown by the conflicts inside the top executive group (too rapidly described as 'Franco-German' competition), but this is often the case of MNCs facing a crisis (Barmeyer and Mayrhofer, 2007).

12.2.3   Renault-Nissan: a Franco-Japanese company?
Rather the triumph of industrial rationale

The case of the Renault-Nissan alliance is emblematic of a wrong analysis of MNCs based on cultural conflicts. When this alliance was formed, the economic press did not believe in it. Following a purely culturalist analysis, newspapers drew up a list of obstacles: how could a long state-owned French company win over a private Japanese company? Cultural distance appeared to be too important. However, when Renault formed this alliance, the objective was clear: to put new life into Nissan, a 'sleeping' car manufacturer. Carlos Ghosn, CEO of Nissan, arrived in Tokyo in 1999, with a trusted team of French managers. Many intercultural consultants, specializing in Japanese management, rushed to make offers for consulting to Renault, but Carlos Ghosn rejected them. Also settling down in Tokyo did not generate a lot of enthusiasm among spouses, and the French group rapidly found out that very few people spoke English in Japan. Intercultural surprises were legion.

But the higher common principles were clearly those of the market and industrial worlds: it was necessary to improve profitability and to boost the industry. The universe in which everybody would work was the automotive industry. According to Dominique Thormann, vice-president of Renault-Nissan, 'Ghosn does not believe in culture clashes; he wanted to see Nissan only as a car manufacturer and work on that basis' (in Magee, 2003, p. 70).

If we continue to use the worlds analysis, we can say that the market and industrial worlds struggled for priority. The executive team launched the Nissan Revival Plan in October 1999, which aimed at drastically cutting expenses and regaining growth (purchase concentration, rationalization, general cost reduction, sales network revitalization).

Diversity was organized within the industrial world: cross-functional teams were set up in order to provide innovations (this concept had been developed by Michelin in North America under the leadership of Ghosn six years earlier). In the industrial world, the new top management team had many assets, including years of industrial experience and former foreign responsibilities. On the Nissan side, the technical competence was obvious. A dialogue was rapidly initiated, even if it held surprises for both sides on the issue of working methods.

Common principles were established: mutual respect and mutually recognized professionalism. According to the market world, the new team had a number of assets: commercial experience, shareholder support, complementariness of sales networks, and so on.

The pace was determined by the industrial world; it was necessary to act rapidly, to launch new products rapidly, and so on. What was crucial was the test-type, which would be used as a reference. The market test was the first, since profit returned in 2001, with the Nissan operational margin being the highest in its history. The other test was industrial: would the two partners be able to create a new model, built on a common basis? Such was the case with Infiniti G35, launched in 2002. These two tests were well perceived by public opinion (the reputation world is not far away when business is prosperous). The Japanese press voted Carlos Ghosn, a foreigner, Manager of the Year, because he saved Nissan from bankruptcy.

The new organization challenged principles deeply rooted in the Japanese industrial tradition, and on which a number of specialists discoursed, harping on their link with Japanese culture. It concerned, for example, the strong links between the large company as a contractor and the myriad subcontractors, or life-long employment, or the absence of redundancies. The industrial world that the new executive team had in mind referred to another rather universal model, consisting of a drastic reduction in the number of suppliers in order to simplify the circuits and obtain better prices. The purchasing function was centralized and the *keiretsu* system (a set of companies with interlocking business relationships and shareholdings) was stopped. Nissan had previous involvement with 1394 companies; it kept only four. Management tools and performance indicators in the industrial world were defined. Compromises were found and partners avoided power relationships. In the case of disagreement, common principles (profitability, efficiency) were reiterated and both sides made efforts to integrate (Barmeyer and Mayrhofer, 2009).

Does this mean that beliefs and representations, especially political ones, were the same on both the Japanese and French sides? Of course not; but what counted was the applied common principle and the nature of the resulting test. The civic world did not prevail. Communication and interaction modes and the values of the society may be analysed, thanks to a cultural approach: the principles applied by the Nissan-Renault alliance belonged to another world, and were adapted to clear criteria and evaluation methods, those of the automotive industry in a competitive market in the 2000s: profitability, production flexibility, rapid adaptation to the market.

12.2.4   Danone-Wahaha: When a commercial partner becomes a rival

Perceived as a well-performing joint venture, associating a large group of the agri-food industry and an important Chinese private company, in 1996, this alliance ended with Danone's retreat in October 2009, after a violent dispute.

Danone had long established itself in the Chinese market, a critical one for the group. The alliance with Wahaha was profitable, and both partners benefited from it: Danone used a leading trademark and entered the fruit juice and dairy beverage markets; Wahaha was looking for technological and commercial support from a renowned company. Danone made considerable efforts to adapt to the Chinese context: some of its expatriate managers went to great lengths to learn about Chinese culture.

However, the Danone President for Asia, a young financial manager who had graduated from Hautes Études Commerciales (HEC) in Paris, and who was at ease with numbers, was confronted with an older pragmatic self-made entrepreneur, Qinghou Zong, founder and CEO of Wahaha. Inside the market world, while positive relationships were built initially, there came a point when both partners felt they had been cheated.

Danone discovered, in 2006, that Qinghou Zong was distributing identical products on his own account, through companies managed partly by his daughter and registered in the Virgin Islands, a tax haven. The loss for Danone was estimated at 100 million US dollars. Qinghou Zong argued that the Danone group was too slow to make the required investments. To solve the problem, Danone offered to buy 50 per cent of Wahaha, but the Chinese considered the amount offered was insufficient.

Qinghou Zong, meanwhile, had discovered that his joint venture partner was not a Franco-Chinese company as at the beginning, but was now Danone alone, which had bought the shares of its first partner. He considered that the Wahaha interests were no longer protected. The conflict escalated verbally and judicially in 2007, leading to Qinghou

Zong's dismissal. Chinese employees and managers rallied in the streets of Shanghaï to support their boss and to ask Danone leaders for an apology. Danone took legal action and lost its 24 cases in the Chinese courts, and then denounced Qinghou Zong's behaviour as unfair. The group also discovered that the transfer of the Wahaha trademark to the joint venture had never been authorized by the Chinese authorities. Finally, a compromise was found in October 2009: Danone withdrew from the joint venture and sold its share to Qinghou Zong, for an amount kept secret.

A number of factors explain the conflict (legal errors, lack of control from Danone, and so on). The cultural dimension was present: different management methods, the Chinese concern not to lose face, and so on; but the components of the conflict were essentially commercial, and a struggle for power took place inside the market world. The civic world prevailed during media confrontation, with the Chinese defending their nation in the face of the 'tyranny' of foreign MNCs. But it was merely a tactical move in a business conflict of interests, in which large investments were at stake (one of the largest private fortunes in the country).

The domestic world probably also played an important role, because Wahaha was a family-owned business with poor personal relationships with MNC delegates. However, these cultural differences might also have existed in Europe between the same types of companies. The market test was clear: convergence between commercial interests was obvious, as was confidence in signed agreements and the balance of power was established – until it was disrupted and a dispute broke out. Other justifications were put forward later by the parties, such as the value of signed agreements, legal transfer of the trademark, political interventions, and so on, but only after the commercial conflict began.

12.3 Discussion

These four cases are not representative as they illustrate MNCs resulting from recent alliances, having one or several European partners. Other cases of alliance strategies should be studied, with the same objective, which is to define the role of national culture in the strategic decisions of MNCs.

In the Alcatel Lucent case, concerns about price and technical efficiency took precedence over questions about intercultural relationships; opinion may be considered as a secondary reference because of the

Table 12.3   The worlds in the four cases

	Main referent world	Secondary referent world
Alcatel-Lucent	market	opinion, civic
EADS	industrial, market	civic, domestic, opinion
Renault-Nissan	market, industrial	opinion
Danone-Wahaha	market	civic

importance given to this cooperation at the beginning by the media. This was also the case of EADS, a group with high media coverage due to governmental interest in such a large company operating in a strategic industrial activity. Renault and Nissan agreed on market and industrial criteria, under the tight scrutiny of public opinion in both countries to begin with. Danone and Wahaha agreed and then separated on price and market questions, civic concerns being put forward by the Chinese side (see Table 12.3).

The conducted analysis shows that the anthropological approach, mainly relying on national culture, is not sufficient in itself to explain critical events taking place in MNCs. The specialized literature has often operated a hasty transfer of cultural phenomena to the organizational level.

Values, representations, routines inherited from a social group have an impact on communication and relationship modes (especially in the domestic world, if we use our theoretical framework). But sticking to the micro-sociological level is limited. In the economic environment current at the time of writing, industrial and market principles are dominant and provide the common framework in which actors are struggling.

The exclusive national culture approach hardly integrates the weight of conventions and the strength of free-market world economic institutions. This approach may underline how misunderstandings can occur within intercultural interactions, but it misses the essential point: isomorphic factors (Powell and Di Maggio, 1991), that is, codes, principles and institutions which transcend nationalities. The factors that explain the universal importance of industrial, market and network common references are well known: ideological domination of free-market capitalism, unifying role of large consulting companies, emergence of an interchangeable top executive class, having the same training, experience and decision criteria, and so on. This is the case, for example, of Carlos Ghosn (Nissan), Philippe Camus (EADS and Alcatel) and Emmanuel Faber (Danone). It is worth noting that studies examining cultural differences in organizations and strategic decisions, were conducted in the 1980s (e.g., the famous surveys conducted by Laurent in 1983 and Hofstede in 1982), or in the 1990s (Schneider and Meyer, 1991) therefore underestimating the trend towards homogenization (Irrman, 2008).

12.4   Conclusion

National culture differences do not play a major role in the alliances discussed in this chapter. The analysis would have been different if other situations had been studied closer to the ground level of these organizations, or if small and medium-sized enterprises had been dealt with. But the codes and institutions concerning MNCs tend to point to a managerial homogenization at the executive level.

To take the example of China, it is always possible to discuss Chinese culture at length; indeed excellent books have been written on that subject. But in 1993, China adopted a new Charter of Accounts, which implemented the classical accounting categories similar to those of Western countries; Chinese managers graduate, having been awarded Anglo-American Masters of Business Administration (MBA); family business leaders try to accumulate as much wealth as possible and use tax havens. It would be difficult today to find significant cultural differences in the strategy of Chinese companies. Chinese groups starting up in the world market have to deal with the questions that European or North American MNCs had to face before them: finding a balance between international managers and headquarters, sometimes too tight control of foreign subsidiaries, renewal or maintenance of local teams, and so on. But there are many success stories (Huawei, Beijing automotive, for example) with strategic 'recipes' which are not especially Chinese, but are well known, such as a dynamic operation on new markets, agreed investments, know-how acquisition, and so on.

The first practical conclusion that can be drawn from this analysis is that we must take into account organizational or decisional levels when we consider cultural factors in MNCs. At some levels, domestic (relational) or civic justifications are more crucial. At other levels (the most important ones in the four cases), industrial, market and network ones are critical.

This analysis of different levels can be completed by the analysis of the different types of involvement mentioned earlier in this chapter. Numerous actors, whom we have described as plural, may simultaneously experience several frameworks. An employee or a manager may operate at the same time in different worlds, either local or global ones. This reminds us that the cultural analysis may also be used as a tactical argument by the actor to account for success or failure. According to what suits them best, they can be a strict manufacturer, a citizen showing solidarity, a performing salesman, a faithful friend, a brilliant independent innovator, and so on.

Different types of behaviours, that cultural analysis hardly explains, are understandable if we consider the plurality of frameworks that individuals can use according to specific situations. The objective of this study is less to downplay the role of culture than to put into perspective its impact on some important strategic decisions and to show the tactical use that individuals can make of it in certain circumstances.

The study of the management of international alliances stresses the essential difficulty of any culturalist rationale, which is using a sensitive concept too easily especially when it takes the form of an independent variable. Contrary to what has been put forward in the intercultural management literature for a long time, national culture does not form an isolated block, which can be measured in terms of strategic impact. Studying MNCs requires a multi-level analysis of the context in which they operate, taking into account economic, geographical, historical, socio-political, legal and cultural aspects. In that respect, Table 11.3 proposed by Moalla and Triki in Chapter 11, dealing with the success factors of alliances, moves in this direction. It is a more complex, but richer and more realistic approach.

References

Amblard, H., Bernoux P., Herreros, G. and Livian, Y.-F. (2005) *Les nouvelles approches sociologiques des organisations*, 3rd edn (Paris: Le Seuil).

Barmeyer, C. and Davoine, E. (2006) *International Corporate Cultures: From Helpless Global Convergence to Constructive European Divergence* (Wiesbaden: Gabler).

Barmeyer, C. and Mayrhofer, U. (2004) 'Le changement organisationnel dans les fusions internationales: le cas EADS' in T. Froehlicher and B. Walliser (eds) *La métamorphose des organisations* (Paris: L'Harmattan) pp. 11–32.

Barmeyer, C. and Mayrhofer, U. (2007) 'Culture et relations de pouvoir: une analyse longitudinale du groupe EADS', *Gérer et Comprendre*, 88, 4–20.

Barmeyer, C. and Mayrhofer, U. (2009) 'Management interculturel et processus d'intégration: une analyse de l'alliance Renault-Nissan', *Management & Avenir*, 22, 109–31.

Boltanski, L. and Chiappello, E. (1999) *Le nouvel esprit du capitalisme* (Paris: Gallimard).

Carr, C. and Harris, S. (2004) 'The Impact of Diverse National Values on Strategic Investment Decision in the Context of Globalisation', *International Journal of Cross Cultural Management*, 4 (1), 77–99.

Chevrier, S. (2003) *Le management interculturel* (Paris: Presses Universitaires de France).

De Singly, F. (2003) *Les uns et les autres* (Paris: Armand Colin).

D'Iribarne, P. (1998) *Cultures et mondialisation* (Paris: Seuil).

D'Iribarne, P. (2008) *Penser la diversité du monde* (Paris: Seuil).

Dubet, F. (1994) *Sociologie de l'expérience* (Paris: Seuil).

Hofstede, G. (1982) *Culture's Consequences* (London: Sage Publications).

Hofstede, G., Hofstede, J. and Minkov, M. (2010) *Culture et organisations. Nos programmations mentales*, 3rd edn (Paris: Pearson Education).

Irrman, O. (2008) 'L'analyse interculturelle en gestion: une approche interactionniste' in E. Davel, J.-P. Dupuis and J.-F. Chanlat (eds) *Gestion en contexte interculturel, Approches, problématiques et plongées* (Québec: Les Presses de l'Université de Laval) pp. 119–62.

Laurent, A. (1983) 'The Cultural Diversity of Western Conceptions of Management', *International Studies of Management and Organization*, 13 (1–2), 75–96.

Livian, Y.-F. (2010) *De nouveaux cadres théoriques pour de nouveaux comportements*, 21st Conference of the Association francophone de Gestion des Ressources Humaines – French-Speaking Human Resource Management Association (AGRH), Saint Malo, 17–19 November.

Magee, D. (2003) *Comment Ghosn a sauvé Nissan?* (Paris: Dunod).

Meier, O. (2006) *Management interculturel* (Paris: Dunod).

Nachi, M. (2006) *Introduction à la sociologie pragmatique* (Paris: Armand Colin).

Powell, W. and Di Maggio, P. (1991) *The New Institutionalism in Organisational Analysis* (Chicago: Chicago University Press).

Schneider, S. and Meyer, A. (1991) 'Interpreting and Responding to Strategic Issues: The Impact of National Culture', *Strategic Management Journal*, 12 (4), 307–20.

Thévenot, L. (2006) *L'action au pluriel* (Paris: La Découverte).

13
The Construction of Networks by MNCs: An Analysis of the Banking Sector

Paul Marc Collin

Globalization is an opportunity as well as a necessity. Clients move and ask companies to follow them. That is why a proactive international strategy represents an appropriate response to globalization. Multinational companies (MNCs) have emerged from the design and implementation of such policies. Among MNCs, there are industrial as well as service companies. Both are characterized by a complex management system due to the diversity of countries of operation (Colovic and Mayrhofer, 2011; Hennart, 2009).

One of the specifics of services is their strong intangible dimension. Service MNCs cannot remain isolated. They need partners, especially in an international context, and thus form international alliances and/or networks. There are several types of networks: physical networks (railway, for example), computer networks (Internet) and social networks (Facebook, for example). One of the social networks is called socio-technical network and includes inter-individual and inter-organizational dimensions. This concept is useful for the development of service MNCs because it helps to build the infrastructure that will allow them to provide services across borders.

In this chapter, some observations will first be made on the banking sector, before discussing the conditions of sustainability of inter-organizational networks. We will also analyse the case of the banking sector, focusing on the spread of international bankcards. In the banking sector, one of the priorities of networks is to implement the interoperability of infrastructures among partners.

The study which forms the basis of this chapter involved a case study approach (Eisenhardt, 1989; Yin, 1990). Data collection was based on secondary data as well as interviews. Project leaders were interviewed, as well as clients and partners of MNCs in the field of payment systems. Other stakeholders were approached: banks, regulation officers, merchants.

13.1 Building the inter-organizational network of MNCs

After identifying the most relevant partnerships, MNCs have to sign and manage global and local agreements. This requires a high level of skills which can be achieved through recruitment and development of competence. Dispatching responsibilities between local partners (local operational marketing agencies, for example) and global partners (international advertising agencies, for example) is a strategic decision.

13.1.1 Specifics of service MNCs

The globalization of services is a recent and important phenomenon. Sometimes the pro-activeness of economic actors is offset by social activism calling for a break in the liberalization of investments (anti-globalization movements, for example). However, the main trend is to integrate more members into the World Trade Organization (WTO): China in 2001, Russia in 2011. If the financial crisis seems to slow down this process, it can be observed that most countries understand the value of supporting this trend.

Among recent movements can be mentioned the emerging economic diplomacy of countries such as Brazil, looking for a multi-polarization of power. Globalization is necessary for many companies in order to follow their clients' foreign direct investments (FDI), ensure economies of scale and face hyper-competition on international markets, but it cannot be built without the emergence and development of a specific capability, namely, networking.

In strategic management, a capability is the capacity of an organization to develop and change competencies, in order to respond to a versatile environment. Resources support the development of an MNC's competitive advantage. Regarding networking as a resource, the offer of MNCs needs to become legitimate to provide constructive help in each country of operation: the home country and foreign countries. To meet this objective, two methods are available: independence (e.g., American Express strategy) or partnership (e.g., Visa, MasterCard with host countries' local banks). In the first example, American Express took a hundred years to build *ex nihilo* an international network of agencies. In the second case, Visa and MasterCard decided to seek the support and participation of local banks to gain time and money.

When Moneta, an international network for payment means, planned to enter the European market, it turned to banker friends in England and Italy, in order to test pilot projects of new banking services, before using these partners as major allies in their European expansion strategy. In China, the Moneta network used HSBC to launch its cards.

This networking flexibility was theorized by Campbell and Verbeke (1994) in an article about the globalization of service MNCs and their dynamic capability to establish networks with local actors. The authors explore the link between international strategy, measured by the choice between country-by-country reactivity and centralized innovation, and networking capabilities.

We observe a tendency for service MNCs to develop *consortia*. Starting with business partnerships (e.g., clubs of airline companies, software companies), MNCs try to develop a common good. A relevant example is the electronic reservation system for airline tickets (Amadeus). This infrastructure is available to each firm involved in this particular industry.

The emergence of a social network is achieved through friendly core business relationships ready to imagine today's cooperation and to develop tomorrow's services. Spiral innovation thrives on the exchange of ideas between executives of a same club. Moreover, MNCs establish advisory committees, think tanks or steering committees for innovative projects. The goal is to guarantee the success of projects, the structure of the services' offer, thanks to a shared infrastructure built upon incremental agreements between club members.

The common good created by the emergence of a local network is characterized by the credibility of the profession with certain segments of clients. The network established between Moneta and French banks reassures the French client. The relationship with Moneta is embedded in the relationship with the banker. The client knows whom to contact if a problem occurs. On the contrary, American Express's positioning seems more distant. It focuses on business travellers and not on the regular client of a retail bank.

In summary, the high number of partners necessary to build an international service offer requires the emergence of a networking capability. Mainstream capabilities must be completed with a high level of formal and informal, individual and collective, intra- and inter-organizational network flexibility.

As has already been observed, the internationalization of services very often requires an inter-organizational infrastructure. This includes efforts to standardize support systems. Individuals design and use these systems. However, in a very normative context, there is always an important part dedicated to inter-individual networking, and this part should remain marginal. Inter-organizational flows are by nature more complex than inter-individual ones (Zaheer and Usai, 2004). At the individual level, and even at the intra-organizational level, it is easier to identify the content of the link, the individual being the only respondent. These flows include affect, advice and friendship (Krackhardt and Brass, 1994; Shah, 1998).

These links involve numerous individuals, and a simple link may include a series of processes such as communication, conflict resolution, trust, inter-individual affect. This makes correlation difficult. As an example, trust might mean collectively trusting the other organization (Gulati, 1995), or simply being familiar with the organization's routines (Zollo et al., 2002).

Individuals influence the development of inter-organizational cooperation. It is clearly the case when partnerships between MNCs are established, often thanks to friendships, or close ties. It is less obvious in later stages, because then the optimization of technical procedures and the logic of problem-solving take precedence over inter-individual relationships. The influence becomes more direct in the phase of reinforcement of the created inter-organizational network, contributing to its irreversibility.

For all these reasons, it is considered that the actor-network approach contributes to a better understanding of construction processes concerning service offers in an international context. For instance, the conditions for using new resources help the understanding of the business development dynamics of the organization. This interpretation thus allows the creation of propositions aiming to reinforce the network under construction.

Finally, the main challenge is related to the irreversibility of the network to its sustainability, thanks to the actors' adhesion. This is why this chapter proposes an analysis of the conditions under which the interoperability is built between networks, before identifying its impact in the case of international networks. Then, some elements of discussion on the reinforcement phase will be introduced.

13.1.2 Allowing the network to emerge

13.1.2.1 Network interoperability as a resource

The international strategy of an MNC needs the resource of network interoperability. The international offer builds itself incrementally, starting from a pivotal firm and adding partnerships: co-branding agreements with other client-oriented companies ('carte bleue' Visa of Crédit Lyonnais, for instance), agreements with third-party suppliers, licensing agreements with distributors in foreign countries.

The technical dimension of services requires technical interoperability between partners. Isolated and closed systems are the worst-case scenario. For example, an international bankcard must be accepted everywhere internationally ('We are everywhere you want to be', as mentioned in an advertising campaign), by merchants and automated teller machines (ATMs). The registered transaction is then sent from computer to computer to the cardholder's bank. The service quality (speed, reliability, security) needs fluidity in the communication between systems. This can be achieved through the negotiation of cooperation arrangements between banks and merchants, within France as well as abroad.

MNCs deal with cross national and strategic borders; therefore, bankers and merchants need telecommunication operators to exchange data in a secured way. The network organization often extends its borders to include a larger number of stakeholders. For instance, the French state has made a comeback in a previously highly deregulated field, in order to discipline actors along financial security requirements.

Interoperability is one of the 'convergent development' modes expected by MNCs in the field of global electronic payment systems (banks, merchants, computer service companies, telecommunication operators). Our study develops some promising avenues towards understanding the construction of an international offer. After the socio-technical network has been defined, the concept of interoperability will be presented and illustrated.

The network is a continuum organization mode between market and hierarchy (Williamson, 1981). It links individual and collective players for an economic purpose. The goal is critical. The social network implemented by economic sociology (Steiner, 1999) describes a form of social interaction which puts players in contact with one another: transactions in a market, exchanges of services among individuals of a same district, participation of groups of companies in executive committees.

The notion of player takes different forms. The player might be an individual in a market, an MNC or a nation. The actor-network theory focuses on relationships among players more than on players themselves. Regarding the socio-technical network, according to Callon's definition (1986), the coexistence of human and non-human players can be observed, as can a focus on the content of the relationship (e.g., controversy around the definition of a new service). The perspective developed by Callon (1986) is closer to the player, is more human and oriented towards international project management.

13.1.2.2 Operating the network

The implementation phase is a real challenge. Among the key success factors is the strategic compatibility between partners of MNCs in the network. The physical network represents a mandatory entry point. For instance, the key to the success of a dynamic socio-technical network such as Moneta is the quality of its interoperability which results from the compatibility in the design of equipment and cross-border procedures.

External players are invited to participate in think-tank meetings or to join local pilot experiments, before being formally integrated into the economic interest group, the *Groupement d'Intérêt Economique* (GIE). Each player is a representative of the home organization and/or profession. For example, the fast food restaurant industry has been involved in the pilot project concerning payment by debit cards. Each player brings resources and questions the goal and the boundaries of the group's work. After a while, the group is formally structured and acquires legitimacy in the eyes of the outside world.

The simultaneous construction of such groups can be observed, each one being supported by strategic groups (blue Visa banks against green MasterCard banks in France, for example), or taking contradictory or complementary technological options. Regarding payment security systems via bankcards on the web, a battle of standards has been waged between supporters of secured electronic transaction (SET) and those of secured socket layer (SSL).

In the SET universe, Cyber-Comm is the outcome of the merger of two initiatives of SET applications to smartcards, CSET (a consortium associating international organizations such as Visa, Mastercard and Europay) and E-COmm (a consortium uniting Banque Nationale de Paris (BNP), Société Générale and Crédit Lyonnais). Observing the behaviour of these MNCs is very thought provoking and helps other MNCs prepare their own international service development; for example, car manufacturers, with after sales service and assistance contracts.

Ties among engineers help to build teams in charge of screening potential technical solutions. Later, member organizations may integrate these solutions into their respective strategies. Project teams are called upon to transmit the decisions to business developers who will use these results as levers for new service development. As an example, Moneta has developed a platform of services on the Internet (after sales service, assistance, and so on).

Interoperability allows cross-border services to be implemented more easily. It includes capacity modularity issues. To succeed, interoperability must involve a combination of human players and resources offered by non-human players (actants). Then, each essential dimension of the new service (e.g., ticket reservation software, the chip on a smart bankcard, the hologram on a banknote) is offered through a wide range of media such as software beta-test version, simulation package, user requirements, or presentation of software functions for a client. Clients are disseminated throughout the network, on the Internet or in a videoconference between headquarters, subsidiaries and external partners.

Partners of such a network include software developers, card imprinters, website managers, service quality auditors and consulting companies. These are collective entities, but it can be observed that the choice of a partner is dependent upon the presence of a trustworthy person inside the entity.

Moreover, the selection of members for project teams takes into account the relational capabilities of these individuals, in view of the project's final goal. For instance, the project called Development of a *de facto* Standard, created by the International Organization for Standardization (ISO), concerned individuals with significant experience in the working groups of the ISO.

It became obvious for players that they had to develop a common platform as a lever for international services. The reason is the very high cost of developing proprietary solutions. Developing specific software for each company would prove too costly, given the budget constraints of many MNCs, especially in this time of economic crisis.

13.1.3   Sharing resources and know-how

A large number of players necessitates the finding of solutions agreeable to all and the focusing on shared technical and social infrastructures. For example, social infrastructure includes hiring and training employees in charge of handling complaints. Eventually, compliance with international standards is required via ISO and International Financial Reporting Standards (IFRS) and leads to a total compatibility of systems for each link of the value chain. The goal is to achieve service reliability and fluidity, in both front office staff (those in contact with the public and who develop close ties with clients) and back office staff (those responsible for software and technical support).

The Moneta project 'Global Platform', resulting in the creation of an exchange forum, is, at the time of writing, in progress. It reported, after the meeting of an advisory committee (genuine club of experts in electronic banking), the development of multiple incompatible technical solutions. Members of this forum understand that solutions include the convergence towards a de facto standard.

However, no player can decide for everybody else. Players understand that they are not a normative body and therefore not authorized to impose solutions on others. That is why they first try to understand each player's respective position, banks, merchants, software developers, telecommunication operators, consumer representatives, public authorities, and then provide these players with guidelines.

To achieve this goal, they need to become legitimate (Kostova and Zaheer, 1999), by reducing the distance between the perceptions of the different national players. The MNC (Moneta, in this case) has to anticipate the question of legitimacy in the host country's environment.

The actor-network approach helps to understand many dimensions of international banking strategies, but also raises interesting methodological questions regarding the link between content and context of the relationship for instance. The challenge is to compare networks with diverse contents, to select the relevant content after a qualitative analysis and to combine case studies and structural analyses.

13.1.4   Understanding strategic moves of banks from the actor-network perspective

The actor-network theory is a sociological approach to the actor, which also includes technical objects. Service networks are structured around actors, whether individual or collective, internal or external. These actors operate as points of entry into the networks, not only from a competitive advantage point of view, but also from a partnership and service offer development point of view, via the design of technical solutions.

An analogy with alliances of car manufacturers around common technical platforms will be proposed. In the service industry, cooperation between MNCs is quasi-obligatory, because services require communication between organizations. For instance, a travel reservation system must be able to communicate in real time with each airline company, be it a flagship or a low cost carrier.

The actor-network is structured by the positive consumer benefit offered by the service (easy price comparison and flight reservation). The actor-translator emerges during a problematic situation, whenever there is an inter-organizational tension between what unites and what separates positions. The translator acts in a context of dialectic tension and contributes to the contextualization and problematization of the network. As in every management change situation, problematization can only be achieved thanks to a translator.

Between actor-network and translation theories, the research object is the same: change in systems of action. The two schools aim at understanding the behaviours of the actors. Their key constructions are compatible, like the terms 'network' and 'system', for example. Similarly, actants and actors are close concepts, even though innovation sociologists consider they are the only ones to be free from anthropocentrism. The actant includes the human actor without destroying it. The strategic analysis (Crozier and Friedberg, 1977) is dissolved in the actor-network theory. It is amended, replicated, but never rejected.

The individual or collective legitimacy of the actor comes from his technical expertise, his current job experience, or from belonging to a specific group of professionals. The size of the actors is variable. Here lies the challenge of the whole change process. The variability of size makes it compulsory to differentiate between spokespersons. In international services' networks, differentiated mechanisms are implemented, to ensure equal representation of small members.

Another element of the actant-translator question is the role in the project team, that is to say the group formed by stakeholders, aiming at translating an organization's strategic intentions into pilot experimentations and new service offers; for example, business cards, new rubbish recycling services, a new fast train service, among others. The team may be composed of persons from other departments during the project, either from inside or outside of the company. Service MNCs have a strong tendency to concentrate on highly important projects in order to shape the future.

The debit bankcard was an international project before becoming a service, and has helped structure international bankcard networks around the world. Today, payment on the Internet and mobile payments seem to be pivotal projects for such networks. For all these reasons, it is suggested that using the actor-network theory as a stimulating approach promotes a better understanding of the innovation processes within inter-organizational networks operating in an international context. Relationships between individuals represent a cascade of interfaces. The construction of these interfaces is characterized by conflicts, consensus building, mediations, reciprocal concessions or unilateral imposition.

The author's research field, the banking sector, illustrates the conditions of emergence of a social capital within an inter-organizational group aiming at becoming a consortium. The interdependence helps to build confidence among members. Ideally, each of them makes resources available to the group. The aim is to develop operational recommendations. The relevance of recruiting can be observed in these types of groups, individuals and organizations with relational capabilities with the outside world; for example, the manager of the Internet platform at Moneta had such a profile. Once set up, the group constructs a common language, a grammar which will become the lingua franca for all the new service's stakeholders. This observation applies to all types of services.

The actor-network is also composed of individual or collective actors (employees, managers, project managers, departments), with different objectives but deriving the same benefits from combining and sharing their resources. The 'bankcard' actant lends its legitimacy as a banker, its skills at benchmarking competitors' practices. On the editorial board of a bank journal, the 'telecommunications operator' representative brings a resource as an active member of an ISO standards' task force. The spokesperson 'retail' will educate the group on the expectations of the cardholder as an end-user of the service.

13.2 Discussion

13.2.1 Managerial questions

The first condition of emergence is the existence of managerial questions about opportunities or modes of cooperation. Decision making in this area not only follows the logics of optimization but also develops a list of criteria for selecting an ideal partner. A prerequisite to the discussion is the creation of a favourable context when it comes to deploying capabilities in line with the organization's strategic intention. The MNC identifies the resources it is looking for and those which are missing. It is then in a position to anticipate the ways to convince stakeholders to make their resources available. Resources are related to information, social capital, solidarity and the spirit of resource sharing. The social capital is made up of resources which individuals may obtain by socialising through a network, or just by being known or enjoying a good reputation.

There are numerous definitions of social capital. They share the philosophy according to which a positive attitude towards others may lead to value creation, and economic benefits can result from belonging to such social networks. Identifying potential partners requires a constant presence in the organizational field, through participation in socio-professional associations such as Rotary, Lions Club, Prisme club in France, employers' associations and/or chambers of commerce. On the interface between transaction and 'gift-counter gift' (Mauss, 1980) logics, the contextualization of the network requires tenacity and a combination of focused intention and flexibility in implementation.

The managerial question, sometimes obsessive, concerns the performance improvement of MNCs, thanks to their strategic intention. The combination of resources has a goal. The intention, the willingness of the senior manager, of the project leader, is sometimes obvious in a procedure or in a process. The procedure, or modus operandi, reveals the deliberate nature of this approach.

The process takes into account the emerging nature of sharing resources. That is why the process approach is a condition of emergence of the inter-organizational network relying on social capital. Eventually, the condition of emergence of such a network is related to the content of the relation. In the Moneta example, the relationship leads to the emergence of technical propositions which trigger controversies among more or less specialized actors, hence the relevance of using such a perspective to analyse innovation processes.

We must dialectically link the relationship content and the project leader's strategic intention. Sometimes, it is positive to leave space for expert controversies. At other times, it is best to impose the acceptance of a compromise on a majority of network members. This is why the main steps of an actor network's development will now be presented (Callon, 1986).

The actor-network – the project leader or the person responsible for a discussion forum – analyses the main actants, their stakes in the process and their degree of convergence by topic, and building on the awareness of what unites and what separates them, the actor-network makes an attempt to transform each individual into a collective representative, take them from an individual position to a cooperating position within a project or more globally.

'Virtual Moneta' London department invites actors to build a transdisciplinary team in order to combine expertise and to screen the potentialities of new web and mobile services. The objective is to understand Business to Business (B to B) and Business to Consumer (B to C) paradigms and to converge towards a shared and interoperable solution satisfactory to all.

The manager of this regional department is aware that the partner's initial skills determine the project success. For this reason, makes an alliance with legitimate actors and creates an attractive club, running the risk of making other actors jealous. According to one of the managers, the team operates as an 'old boys' network, where everyone acts as the spokesperson for a galaxy of resources and interests. For example, a famous tour operator helps the group understand the advantages and drawbacks of each e-commerce solution for travel services.

Once convergence has been implemented, thanks to the synergy of actors' resources, the 'enrolment/alignment' step confirms the success of the project via quantitative and qualitative attractiveness and thanks to the diversity of stakeholders. The final step is the 'reinforcement' or irreversible acceptance of the network. We call it also generalization and institutionalization.

Finally, the actor joins the project group with some social capital, which he combines and values in the project development process. In the transnational logic (Bartlett and Ghoshal, 1991), integration and coordination mechanisms rely on more informal modalities which can bring distant pieces of knowledge together, access resources and promote innovation. If we admit that social capital facilitates information and knowledge transfers, as well as cooperation between individuals, then it is useful to observe and analyse the way this particular form of capital can be produced.

13.2.2   Focusing energies and piloting the network

Following Jones et al. (1997) and Philips et al. (2000) inter-organizational network is shown to be a set of relationships between legally distinct organizations characterized by continuity, complexity and reciprocal adaptations, as well as the development of social links in view of designing and implementing a common project. The implementation of the common project, therefore, is the dependent variable of the model. It expresses the intention connected to the inter-organizational network. In the strict sense of a social network, there might be a persistence of the gift and counter-gift logic without seeking performance or strategic implementation.

Inter-organizational networks might appear to be 'disembodied' because of their dimensions. This is the case of research and development consortia established between MNCs. But they bring together individuals who are expected to express their respective talents. Hewlett-Packard is a case in point. The programme, 'Voice of the Workforce', tries to mobilize individuals and to develop a true 'public opinion' forum inside the firm. The network pools individual energies to build a collective force. In banking services, even clients are represented more often, as they participate in think tanks brought together by retail banks and are approached by consumers' organizations for information about potential problems. They can telephone to complain – recent scandals concerning bank services' invoicing are a good example.

Other actors participate in clubs, forums, consortia and economic interest groups which have their own dynamics. These groups include international actors and 'liaison' agents, true network facilitators inside MNCs (McEvily and Zaheer, 2004). Information technology managers meet project leaders and client relationship managers.

The relational logic also inspired the strategic management field. It has become important to focus on resources and competences of MNCs. For this reason, it is suggested that they place network facilitators at the centre of their partnership system and implement a process to identify these facilitators within each organization. The list of sought talents is incomplete: relational capabilities, agenda building, career path diversity, double competence (technical and managerial). 'The innovator must know who, among engineers, administrative personnel or industrial people, speaks on behalf of good actors, who needs to be taken into account' (Latour, 1992, p. 67). This resource may be called 'relevance of an individual representativeness in a group' (ibid.). Innovation aims at developing functionalities by actors for actors. Identifying key actors and representing them accurately is a key success factor in this field.

Networks of MNCs present characteristics which are sometimes far removed from a social network framework. They are often imposed by hierarchy, at least in the early stages of a project. Individual initiative might seem limited. An individual's social capital may be instrumentalized.

Moreover, the development of project groups does not always take into account individuals with the most relevant social capital in relation to a given project, for fear of individual opportunism. Then, the representation within a project team will include a representative from each service. It is, therefore, important to consider social capital as a criterion for participating in a project group, while ensuring consistency and complementariness.

Partnership between MNCs is not a social network because it follows a commercial logic. Its ultimate goal is to overcome competitors, even through cooperation (Hamel and Prahalad, 1994) to the point of creating a 'coopetition' system. Eventually, the partnership is more instrumental. Its objective is to optimize the modes of operation more than to place the individual in the centre. This social capital is most useful when procedures are fluid. If the individuals can convince the MNC that their relational network might be useful, then the firm will take it into consideration. However, priority is given to the value chain, independent of an individual's unique talents. This approach is exacerbated by individuals' mobility, 'people turnover' and the willingness of

MNCs to run their organization independently from individuals. This comment must be considered in the context of small and medium-sized enterprises (SMEs) where individuals' unique qualities (*habitus*, agenda, capabilities, and so on) are very important to a recruiter, who buys the actor's competence to win over new clients and reassure existing ones. Consulting companies work in flexible networks of partnerships. Each individual acts as an ambassador of the company network.

In contrast, however, in MNCs, the focus is on continuity of service, sometimes regardless of people's availability at a given time. MNCs search for an average competence, a standard talent. The social capital on the one hand and the social network on the other appear to carry the risk of both good or bad surprises, contradictory to the search for uniform quality and reliability.

13.2.3 Sustaining the network

The intention describes the strategist's or project leader's desire to focus the attention and resources of the organization's members. It tends to move towards formalized procedures and organization charts. The intention to control leads many MNCs to develop somewhat bureaucratic information technology systems. However, there are some informal areas, either by obligation – unforeseen incidents leading to the implementation of ad hoc solutions – or awareness – the informal part in the socialization of new recruits in MNCs.

This informal part favours the emergence of network facilitators. Their function evolves with events and controversies. Knowledge within a project group is negotiated. Its production raises questions among actors, who develop different points of view. All players, via their standpoint (written evidence of the point under discussion), take into account their rival's point of view, multiplying experiments and modifying the proposed standpoint. This is the way compromises are achieved and how knowledge content and the identity of social groups involved are impacted in the negotiation. The group is transformed by the construction of a common good or a new technical standard, for example. The team acquires a certain degree of autonomy from the contribution of the respective attributes of members.

Eventually, project teams and inter-organizational instruments all have intentions, usually normative. The actor's individual freedom will have trouble expressing itself, which is why the perspective of the strategic actor (Crozier and Friedberg, 1977) seems relevant. Individual actors having to identify the hierarchy of the organization's intentions may place their own career path. It is up to them to multiply initiatives in a formalized area, though open to propositions. The inventor of the Smartcard, Roland Moreno, started up his own company in order to promote solutions for large 'prescriptive' MNCs. Simplicity, reliability and a relational network were strong points in his approach. He had to be tenacious, but it finally worked out well.

At the beginning, the strategic intention is not always present, or may be only as a type of experimentation without any performance-related expectations. Engineers exchange ideas and develop a service prototype. If the first steps are promising, then respective organizations start to get interested in the idea. Their involvement translates into a formal investment (Boltanski and Thévenot, 1987). It might take the form of a project team start-up, with a related mission statement, or even the creation of an economic interest group or consortium.

In the latter case, the intention is to be a pioneer in establishing and maintaining a competitive advantage, or to paralyse competition in order to establish a monopolistic position. At this point, it could even be considered that the social network is utilized in order to establish a monopoly, while inter-organizational agreements reinforce access restriction to the market. The creation of a common good is another type of strategic intention. Priority is given to balanced and fast business development. Internet actors have rapidly understood that general interest requires a reduction in the perceived risk for bankcard payments on the web.

Some network facilitators, especially the ones well connected to influential groups, have decided to bring together specialists to develop a solution acceptable by everyone. Having been approved, this solution has become an obligatory step for every member of the international network.

The strategic intention of international service networks may be analysed as a willingness to deploy 'black boxes'. As an example, the strategy of standardization of services and technical supports involves a dimension of relationship development around a 'black box', that is a dimension in the form of a unique solution that actors must accept. Here, actors are not worth what they bring, but their approval is needed because of their central position. The goal is to 'naturalize' the chosen scenario. The social network becomes a solution-legitimatizing tool. But the solution has been built by actors, helped by facilitators. This type of network is characterized by a high level of interactivity, with a constant search for balance.

The organization's intention aims at satisfying stakeholders. In cooperation between MNCs, the goal is to produce a common good, an infrastructure, fuelling the development of the entire industry. An example of a common good is the opening of every ATM to cardholders of all banks. Portugal has succeeded in this project. Another common good is the security of inter-actor transactions, from merchant banks to cardholders' banks. This has been built by actors. It is also a product which facilitates the development of transaction flows.

13.3   Conclusion

MNCs need to build and sustain networks, because they allow weaknesses of resources and competencies to be offset. The challenge is how to select relevant global, but also local partners, to ensure fluidity in service. Stakeholders move from a competition to a cooperation logic, under certain specific conditions. The network permits organizational learning with a positive effect by sustaining the most efficient networks.

The analysis in this chapter, even if it is not a model to be followed *in extenso*, offers interesting insights for decision makers involved in building international cooperation strategies. The network effect accompanies the development of MNCs and helps managers experiment multiple strategic situations.

References

Bartlett, C. and Ghoshal, S. (1991) *Le management sans frontières* (Paris. Editions d'Organisation).

Boltanski, L. and Thévenot, L. (1987) 'Les économies de la grandeur', *Cahier du centre d'études de l'emploi* (Paris: Presses Universitaires de France).

Callon, M. (1986) 'Eléments pour une sociologie de la traduction', *L'Année sociologique* (Paris: Presses Universitaires de France).

Campbell, A. and Verbeke, A. (1994) 'The Globalisation of Service Multinationals', *Long Range Planning*, 27 (2), 95–102.

Colovic, A. and Mayrhofer, U. (2011) 'Optimising the Location of R&D and Production Activities: Trends in the Automotive Industry', *European Planning Studies*, 19 (8), 1481–98.

Crozier, M. and Friedberg, E. (1977) *L'Acteur et le Système* (Paris: Le Seuil).

Eisenhardt, K. (1989) 'Building Theories from Case Studies Research', *Academy of Management Review*, 14 (4), 532–50.

Gulati, R. (1995) 'Social Structure and Alliance Formation: A Longitudinal Analysis', *Administrative Science Quarterly*, 40 (4), 619–72.

Hamel, G. and Prahalad, C. K. (1994) *Competing for the Future* (Boston, MA: Harvard University Press).

Hennart, J. F. (2009) 'Down with MNE-Centric Theories! Market Entry and Expansion as the Bundling of MNE and Local Assets', *Journal of International Business Studies*, 40 (9), 1432–54.

Jones, C., Hesterly, W. S. and Borgatti, S. P. (1997) 'A General Theory of Network Governance: Exchange Conditions and Social Mechanisms', *Academy of Management Review*, 22 (4), 911–45.

Kostova, T. and Zaheer, S. (1999) 'Organizational Legitimacy under Conditions of Complexity: The Case of the Multinational Enterprise', *Academy of Management Review*, 24 (1), 64–81.

Krackhardt, D. and Brass, D. (1994) 'Intraorganizational Networks: The Micro Side' in B. Wasserman and J. Galaskiewicz (eds) *Advances in Social Network Analysis: Research in the Social and Behavioral Sciences* (Newbury Park: Sage Publications), pp. 207–29.

Latour, B. (1992) *Ces réseaux que la raison ignore* (Paris: L'Harmattan).

Mauss, M. (1980) *Essai sur le don. Sociologie et anthropologie* (Paris: Presses Universitaires de France).

McEvily, B. and Zaheer, S. (2004) 'Architects of Trust: The Role of Network Facilitators in Geographical Clusters' in R. M. Kramer and K. S. Cook (eds) *Trust and Distrust in Organizations* (New York: Russell Sage), pp. 207–29.

Philips, N., Lawrence, T. B. and Hardy, C. (2000) 'Inter-Organizational Collaboration and the Dynamics of Institutional Fields', *Journal of Management Studies*, 37 (1), 23–43.

Shah, C. K. (1998) 'Who are Employees' Social Referents? Using a Network Perspective to Determine Referent Others', *Academy of Management Journal*, 41 (3), 249–68.

Steiner, P. (1999) *La sociologie économique* (Paris: La Découverte).

Williamson, O. E. (1981) 'The Economics of Organization: The Transaction Cost Approach', *American Journal of Sociology*, 87 (3), 548–77.

Yin, R. K. (1990) *Case Study Research: Design and Method* (Newbury Park: Sage Publications).

Zaheer, S. and Usai, A. (2004) 'The Social Network Approach in Strategy Research: Theoretical Challenges and Methodological Issues', *Research Methodology in Strategy and Management*, Vol. 1 (Oxford: Elsevier), pp. 67–86.

Zollo, M., Reuer, J. J. and Singh, H. (2002) 'Interorganizational Routines and Performance in Strategic Alliances', *Organization Science*, 13 (6), 701–13.

14
Partnerships between French MNCs and Chinese Companies: Win-Win Relationships?

Maha Raïs and Simin Lin

The report of the United Nations Conference on Trade and Development (UNCTAD, 2010) indicates that China is the second most popular destination for investments of multinational companies (MNCs), behind the US. In 2009, investments in China amounted to 95 billion US dollars. For many MNCs, entering the Chinese market represents an important strategic challenge (Allouche et al., 2008). Attracted by the market's size, growth prospects and low production costs, MNCs increased their investments in China (Jaussaud and Schaaper, 2006). France is one of the top ten investors in China; almost all large French Groups are present in the country: Carrefour, Lafarge, Areva, PSA Peugeot Citroën, L'Oreal, Danone, Electricité de France (EDF), and so on

In order to develop in the Chinese market, many French MNCs have established partnerships with Chinese companies. Business practice shows that the performance achieved through cooperation often provides mixed results. In this chapter, we will discuss the benefits of Franco-Chinese partnerships. First of all, we will examine the attractiveness of the Chinese market for French MNCs and the development of partnerships between French MNCs and Chinese companies. Then, we will examine the benefits of these partnerships for both French and Chinese companies. Finally, we will discuss how Chinese authorities have adapted to the presence of MNCs in China.

14.1   China: A priority market?

14.1.1   The attractiveness of the Chinese market for French MNCs

The appeal of the Chinese market for MNCs is the result of the economic openness and reform policy that the country has pursued since the late

1970s. This policy includes tax incentives, customs duties abatement on imports and tax reduction. MNCs' increased investments in China also reflect the growing importance of the Chinese market; indeed, many MNCs consider that China offers the world highest growth potential (Story, 2004).

For a large number of French MNCs, China has become a strategic market. For example, the Alstom group holds a strong position in China and achieves more than 35 per cent of its turnover in the Chinese market. Lafarge group, ranked among the top ten cement producers in China, has also benefited from China's rapid development, especially in the central part of the country where many cities have a popula-tion of over 32 million people. The Chinese market has provided huge opportunities for this group as urbanization continuously developed. According to Population Reference Bureau (PRB) forecasts (2010), 48 per cent of the population now lives in cities, and this figure could reach 59 per cent by 2025. In a period of economic crisis, the importance of the Chinese market may enable companies to offset business losses in other regions, particularly in Europe and the US. For example, luxury goods groups LVMH and Hermès registered a 20 per cent annual growth rate of activities in China (see Box 14.1), and the same rate exceeded 40 per cent for the Sanofi group (Allouche et al., 2008).

Many empirical studies on the international expansion of companies show that labour costs are critical to the decision of doing business abroad. Numerous companies are attracted by countries like China, where labour costs are relatively low (Kaufmann and Korte, 2010). For example,

Box 14.1   LVMH and Hermès in China

In 2009, the LVMH group's presence in China enabled it to limit the negative effects of the financial crisis on its performance: the Chinese market represented six per cent of its sales, a 15 per cent increase com-pared with 2008. At the beginning of 2010, the world number one leader in luxury goods registered a 13 per cent drop in profits since the financial crisis. The group's managers reported that without Chinese consumers, the situation would have been much worse. In fact, the Chinese have become the number one consumers of Hennessy's cognac and the number two consumers of Louis Vuitton's products in the world. According to the Chinese Ministry of Commerce, China may become the world number one purchaser of luxury goods by 2012. The potential clientèle is estimated at more than ten million people. The Hermès Group was able to withstand the financial crisis thanks to sales growth in China. It entered the Chinese market in 1997 and has opened 20 shops in China's major cities; it plans to further increase its market penetration. It improved its sales by 18 per cent in the fourth quarter of 2009, and the strongest gains were recorded in China, Macao and Hong Kong (29% for the year 2009).

Source: Le Figaro, 6 February 2010.

Maped, a French MNC specializing in school supplies, established itself in China mainly in order to reduce its production costs.

14.1.2 The development of partnerships between French MNCs and Chinese companies

Partnerships established between French MNCs and Chinese companies have changed considerably since the beginning of China's policy of economic openness. Like other foreign companies, French MNCs initially formed joint ventures, holding minority stakes before taking majority stakes. In the past, Western MNCs were forced to create joint ventures with local partners in order to enter the Chinese market (Plantade and Plantade, 2006). Indeed, at the beginning of its market openness, the Chinese government had imposed strict rules to compel all foreign investors in China to partner with a local company. Thus, many joint ventures were established by MNCs during the 1980s (Jaussaud and Schaaper, 2006).

Since the early 1990s, Chinese authorities have become accustomed to the presence of foreign MNCs in China. They began to trust them and encouraged them to take majority stakes or even acquire the joint venture's entire capital. Chinese authorities became aware of the crucial role played by MNCs in the country's rapid development. The opportunity to increase their financial share in joint ventures led MNCs to devote more resources and give more importance to their subsidiaries in China. Joint ventures controlled by MNCs generally performed better than those controlled by local companies (Jaussaud and Schaaper, 2006).

However, an international joint venture is potentially unstable since the relationship and the negotiating power between partners may fluctuate over time (Schaaper, 2005). The degree of instability can be higher in a joint venture with a Chinese company because of the large cultural differences and the local institutional environment (Buck et al., 2010).

Moreover, it is important to point out the managerial difficulties, the risk of abuse of intellectual property rights and the lack of commitment on the part of the Chinese partner. To overcome these difficulties, several MNCs have chosen to acquire the financial capital owned by their local partner and have thus regained their independence. This has been the case for Schneider Electric and Sanofi-Aventis. Finally, it is interesting to note that the type of partnership established by MNCs depends on its objectives. If the aim is to produce locally at a competitive price and to launch products onto the Chinese market, multinationals companies often establish joint ventures to benefit from their local partner's commercial networks and expertise. On the contrary, if the subsidiary's local production is to be exported to other regions, MNCs often prefer to control the joint venture (Schaaper, 2005).

14.2   The benefits of Franco-Chinese partnerships

Many MNCs have developed partnerships with local companies, in order to enter the Chinese market. Therefore, it seems necessary to consider the benefits of these partnerships both for MNCs and Chinese companies.

14.2.1   Advantages of partnerships for MNCs

The partnership between an MNC and a Chinese company often aims at better access to local resources: human resources, distribution networks, and so on. By referring to transaction cost theory and the resource-based view, Schaaper (2005) explains that a partnership can reduce the risk of local opportunistic collaborators and provide faster access to local resources. Many empirical studies confirm that the creation of a joint venture with a local partner usually facilitates the establishment of an MNC (Jaussaud and Schaaper, 2006). Indeed, the MNC may benefit from the joint venture when dealing with the Chinese administration and political authorities, which is an essential requirement when entering the market (Allouche et al., 2008). For example, in order to establish itself in China, Alstom chose to develop a partnership with a local company in the steam turbines sector. The cooperation enabled Alstom to expand more easily in the local market, to benefit from the local company's experience and to better understand the needs and expectations of Chinese customers. When an MNC plans to do business in markets in transition with significant differences, it often associates with a local company, in order to benefit from its networking activities, especially with the national government (Johanson and Vahlne, 2009).

The collaboration with a local partner allows the solving of problems related to geographical and cultural distance (Shan, 1991; Ellis, 2007).

Beside access to resources, collaborating with a local company allows MNCs to benefit from its relationship network and achieve an easier market penetration (see Box 14.2), mainly for two reasons. The first

Box 14.2   Sanofi-Aventis and PSA Peugeot Citroën in China

The Chinese market for consumer health care is the second largest market worldwide after the US and was valued at 12 billion Euros in 2010. The French Sanofi-Aventis group entered the market in the 1980s. It forecasts sales of two billion Euros in the country until 2015, after achieving a turnover of 512 million Euros in 2009 (29%). In 2010, the group targeted the Chinese market for vitamins and mineral supplements, currently the largest health care sector in China. At the beginning of its presence in China, Sanofi-Aventis conducted a partnership strategy by establishing a joint venture with the Chinese laboratory Minsheng, in which it held a majority stake. During the same year, the group opened a new research and development centre in Shanghai in view of taking advantage of the booming Chinese demand and meeting the needs of the Asian-Pacific market.

PSA Peugeot Citroën established its first joint venture in China with Dongfeng Motor Group in 1992 and it is still seeking to strengthen its position in the Chinese automobile market. In 2010, the group decided to create a joint venture, owned in equal parts with the Harbin Hafei Automobile Industry Group, a subsidiary of China Changan Automobile Group. This venture is intended to produce and market light-duty and passenger vehicles in China: the launch of the first vehicle is scheduled for the second semester of 2012. PSA Peugeot Citroën has already built Peugeot 408 and Citroën C5 in partnership with Dongfeng Motor Group, but it remains behind most foreign car manufacturers, due particularly to a limited range of vehicles. The first joint venture produced only 175,190 cars in the first semester of 2010, that is to say one third of Hyundai Motor and Kia Motors' sales and 15 per cent of General Motors' sales over the same period. Thanks to this new joint venture, the French brand plans to sell two million vehicles per year in China and gain a ten per cent market share.

Source: *Les Echos*, 7 April 2010; *La Tribune*, 9 July 2010.

is because MNCs wish to grow externally, a policy pursued by many French companies such as the Schneider group, which has acquired several Chinese companies over the past few years. The French Groupe SEB is also a case in point: it has acquired a 52 per cent equity stake in Supor, the number one cookware manufacturer in China, after a long procedure (see Chapter 8). Secondly, because MNCs have to establish joint ventures in areas defined as strategic by Chinese authorities, such as aerospace, energy, transport and insurance. The collaboration between MNCs and local companies may also lead to technology transfer. The case of Lafarge illustrates this aspect: its partnership with the Chinese group Shui in 2005 strengthened its presence but also helped the Chinese company to benefit from the transfer of technological know-how. It should be noted that Lafarge group learnt from its Chinese partner how to open a production site in 18 months, while the average time for the group to establish a production site in China was 36 months. It is also worth mentioning that the MNC may not only transfer technology to the joint venture's partner companies but also to other local companies it works with. In this context, the transfer is less direct: from the MNC to local suppliers or buyers, competitors or complementary businesses in the same industry.

14.2.2   Advantages of partnerships for Chinese companies

Many studies show that Chinese authorities seek to attract MNCs because they are significant sources of new technologies and can improve Chinese workers' skills (Spencer, 2008).

14.2.2.1 *Technology transfer and training*

The size of the population, with over 1 billion, 330 million inhabitants, means that China has an important reservoir of labour. However, we must bear in mind that the country faces a general problem of unqualified workforce. In 2005, McKinsey Global Institute (MGI), a consulting firm, published a report entitled 'Addressing China's Looming Talent Shortage', dealing with the lack of Chinese skilled employees. This study shows that only ten per cent of three million new Chinese graduates were qualified and competent enough to work in foreign companies operating in China. This could be explained by the divergence between the graduates' education and the needs of the foreign companies. Indeed, most of the education provided in China is very theoretical and does not meet the expectations of MNCs, who seek employees with work experience, team spirit and language skills, particularly a good command of the English language. Recruitments by MNCs can provide a solution to these shortcomings by gradually supplying the local labour market with more qualified employees.

Another indirect way to transfer technology is through qualified workers' migration from MNCs to local companies or company start ups. Technology transfer from MNCs to local companies promotes the efficient use of resources in the host country and provides information to help improve products and local workforce. All this tends to provide support for the development of local companies and encourages innovation and investment in research and development. Thomson group is a case in point (see Box 14.3).

Since it is difficult for MNCs to find experienced and qualified local managers in China (Schaaper, 2005), internal training of local employees may provide an alternative. This policy aims not only to improve employees' skills and performance, but also to encourage them to adapt to MNCs' needs and meet their expectations. For example, the automotive supplier Valeo applies this practice to all engineers, who receive

Box 14.3   Thomson Broadband R&D

Thomson, a world leader for digital video technology, has been present in China since 1968. In 2004, it opened a new research and development (R&D) centre in Beijing. Approximately 400 young Chinese researchers worked there, supervised by 20 visiting expatriate experts and 10 permanent managers. In 2006, two years after its creation, the centre had already registered over 60 patents in China and had opened three laboratories: the first specialized in medium- and long-term technology, the second developed innovative technological products sold to large international or Chinese companies (home routers, digital television decoders, and so on) and the third focused on the development of integrated circuits.

Thomson's research centre developed rapidly in Beijing, expanding from 56 employees in 2004, to 600 at the end of 2007. It brings together young dynamic and voluntary Chinese researchers who are attracted by Thomson's high-level and well-supervised research in the heart of a pleasant high tech environment. In addition, Thomson ensures that its researchers feel part of a real MNC and are able to develop their talents.

Source: Chambre de Commerce et d'Industrie Francaise en Chine (CCIFC), 2007.

a six-month training in Europe immediately after being hired, and therefore they become familiar with software and production processes.

14.2.2.2   *Productivity and access to resources*

The MNC is viewed as a rich source of technology and knowledge transfer by the host country and therefore as critical to the improvement of productivity by local companies. Sachwald and Perrin (2003) show that the introduction of new entrants and new technologies affect the production and dissemination of knowledge in local companies. This may foster research and development and contribute more generally to higher productivity. For example, France Télécom was attracted by the boom in the telecommunication market and the development of innovation in China.

The company opened its first R&D centre in Beijing in 2004 and developed industrial and academic cooperation with Chinese partners. With cutting-edge R&D, as well as technical and business skills, the French MNC provided its Chinese partners with the necessary technology and expertise to offer new mobile services such as new musical services, video loadings, online payment, games, and so on. It may also be noted that the presence of MNCs fosters competition between local companies, and therefore encourages them to improve their learning capacities and to develop.

Networking with MNCs may provide an important advantage to local companies. Indeed, pooling resources allows the emergence of new skills which would be much more difficult to achieve separately (Mayrhofer, 2007). It allows Chinese companies to access multiple resources and skills of MNCs as well their production capacities. These collaborations may also be of other practical interest such as information sharing, networking, or reducing the risks linked to the application of new technologies (Spencer, 2008). Through these partnerships, Chinese companies can more quickly access the resources and expertise they need to develop and lower the cost of new market access, which might have been hardly feasible as individual companies.

14.3   The Chinese government policy towards MNCs

14.3.1   Towards a more selective policy for the establishment of MNCs

Within the framework of its openness and reform policy, China has provided considerable assistance to foreign investors, in order to attract them and promote economic growth. Indeed, foreign companies have benefited from tax cuts, favourable recruitment conditions, autonomy, and so on. However, since 2006, the Chinese authorities have begun to take into consideration the economic importance and the influence of MNCs, as well as the need to protect the Chinese economy. After several years of economic openness, China's dependence on foreign companies, especially on MNCs, became an important issue: in 2007, 60 per cent of its exports were made by foreign companies and two thirds of the Chinese patents originate from them. The local added value did not exceed 30 per cent of the average total production value (Allouche et al., 2008). This situation prompted the Chinese authorities to change the political and legal framework which used to be favourable to the established MNCs. The Chinese government adopted a specific procedure to authorize the establishment of MNCs in major industries of the country. When Groupe SEB acquired an equity stake in Supor, China's leader in cookware, this policy applied.

In 2007, a new tax policy was implemented. This reform ended the preferential tax rates granted to MNCs (15% on profits of foreign companies, against 33% for Chinese companies). It aimed to make all taxable companies in China pay a standard rate of 25 per cent after five years.

14.3.2 The undervaluation of Chinese currency and its impact on production costs

According to a survey among MNCs conducted by the consulting company Booz Allen Hamilton, 54 per cent of foreign companies in China believe that China's attractiveness is decreasing (Booz Allen Hamilton, 2008). There are several reasons for this, including increased production costs, the yuan's appreciation against the dollar, domestic inflation, and so on. In fact, wages rise each year at a rate of 9–10 per cent and the costs of raw materials increase by an annual rate of seven per cent. Some of the interviewed companies claimed they intended to move to neighbouring countries such as India, Vietnam or Thailand, where production costs are lower (Bouveret-Rivat and Mercier-Suissa, 2010).

14.3.3 The problem of counterfeiting

Despite its various advantages favouring foreign investment in its territory, China's reputation is unfortunately marred by the prevailing presence of the 'counterfeiting industry'. The country has even become the world leader for abuses of property rights and intellectual property rights. The Ministry of Foreign Economic Relations confirms that the counterfeiting market in China represents 15–30 per cent of the country's industrial activity, 8 per cent of the Gross Domestic Product (GDP) and three to five million jobs (Jejcic, 2006). In some regions, counterfeiting has even become the main activity and the foundation of the local economy. This phenomenon is an embarrassment to local authorities and a threat to foreign MNCs.

Counterfeiting has become critical to China's future relationships with foreign partners. In fact, foreign companies may be reluctant or cautious when it comes to investing and establishing their R&D centres in China because of the weak protection of intellectual property and the high probability of technological leakage (Buck et al., 2010).

MNCs which invest in an environment where intellectual property rights barely exist, and where the activity related to counterfeiting is growing, are concerned about the decline of their market share and indicate their dissatisfaction to Chinese authorities. Since the implementation of the openness and reform policy, the Chinese government had encouraged local companies to take advantage of their exchange with foreign partners. However, copying techniques, know-how and imported technologies is almost considered as 'normal' by many Chinese companies.

There are many examples of French MNCs affected by imitation or counterfeiting by Chinese companies. A case in point is the dispute in 2007 between Michelin and its Chinese partner, in which the French group accused its partner of producing counterfeit lorry tyres in its factories. The Danone group suffered a similar misfortune with its Chinese partner Wahaha and had to sell its 51 per cent equity stake (see Chapter 12).

Box 14.4   Valeo R&D: Counterfeiting and market surveillance

In order to fight counterfeiting, Valeo adopted a specific approach in terms of R&D. All patents are duly registered and confidentiality agreements are signed with customers, suppliers and employees. However, these preventive actions cannot solve all problems, so Valeo has set up a market surveillance system designed to identify counterfeiting. The company is supported by the Chinese government which has made considerable efforts in this respect. For example, Valeo and most of its international competitors cooperate with the Chinese customs which operate a 'hot line'. Any Valeo-branded product going through customs is reported and its serial number is checked to ensure its authenticity. This kind of checking is an effective way of fighting the export of fake products.

Source: Chambre de Commerce et d'Industrie Francaise en Chine (CCIFC), 2007.

To address this issue, the Chinese authorities had to consider the important economic weight of counterfeiting, but also the complaints and pressures of MNCs. They have attempted to take restrictive measures, yet insufficient from the viewpoint of MNCs. As a result, MNCs put in place more sophisticated protection strategies to fight counterfeiting and industrial espionage. An example is provided by the Valeo group (see Box 14.4).

14.4   Conclusion

Driven by economic globalization, MNCs strengthen their presence in the world market. Attracted by the flexibility of political reforms, low production costs and market size, most MNCs regard China as a priority destination. In this chapter, we have presented organizational structures that can be adopted by MNCs that wish to enter the Chinese market, and we have studied the benefits of partnerships with local companies. We observe that, despite various expectations of both parts, namely the maximization of profits and the gain of market share for MNCs and the access to technology and the development of employment for Chinese companies (Poncet and Madariaga, 2006), relationships can be built in the mutual interest of both parties. Indeed, MNCs can provide local companies with resources in terms of technology, training, productivity, and so on. Meanwhile, local companies can provide multinationals with various advantages, such as easy access to local networks, the reduction of risks associated with investments made on an unknown market, and so on.

If partnerships are to result in a win-win situation, it is important to note the emergence of Chinese MNCs, such as Huawei in the area of telecommunications and Lenovo in the area of information technology. These new MNCs enjoy crucial competitive advantages, especially in terms of costs, and can be leaders in their local markets. Chinese MNCs recognize the benefits of cooperation with foreign MNCs (Ghemawat and Hout, 2008), but they are also fierce competitors both in their home country and abroad. This new competitive environment may eventually change the relationship between foreign and Chinese companies.

References

Allouche, J., Domenach, J.-L., Froissart, C., Gilbert, P. and Le Boulaire, M. (2008) 'Les entreprises françaises en Chine. Environnement politique, enjeux socioéconomiques et pratiques managériales', *Les Etudes du CERI*, 145–46.

Booz Allen Hamilton (2008) *China Manufacturing Competitiveness Study 2007–2008* (McLean, Virginia: Booz Allen Hamilton).

Bouveret-Rivat, C. and Mercier-Suissa, C. (2010) *PME: Conquérir des parts de marché à l'international* (Paris: Dunod).

232 Partnerships between French MNCs and Chinese Companies

Buck, T., Liu, X. and Ott, U. (2010) 'Long-Term Orientation and International Joint Venture Strategies in Modern China', *International Business Review*, 19 (3), 223–34.

CCIFC (Chambre de Commerce et d'Industrie Française en Chine) (2007) 'La Chine, laboratoire du monde?', *Les Connexions*, 37, 45–55.

Ellis, P. D. (2007) 'Paths to Foreign Markets: Does Distance to Market Affect Firm Internationalization?', *International Business Review*, 16 (15), 573–93.

Ghemawat, P. and Hout, T. (2008) 'Tomorrow's Global Giants: Not the Usual Suspects', *Harvard Business Review*, 86 (11), 80–8.

Jaussaud, J. and Schaaper, J. (2006) 'Entre efficience, réactivité et apprentissage organisationnel – une étude qualitative sur le cas des filiales françaises en Chine', *Management International*, 11 (1), 1–14.

Jejcic, V. (2006) 'La Chine est devenue l'empire de la contrefaçon', *Balkans-Infos*, 116, 4–7.

Johanson, J. and Vahlne, J.-E. (2009) 'The Uppsala Internationalization Process Model Revisited: From Liability of Foreignness to Liability of Outsidership', *Journal of International Business Studies*, 40 (9), 1411–31.

Kaufmann, L. and Korte, P. (2010) 'Responses of Advanced Country MNEs to Low-Cost Country Imports in their Home Markets', *Management International Review*, 50 (2), 241–62.

La Tribune (2010) 'PSA concrétise son alliance avec le chinois Changan', 9 July.

Le Figaro (2010) 'LVMH mise sur la Chine pour sortir plus vite de la crise', 6 February.

Les Echos (2010) 'Sanofi-Aventis se renforce dans l'automédication en Chine', 7 April.

Mayrhofer, U. (2007) 'Les rapprochements d'entreprises: perspectives théoriques et managériales', *Management & Avenir*, 14, 86–103.

MGI (McKinsey Global Institute) (2005) *Addressing China's Looming Talent Shortage* (Chicago: MGI).

Plantade, J.-M. and Plantade, Y. (2006) *La face cachée de la Chine, toute la vérité sur la plus grande jungle économique du monde* (Paris: Collection Bourin Editeur).

Poncet, S. and Madariaga, N. (2006) 'L'impact des IDE sur la croissance: application au cas chinois' in Y. Shi and F. Hay (eds) *La Chine: forces et faiblesses d'une économie en expansion* (Rennes: Presses Universitaires de Rennes), pp. 327–46.

PRB (Population Reference Bureau) (2010) *Fiche de données sur la population mondiale 2010* (Washington: Population Reference Bureau).

Sachwald, F. and Perrin, S. (2003) *Multinationales et développement: le rôle des politiques nationales* (Paris: Agence Française de Développement).

Schaaper, J. (2005) 'Contrôle multidimensionnel d'une filiale à l'étranger: construction d'un modèle causal à partir du cas des multinationales européennes et japonaises en Chine', *Finance Contrôle Stratégie*, 1, 159–90.

Shan, W. (1991) 'Environmental Risks and Joint Venture Sharing Arrangements', *Journal of International Business Studies*, 22 (4), 555–78.

Spencer, J. W. (2008) 'The Impact of Multinational Enterprise Strategy on Indigenous Enterprises: Horizontal Spillovers and Crowding Out in Developing Countries', *Academy of Management Review*, 33 (2), 341–61.

Story, J. (2004) *Chine, un marché à conquérir* (Paris: Pearson Education).

UNCTAD (United Nations Conference on Trade and Development) (2010) *World Investment Report 2010* (New York/Geneva: United Nations Conference on Trade and Development).

15
Implementing Corporate Social Responsibility in MNCs: Google Incorporated

Aline Pereira Pündrich and Sylvaine Mercuri

The economic weight of multinational companies (MNCs) is now well established. In some cases, the revenues they generate largely exceed the budgets of the poorest countries in the world. Over the years, the scope of their activities has expanded, and not only their networking characteristics but also malevolence, has caused worldwide scandals. At the end of the 1980s the international community urged MNCs to demonstrate greater transparency and to respect the needs of people without compromising the needs of future generations. This was the subject of the Brundtland Report, published at the request of the World Commission on Environment and Development (United Nations) (WCED, 1987) which first mentioned the concept of sustainable development. At the same time non-governmental organizations (NGOs) and groups fighting inequality across the world maintained their commitment to denouncing the harmful effects of economic activities developed by MNCs (Doh and Guay, 2004). These factors have led people to question certain processes used by MNCs to meet their needs, and such trends in consumer attitudes have led MNCs to either change or strengthen their way of doing business.

Given this turbulent background, MNCs have to reconsider their behaviour by being more responsible or, in other words, by assuming the consequences of their actions. But how should they proceed? Does this concern the various partnerships they develop? What new problems do they have to face? Corporate social responsibility (CSR) could be the answer. As Capron and Quairel-Lanoizelée (2010) explain it, 'CSR can be used by companies (or larger economic entities) to meet social demands because it helps developing strategies, management systems, change management. It also encourages methods which integrate (in principle) new performance concepts such as monitoring, controlling, evaluation and accountability' (p. 16). To elaborate this crucial and emerging concept, we will first focus on the environment which forces MNCs to question their responsibilities, with particular attention paid to stakeholders. In the second section of the chapter, we will present and analyse several strategies that MNCs may use to meet social demands. Finally, in the third section, the case of Google Incorporated will be introduced, to show how an MNC can implement CSR.

15.1   Corporate social responsibility: A shared concept

In recent years, CSR has been promoted by international institutions such as the United Nations and has been widely discussed by researchers (e.g., Clarkson, 1995; Carroll, 1999; McWilliams and Siegel, 2001; Gond and Igalens, 2010). This concept already existed in some companies, but was not called corporate social responsibility (Capron and Quairel-Lanoizelée, 2010). It was formalized and implemented in companies of different sizes, activities and cultural backgrounds. Such diversity in application complicated the model and CSR now has a multitude of definitions. In the Green Paper published by the European Commission (2001), CSR is defined as 'a concept whereby companies integrate social and environmental concerns in their business operations and in their interaction with their stakeholders on a voluntary basis' (p. 6).

Corporate responsibility is often organized around two areas: social responsibility and environmental responsibility. Although efforts in social responsibility have rapidly been made by MNCs (e.g., the eradi-cation of child labour or social restructuring management), the environmental aspect has been undermined. As Mazerolle (2006) reminds us, 'at first, MNCs aimed to avoid responsibility by relocating their polluting activities in third world countries, then secondly, global awareness of environmental issues led them to fully assume their environmental responsibilities' (p. 174). In general, the scope of CSR is very broad. Deresky (2008) argues that 'CSR's areas of interest are poverty, lack of opportunities in the world, environment, consumption, safety and employees' welfare' (p. 34).

The globalization of the economy has led many organizations to take up the new challenge of assuming the consequences of their decisions. For that reason, CSR has been at the centre of multiple interests involv-ing new actors in the field of MNCs.

15.1.1   CSR in MNCs: A response to the demands of stakeholders

Being economically viable and assuming the consequences of their actions are what stakeholders demand of MNCs. However, the balance is not always the same for each stakeholder (Clarkson, 1995); for example, some of them demand higher profits whereas others ask for more transparency. MNCs should therefore be able to pursue these new collective goals which continuously vary according to individual interests, especially when dealing with environmental and social issues worldwide (Svensson et al., 2010).

In mature markets, environmental and social issues have become daily concerns for consumers who are increasingly demanding green practices (Giaretta, 2005). Technological tools and better access to information have enabled consumers to get more involved in business. MNCs have been widely affected by these new practices, especially when some of them faced global fiascos (e.g., Monsanto, Enron, Nike). Today, people want to be considered as world citizens rather than mere consumers.

Since they no longer consider only shareholders, many MNCs develop CSR strategies to meet the diverse expectations of stakeholders. These individuals or groups of individuals who can influence or be influenced by the achievement of the goals of the organization (Freeman, 1984) are the dominant framework of CSR theories; they aim to align the goals of companies and the expectations of stakeholders (Capron and Quairel-Lanoizelée, 2010). Thus MNCs have engaged in multiple negotiations, starting from a dual vision point to reach a multi-pole approach of their relationships with stakeholders (from a shareholder approach to a stakeholder approach). Therefore, MNCs should not only take into account the expectations of investors, but also those of other stakeholders. This attitude may, as mentioned by Rodrigo and Arenas (2007), facilitate the implementation of socially responsible strategies, since it may entail stronger commitment from certain categories of stakeholders such as employees.

15.1.2   What responsibilities are we dealing with?

Responsibilities of MNCs are critical because, in seeking performance, their activities may affect their stakeholders. This is a long-term issue, but not all MNCs have 'spontaneously decided to respect and promote ethics. ... It is rather a series of scandals that have revealed the ethical and environmental irresponsibility of some multinational companies' (Mazerolle, 2006, p. 163). To reassure their stakeholders, MNCs, with the help of researchers, have developed several CSR options and configurations.

Carroll (1991), for example, mentions four types of CSR. Despite some criticism (Pasquero, 2005), Carroll's model is often used to highlight the importance of the company's economic responsibilities, as key issues for managers (Branco and Rodrigues, 2006). Thus, to better integrate socially responsible issues and the relationship with their stakeholders, companies should consider four main responsibilities:

1. Economic responsibilities, which underline the classical idea according to which companies have to produce goods and services that consumers need, while maximizing their profits at the same time.
2. Legal responsibilities, which ensure stakeholders that companies operate and get higher profits in accordance with law.
3. Ethical responsibilities, by which companies meet, with full transparency, expectations of society; in this case, non-statutory laws, rules of conduct and implicit values prevail as far as companies and stakeholders are concerned.
4. Philanthropic responsibilities, which are those expected in general by stakeholders, and lead companies to make financial and humanitarian contributions, for example; in this case, companies are expected to be good citizens.

Carroll (1991) depicts these responsibilities in the form of a pyramid. Economic responsibilities form the base of the pyramid and ensure the company's viability; it enables the development of other responsibilities (in this case, legal, ethical and philanthropic). Socially responsible actions are not the only positive aspects that an organization can bring to society: its economic viability is in itself a benefit for the community (Carroll, 1999). The question is how to combine these two major factors (social and economic) within organizations in a balanced and efficient manner.

To achieve this, strategies have to be defined by organizations. Nowadays, in a world where markets are opened and actors are becoming more aware of their strong interdependence (Milliot and Tournois, 2010), organizations have to define their strategies while keeping in mind that there is no consensus on the meaning and the implementation of social responsibility (see Box 15.1). The only valid consensus is the growing population and the declining availability of resources. An agreement on CSR is therefore necessary, since there is a global organizational culture that requires specific practices in each country and each culture (Deresky, 2008). In fact, a company tends to emphasize socially responsible actions it considers important in its environment. Thus, since there is a multitude of cultural and economic contexts, the definition of a single socially responsible approach will not suffice, because each organization has its own characteristics and its own way of integrating this type of action (Holme and Watts, 2000).

Box 15.1   CSR in France and Brazil

In France, since the law on New Economic Regulations (NER) of 15 May 2001, French listed companies must include social, environmental and financial information in their annual reports. As in Brazil, French companies most concerned by CSR are those that have a significant impact on the natural environment, and that receive strong pressure from their stakeholders. In Brazil, thanks to the growth and stabilization of the economy in recent years, social responsibility and sustainable practices are the focus of discussions. The banking and financial systems, for example, underwent severe modifications (more regular checks of monetary exchange, better protection for savers, and so on). Despite this trend, most Brazilian companies consider that reporting represents an additional cost rather than a real opportunity (KPMG, 2008).

In the framework of socially responsible strategies, NGOs have been important promoters of CSR (Dunning and Lundan, 2008), and they focus particularly on MNCs and codes of conduct. Among these, Standard 26000 of the International Organization for Standardization (ISO) is an example on which MNCs can build. This is not a management system standard and it cannot deliver an ISO certification, but it aims mainly to regulate business–society relationships (Capron and Quairel-Lanoizelée, 2010). NGOs also influence international agreements, and MNCs trust them to establish responsible strategic partnerships (Doh and Guay, 2004; Milliot and Tournois, 2010).

Regarding the tools used by companies to communicate their socially responsible practices, the social report is a means for stakeholders to measure the social, environmental and economic performance of an organization (Meier and Schier, 2005; Gond and Igalens, 2010). This document is often prepared in accordance with the instructions of international organizations such as the Global Reporting Institute (GRI) which receives, evaluates and archives more than 3000 reports on corporate social responsibility every year throughout the world.

15.2   Strategies for social responsibility in MNCs

CSR strategies vary from company to company, although they are all part of a larger integrative perspective. For that reason, MNCs must adapt their CSR strategies at the local level, to meet the demands of local communities. At the same time, they have to consider more general standards referring to society as a whole (Husted and Allen, 2006). But how do these strategies emerge in an international context? Deresky (2008) points out that stakeholders vary from country to country. Therefore, MNCs must be able to consider stakeholders in a different way, whether they come from the headquarters, the subsidiaries or society. Such a complex environment is made up of different cultures and standards which MNCs have to deal skilfully with, notably when they build partnerships with local actors. The presence of MNCs creates expectations from local stakeholders, especially economic ones: communities expect these large companies to use their capital and/or their skills to play a proactive role in the welfare of countries where they operate. MNCs must therefore know how to meet such expectations. They must pay more attention to certain categories of stakeholders who must be considered as members of both headquarters and subsidiaries. This is particularly true for employees. They may have opposite perceptions of what CSR is within MNCs and also have different practices, even if they are part of the same organization (Rodrigo and Arenas, 2007). Other stakeholders, for their part, are quite different whether they belong to headquarters or to subsidiaries.

Since 1990, and more significantly as the new millennium approached, several companies have tried to develop socially responsible strategies (Capron and Quairel-Lanoizelée, 2010). Several experiences have shown that the introduction of these strategies could provide significant benefits. In addition to new markets that opened up for companies and led them to innovate, legitimacy and reputation have also been frequently referred to in such a context (Branco and Rodrigues, 2008). Mazerolle (2006) proposes a breakdown of motivations that helps companies engage in responsible practices, and that may represent potential benefits for them. Mazerolle highlights the efficiency gain, the anticipation of customer expectations, new markets, the mobilization of internal and external stakeholders and market valuation.

In general, socially responsible strategies allow companies to review their processes and to better integrate their stakeholders (Gond and Igalens, 2010). They entail advantages that may subsequently be evaluated by MNCs, such as performance. Tools for performance evaluation concern local impact, human resources and business practices or, in other words, all territorial indicators as Mazerolle (2006) noted.

15.2.1 Motivations of MNCs

Several criteria allow a better understanding of the commitment of MNCs towards CSR. Mazerolle (2006) identifies two of them: first, 'pressure put on companies' by NGO's, public opinion, law and regulations; and, second, 'the attitude of organizations themselves', from CSR perceived as a constraint to CSR perceived as an opportunity (p. 166). Using such standards, Mazerolle developed a typology of MNCs:

- strategists, under strong pressure from society and see an opportunity of development in social responsibility;
- committed, facing moderate to weak pressure and consider CSR as the spearhead of their strategies;
- concerned, facing strong external pressure and are more reluctant to integrate CSR principles;
- proactive, not really subjected to external pressures but still care to engage in socially responsible attitudes;
- ideal targets, exposed to very strong pressure and adopt CSR strategies in order to try to reduce the risk of reprisals;
- entrant, facing moderate pressure in terms of CSR, and adapt to meet external expectations in a moderate way.

From a similar viewpoint, Capron and Quairel-Lanoizelée (2010) suggest a four-dimension typology considering different strategic behaviours for companies: 'the company's economic interest (risk, opportunity) and the management board's focus on one side; media exposure and stakeholders' pressure on the other' (p. 77).

Different criteria can be used to better comprehend the priorities of an organizational strategy regarding the adoption of social responsibility. In order to inform the reader about research on CSR in MNCs, in the next section we will present a gradual approach of social responsibility and its application in the context of MNCs.

15.2.2 A gradual approach to corporate social responsibility strategies

Studies on CSR strategies have widely explored the case of MNCs as well as other forms of organization. Some of the studies have shown gradual approaches to CSR, like Clarkson (1995), for example, who designed a performance scale according to specific strategies (reactive, defensive, resigned or proactive). Martinet and Payaud (2008, p. 204) identified the following CSR strategies:

- The cosmetic CSR, characterized by superficial CSR practices where there is rarely a willingness to build long-term projects with stakeholders. It is a minimal response to legal requirements as well as specific and ad hoc partnerships.

- The additional or peripheral CSR, whereby the company engages in committed CSR practices, although these are not directly linked to the organization's activities and competences. Patronage activities are part of this strategy.
- The integrated CSR, which are practices integrated into the organization's monitoring chart (Kaplan and Norton, 2003). Financial indicators are offset by social indicators and CSR activities are directly linked to the organization's business.
- The 'Bottom of the Pyramid' (BoP) CSR, based on Prahalad's (2005) studies and recommendations concerning very poor countries. The concept of Bottom of the Pyramid is used to illustrate organizations effectively involved in CSR, which practices are vital to redesign the economic system in order to make it viable.

Even if such typologies are representative and help to understand CSR within MNCs, the latter tend to implement responsible practices in different ways. Alberola and Richez-Battesti (2005) remind us that a gradual approach to social responsibility will depend on the organization's objectives, needs and skills. In order to illustrate CSR implementation within an MNC, we will examine Google Incorporated.

15.3   Google Incorporated

In 1995 two young computer science students, Larry Page and Sergey Brin, met at university to develop a project: a search engine which, later, was named after a mathematical concept, Google (Ippolita, 2007). After a great deal of work, the support of some colleagues and friends, as well as a little help from business angels (Vise and Malseed, 2005), the two founders created Google Incorporated in 1998. In the following years, Google was considered to be the basis of a new economic model for the Internet (Battelle, 2005) (see Box 15.2). The search engine offered free services for its users and advertising spaces for its clients. In addition to a combination of digital services associated on a large scale to a search engine, a large diversity of Googleware was offered by Google (Vise and Malseed, 2005). This included advertising space (AdWords), maps (GoogleMaps and GoogleEarth), photo albums (Picasa), and so on.

Thanks to an incredibly fast growth, Google now employs more than 20,000 people worldwide. The company is considered to be one of the best organizations to work at. Since 2007, *Fortune* magazine has ranked Google among the top ten companies. This MNC has a management team whose experience in computer science is highly developed. It has

Box 15.2 Google Incorporated in figures (2009)

Head Office	Mountain View, California, US
Creation	4 September 1998
Subsidiaries around the world	65
Turnover	23.65 billion US dollars
Net profit	6.52 billion US dollars
Number of employees around the world	19,835

Source: Google Inc. (http://www.google.com/about/company) (Accessed March 2012).

its own research and development centre, the Googleplex, located at Mountain View, in California (Ippolita, 2007). Google also contributes to the development of several projects which aim to develop free software, as well as implement philanthropic activities through the 'google.org' platform.

The following section highlights an analysis of Google Inc. (Yin, 2003), which was carried out through a qualitative and exploratory approach (Denzin and Lincoln, 2000). Google was chosen for its use of socially responsible features to manage its staff composed of diverse nationalities. For the analysis, a documentary database was developed through the use of the Internet, of Google's institutional websites and press articles from Brazilian, French and North-American media. Several videos produced in France, Brazil and the US were also analysed for their contents, made up of interviews and testimonials from employees and experts on Google. The material collected was organized following a temporal perspective and is characterized by a longitudinal *a posteriori* research (Forgues and Vandangeon-Derumez, 2007). The use of secondary data draws on the work of Weick (1993).

15.3.1 Google and 'Googlers'

Google has subsidiaries everywhere in the world, and its collaborators speak several different languages. For this MNC, such characteristics reflect the global audience Google serves. With respect to its team, the 'Googlers' (Google Company, 2012a), Google defines itself as aggressively integrated in its hiring process. The company favours abilities over experience, trying to hire the best people. In 2001, Google opened its first international office in Japan, followed by Australia in 2002, Ireland in 2004, and so on.

> We are looking for diversity. We want Google to reflect the diversity of the world that we wish to serve (US manager).
>
> (Cayatte, 2007)

> It is very difficult to find inside Google people having the same kind of experience … We have air traffic controllers, people who have covered the Olympic Games, therapists … They all work together on specific items or in different teams. Since we have people from all over the world, who have worked in many different areas, we can make use of each of their specificities to improve our company (Brazilian manager).
>
> (Life at Google, 2008a)

> I think that the principle of having several people who know the candidate before he is hired is important because it allows us to have different points of view … It is a systematic process which enables us to detect the best mix … there is no science or algorithms for that (French manager on Google's recruiting procedure).
>
> (Cayatte, 2007)

Today, even though they have local characteristics, Google's subsidiaries have similar features, wherever they are. For example, bicycles or scooters are available for employees to go to meetings; and dogs and other pets are welcome in offices. Massage chairs and stretching balls are also available. There are very few individual offices. Portable computers can be found everywhere in the company; snooker tables, volleyball courts and video games are also available. Moreover, the company offers yoga and dance classes, and employees are encouraged to develop association projects (Battelle, 2005).

> These two men have grown up but they have kept their schoolboy spirit (French journalist about Google's founders).
>
> (Cayatte, 2007)

> Working at Google is working in a relaxed environment. If you introduce this culture to a country like Brazil, this feeling will increase. (Brazilian manager).
>
> (Life at Google, 2008b)

As at the beginning of its activities when Google's offices were located in a garage (Ippolita, 2007), the organization has remained informal.

For this MNC, 'commitment to innovation depends on everyone being comfortable sharing ideas and opinions' (Google Company, 2012b).

Even if the creation of this kind of paradise for computer engineers is not new (such working conditions had already been implemented by other high-technology companies such as Apple in the late 1980s and Microsoft a few years later) (Battelle, 2005), such a position has remained critical for Google. The organizational culture, especially at a time when business in Silicon Valley was not very successful (Vise and Malseed, 2005) has allowed Google to attract very good professionals. It has also allowed Googlers to better socialize and feel more comfortable with their superiors in an informal way.

> It is a job where working hours are particular: we can remain six, seven, eight, nine, ten, twelve hours in the office. However, there is a willingness to manage co-workers life-time ... to avoid stress or burn out ... so there is a rather paternalistic attitude ... an innovation of Google in the social area – so to speak. We know this situation here (in France), where there are trade unions within the company ... In the US, they do not exist, that is why Google re-created them (French expert of human resources).
>
> (Cayatte, 2007)

> One thing I love about Google is that you can access almost all information that you need ... you can send it to your customer very rapidly. You don't have to say, 'I have to wait a week, I have to wait for approvals, I have to sign ten papers'. No! I just go to my local guy; I ask him, and he sends me the information (Brazilian employee).
>
> (Life at Google, 2008c)

Another concern for Google in order to improve its employees' well-being is rather simple: food. While most companies do not pay attention to what their employees eat during lunch break, Google not only takes the time to choose real chefs for its canteens (Vise and Malseed, 2005), it also provides free snacks and drinks in offices.

> It is the best gift a company can make to its employees (French journalist about free food).
>
> (Cayatte, 2007)

> We have a kitchen on each floor (French employee).
>
> (Cayatte, 2007)

Another example of the company's informal way of looking at things (Vise and Malseed, 2005) is April Fools' Day. At that time of the year, new products are invented so that employees and users can have fun together all around the world (e.g., the 'MentalPlex', Google's first April Fools' Day joke).

15.3.2   Google's green policies

Google has developed a policy of green attitudes, which consists of developing activities that vary from keeping a vegetable garden in the middle of Googleplex to launching, in 2007, several green initiatives. The company decided, for example, that its employees would have access to hybrid cars, solar panels have been installed in its headquarters, and the company hopes to become completely neutral as far as CO_2 emissions are concerned. In 2009, in order to maintain its green spaces and to reduce the risks of wild fire at Mountain View, Google rented a few goats from a small local company, which allowed to cut carbon emissions.

In order to keep environmentally friendly offices, Google has pledged to help its employees become greener. At Mountain View, for example, bicycles are available for Googlers to ride across the campus. Google also offers daily biodiesel-powered shuttles for its more than 1500 employees and an electric car-sharing system has been developed. Organic waste from Google's canteens is composted and chefs are encouraged to use local and natural products. Among the many examples of green policy, and thanks to a few partnerships with small local companies, Google also offers subsidies to employees who wish to install solar panels at home. In a similar vein, employees who use bicycles or walk collect points that can be transformed into donations and sent to charity institutions of their choice thanks to Google's support.

> Many companies have to adapt their ethics to their core activity. Ours has never changed. It remains as Sergey and Larry defined it when Google started up in 1998 (US manager).
>
> (Cayatte, 2007)

> We would like to have healthy, educated people including animals if they could search the web [laugh]. Actually, we want to build a better world (US director).
>
> (Cayatte, 2007)

Moreover, we noticed that Google was particularly interested in political issues. The company started a petition asking the US government to cut the coal, oil and engine oil consumption up to 40 per cent by 2030. It also created a website dedicated to the North American presidential elections in 2008. Information, videos and photos as well as teaching aids were available to teachers, supporters and electors on this website. Google also created, in 2009, the 'Google centre for elections in India' during the presidential campaign in that country (Google Company, 2012c).

15.4   Conclusion

For a long time, the MNC has been considered as an environmental and social scourge, but it would be unfair to consider it to be solely responsible for social disorders. This has been emphasized by Deresky (2008), who has observed that MNCs have received less criticism over the last few years. Moreover, as Dunning and Lundan (2008) point out, consumerism most commonly related to developed and emerging countries makes every individual responsible for his/her own actions. It is therefore necessary to take into account, and learn from, actions carried out by MNCs within their headquarters and subsidiaries. Strategic partnerships built with NGOs actually allow MNCs to offer solutions to environmental degradation. Such collaborations may well serve as a basis for new questioning. It is also important to remember that MNCs not only develop strategies but are also investing in funds which have ethical, environmental and/or social issues as their criteria (Meier and Schier, 2005). Moreover, questions related to environmental or social issues have a worldwide relevance and cannot be fully analysed unless each and every actor has a say. Such an idea reminds us of the need for global governance.

CSR offers an important challenge for the management of large companies. It may provide several competitive advantages to companies and it is not dictated by current trends. Even though MNCs have received less criticism in the last years, CSR is still not a priority, particularly when it does not concern the core business of large companies (Gond and Igalens, 2010). Thus, there is still some way to go in this area. However, several MNCs have understood the importance of such activities and they are working on their sustainable integration on a daily basis.

References

Alberola, E. and Richez-Battesti, N. (2005) 'De la responsabilité sociétale des entreprises: évaluation du degré d'engagement et d'intégration stratégique', *La Revue des Sciences de Gestion. Direction et Gestion*, 211–12, 55–69.

Battelle, J. (2005) *The Search: How Google and its Rivals Rewrote the Rules of Business and Transformed our Culture* (New York: Portfolio).

Branco, M. C. and Rodrigues, L. L. (2006) 'Corporate Social Responsibility and Resource-Based Perspectives', *Journal of Business Ethics*, 69 (2), 111–32.

Branco, M. C. and Rodrigues, L. L. (2008) 'Factors Influencing Social Responsibility Disclosure by Portuguese Companies', *Journal of Business Ethics*, 83 (4), 685–701.

Capron, M. and Quairel-Lanoizelée, F. (2010) *La responsabilité sociale d'entreprise* (Paris: La Découverte).

Carroll, A. B. (1991) 'The Pyramid of Corporate Social Responsibility: Toward the Moral Management of Organizational Stakeholders', *Business Horizons*, 34 (4), 39–48.

Carroll, A. B. (1999) 'Corporate Social Responsibility: Evolution of a Definitional Construct', *Business and Society*, 38 (3), 268–95.

Cayatte, G. (dir.) (2007), *Google la machine à penser*, France 5 & Dream Way Productions, http://video.google.fr/videoplay?docid=6256146808037867455# (accessed March 2012).

Clarkson, M. B. E. (1995) 'A Stakeholder Framework for Analyzing and Evaluating Corporate Social Performance', *Academy of Management Review*, 20 (1), 92–117.

Denzin, N. K. and Lincoln, I. S. (2000) 'The Discipline and Practice of Qualitative Research', in N. K. Denzin and I. S. Lincoln (eds), *Handbook of Qualitative Research* (Thousand Oaks: Sage Publications), pp. 1–32.

Deresky, H. (2008) *International Management, Managing across Borders and Cultures* (New Jersey: Pearson International).

Doh, J. P. and Guay, T. R. (2004) 'Globalization and Corporate Social Responsibility: How Non-Governmental Organizations Influence Labor and Environmental Codes of Conduct', *Management International Review*, 44 (2), 7–29.

Dunning, J. H. and Lundan, S. M. (2008) *Multinational Enterprises and the Global Economy*, 2nd edn (Cheltenham: Edward Elgar Publishing).

European Commission (2001) *Promoting a European Framework for Corporate Social Responsibility* (Brussels: European Commission).

Forgues, B. and Vandangeon-Derumez, I. (2007) 'Analyses longitudinales' in R.-A. Thietart (ed.), *Méthodes de recherche en management* (Paris, Dunod), pp. 422–48.

Freeman, R. E. (1984) *Strategic Management: A Stakeholders Approach* (Boston: Pitman).

Giaretta, E. (2005) 'Ethical Product Innovation: In Praise of Slowness', *TQM Magazine*, 17 (2), 161–81.

Gond J. P. and Igalens J. (2010) *La responsabilité sociale de l'entreprise* (Paris: Presses Universitaires de France).

Google Company (2012a), *Meet some Googlers*, http://www.google.com/intl/en/jobs/lifeatgoogle/meet/ (accessed March 2012).

Google Company (2012b), *The Google Culture*, http://www.google.com/about/company/culture.html (accessed March 2012).

Google Company (2012c), *Google, Partners Launch India Elections Center*, http://www.google.com/hostednews/afp/article/ALeqM5g90266SPFekCAli4BCi-76c7iX4Q (accessed March 2012).

Holme, R. and Watts, P. (2000) *Corporate Social Responsibility: Making Good Business Sense* (Geneva: World Business Council for Sustainable Development).

Husted, B. W. and Allen, D. B. (2006) 'Corporate Social Responsibility in the Multinational Enterprise: Strategic and Institutional Approach', *Journal of International Business Studies*, 37 (6), 838–49.

Ippolita (2007) *Luci e ombre di Google* (Milan: Feltrinelli).

Jeantet, T. (2008) *L'économie sociale: une alternative au capitalisme* (Paris: Economica).

Kaplan, R. S. and Norton, D. P. (2003) *Le tableau de bord prospectif* (Paris: Editions d'Organisation).

KPMG (2008) *International Survey of Corporate Responsibility Reporting* (Amsterdam: Klynveld Peat Marwick Goerdeler).

Life at Google (2008a), *Working at Google Sao Paulo – Cinthia: Sales Product Specialist*, http://www.youtube.com/watch?v=XSBmAbAQDok&feature=channel (accessed March 2012).

Life at Google (2008b), *Working at Google Sao Paulo – Cynthia: Team Lead, AdSense*, http://www.youtube.com/watch?v=3J5r8byCkTE&feature=channel (accessed March 2012).

Life at Google (2008c), *Working at Google Sao Paulo – Vicente: Creative Maximizer*, http://www.youtube.com/watch?v=iNx8YyGfsN0&feature=channel (accessed March 2012).

Martinet, A. C. and Payaud, M. A. (2008) 'Formes de RSE et entreprises sociales: une hybridation des strategies', *Revue Française de Gestion*, 34 (180), 199–214.

Mazerolle, F. (2006) *Les firmes multinationales* (Paris: Vuibert).

McWilliams, A. and Siegel, D. (2001) 'Corporate Social Responsibility: A Theory of the Firm Perspective', *Academy of Management Review*, 26 (1), 117–26.

Meier, O. and Schier, G. (2005) *Entreprises multinationales, stratégie, restructuration, gouvernance* (Paris: Dunod).

Milliot, E. and Tournois, N. (eds) (2010) *The Paradoxes of Globalisation* (Basingstoke: Palgrave Macmillan).

Pasquero, J. (2005) 'La responsabilité sociale de l'entreprise comme objet des sciences de gestion: le concept et sa portée', in M. F. B. Turcotte and A. Salmon (eds) *Responsabilité sociale et environnementale de l'entreprise* (Québec: Presses de l'Université du Québec), pp. 112–43.

Prahalad, C. K. (2005) *The Fortune at the Bottom of the Pyramid* (Upper Saddle River: Wharton School Publishing).

Rodrigo, P. and Arenas, D. (2007) 'Do Employees Care about CSR Programs? A Typology of Employees According to their Attitudes', *Journal of Business Ethics*, 83 (2), 265–83.

Svensson, G., Wood, G. and Callaghan, M. (2010) 'A Corporate Model of Sustainable Business Practices: An Ethical Perspective', *Journal of World Business*, 45 (4), 336–45.

Vise, D. A. and Malseed, M. (2005) *The Google Story* (New York: Bantam Dell).

WCED (1987) *Our Common Future* (Brundtland Report) (Oxford: Oxford University Press).

Weick, K. E. (1993) 'The Collapse of Sense-Making in Organizations: The Mann Gulch Disaster', *Administrative Science Quarterly*, 38 (4), 628–52.

Yin, R. K. (2003) *Case Study Research: Design and Methods* (London: Sage Publications).

Conclusion

Ulrike Mayrhofer

Throughout its 15 chapters, this book has taken a 'journey' to the heart of French MNCs and of foreign MNCs located in France. The authors have attempted to provide answers to managerial questions raised by MNCs which have become important actors in the world economy, as well as in the French economy.

The different analyses illustrate the diversity of strategies adopted by MNCs to meet the challenges of economic globalization. Their developments show that growth opportunities are numerous, despite the context of economic crisis, but that it is necessary to seize them adequately, considering the sharp increase in competition in many industries. The recent period has been mainly marked by the appearance of new MNCs from emerging markets, which aim to strengthen their positions in the world market. In 2009 three Chinese groups (Sinopec, State Grid Corporation, China National Petroleum Corporation) ranked among the world's 20 largest MNCs (see Chapter 1). According to available estimates, the importance of MNCs from emerging countries is likely to increase in the coming years. To face this new competition it is essential that MNCs focus specific attention on managerial issues which determine, to a large extent, performance gaps between different actors of a same industry.

The insights provided by this book contribute to a better understanding of issues related to the management of MNCs. Today many of them intend to diversify their geographic expansion, focusing mainly on emerging countries, and this trend also applies to French MNCs. The geographic dispersion of their activities implies adapting managerial practices to take into consideration the heterogeneity of the cultural, economic and institutional environments they are exposed to. MNCs thus need to attach particular importance to the management of headquarters–subsidiaries relationships and the management of partnerships with actors located across the world. The authors of this book hope, through their reflections, to have enriched the concepts and tools which may guide managers of MNCs in a fast-changing global context.

Glossary

Acquisition

An inter-firm linkage where one company takes control over another and integrates it, resulting in a loss of independence for the acquired company.

Alliance

A cooperation agreement signed between several companies which choose to share resources (technological, productive, commercial, and so on) in order to achieve common objectives, while maintaining their independence.

BRIC

An acronym referring to the group of emerging countries comprising Brazil, Russia, India and China. These four countries enjoy a strong economic growth rate and relatively low labour costs compared with industrialized countries and a strong demand linked to the size of their population.

Cash flow

The flow of treasury generated by a company's activities.

Competitive advantage

An advantage that provides the company with higher revenue than the average revenue in the industry.

Competitiveness

The capacity of a company or a country to succeed in a competitive environment.

Cooperation

See *alliance*.

Corporate governance

Mechanisms which are likely to limit the discretionary space of managers.

Corporate social responsibility

A voluntary process by which the company integrates economic, environmental and social constraints in its activities and relationships with stakeholders.

Culture

A shared system of values, beliefs and behaviours.

Diversification

A company's development in a new strategic business area.

Economies of scale

A product's lower unitary cost obtained by increasing its production.

Ethnocentrism

A centralized management mode based on the home country culture of the company. Values and managerial practices of a parent company are transferred to its subsidiaries which generally have a limited autonomy.

Foreign Direct Investment (FDI)

An investment in the capital of a company located abroad, with the objective of acquiring decision-making power in order to influence its management.

Geoentrism

A management concept which reflects the willingness of a company to integrate its headquarters and subsidiaries into a global decision-making process. Relationships between headquarters and subsidiaries are characterized by strong interdependence and rely on the logic of cooperation rather than hierarchy.

Globalization

A phenomenon referring to the increasingly interdependent relationships between nations, human activities and political systems worldwide.

Innovation

The development of new processes or new products and services.

Inter-firm linkage

A strategic agreement formed by at least two independent companies which choose to share all or part of their resources (technological, productive, commercial, and so on). An inter-firm linkage may take the form of an alliance or a merger-acquisition.

Joint venture

A company set up by at least two independent companies which share the capital of the newly formed company.

Merger

An operation in which several companies combine their capital to form a new company.

Multinational company

A company which engages in foreign direct investments (FDI) and which owns or, to a certain extent, controls value-added activities in several countries.

National culture
The values, beliefs and behaviours that characterize a country's population.

Organization culture
A set of values, beliefs and behaviours that characterize an organization.

Parent company
A company which owns several subsidiaries.

Polycentrism
A decentralized management concept, in which the parent company grants its subsidiaries a high degree of autonomy, in order to take into account specificities of foreign markets. The control of the parent company on its subsidiaries appears to be limited.

Regiocentrism
An approach based on the division of the world into geographic zones with certain homogeneity (Western Europe, North America, and so on). The management and the control of subsidiaries by the parent company takes place at a regional level; regional headquarters enjoy a high degree of autonomy with regard to the world headquarters of the group.

Specialization
A company's development in a single strategic business area.

Stakeholders
Different categories of partners that are likely to influence the decisions of managers: shareholders, employees, suppliers, clients, and so on.

Subsidiary
A company which is controlled by another company called parent company. The parent company can hold the totality or a majority of the capital (wholly owned subsidiary) or share the capital with another company (joint venture).

Value chain
A tool which enables to divide the firm into different activities, which contribute to creating value: sourcing, technological development, production, services, and so on.

Index

Printed and bound in the United States of America